Talking Science

D1559683

Reverberations
Contemporary Curriculum and Pedagogy

Series Editors

Joe L. Kincheloe and Shirley R. Steinberg

Titles in the Series

Talking Science

Language and Learning in Science Classrooms

WOLFF-MICHAEL ROTH

ROWMAN & LITTLEFIELD PUBLISHERS, INC.
Lanham • Boulder • New York • Toronto • Oxford

ROWMAN & LITTLEFIELD PUBLISHERS, INC.

Published in the United States of America
by Rowman & Littlefield Publishers, Inc.
A wholly owned subsidiary of The Rowman & Littlefield Publishing Group, Inc.
4501 Forbes Boulevard, Suite 200, Lanham, Maryland 20706
www.rowmanlittlefield.com

P.O. Box 317, Oxford OX2 9RU, UK

British Library Cataloguing in Publication Information Available

Library of Congress Cataloging-in-Publication Data

Roth, Wolff-Michael, 1953–
    Talking science : language and learning in science classrooms / Wolff-Michael Roth.
        p.   cm. — (Reverberations)
    Includes bibliographical references and indexes.
    ISBN 0-7425-3706-4 (cloth : alk. paper) — ISBN 0-7425-3707-2 (pbk. : alk. paper)
    1. Communication in science—Study and teaching. 2. Science—Study and teaching. 3.
Language and languages—Study and teaching. I. Title. II. Series: Reverberations
(Rowman and Littlefield, Inc.)
    Q223.R53 2005
    507'.1—dc22

                                                                                                2005006895

Printed in the United States of America

♻™ The paper used in this publication meets the minimum requirements of American
National Standard for Information Sciences—Permanence of Paper for Printed Library
Materials, ANSI/NISO Z39.48-1992.

Contents

Preface

This book is the result of a longtime preoccupation and personal experience with languages in their different forms. As a seventh-grade student, I had difficulties mastering my first language (German) sufficiently to make the next grade. But then I learned two other languages in which I am more fluent now than in my first language. I also learned many special dialects tied to situations and languages—for a long time, I was more fluid speaking physics in German, literature in French, and science education in English, because most of my activities in a field had occurred in one language or another. That is, my general proficiency in each of these languages did not extend to the specialist dialects that I evolved in the course of my particular activities. Only much later did I come to understand, while reading and trying to come to grips with *Monolingualism of the Other; or, The Prosthesis of Origin* (Derrida 1998). Having lived or spent much time in several countries and cultures, I have come to realize that particular ways of thinking are tied to ways of talking, or rather, ways of talking are integral to ways of being. The way we orient to issues, what issues are relevant, the way we orient physically and metaphorically to things and events—all are a function of culture and therefore language. But language is inherently contradictory, constituting an aspect of the world we know and a tool to make this world (and therefore language) the topic of talk. Derrida articulates this in a pair of contradictory statements:

1. We only ever speak one language.
2. We never speak only one language. (Derrida 1998, 7)

The puzzle in this dialectically related pair of statements embodies much of the difficulty in learning science, which uses language that is both the same as and very different from the language we speak pursuing activities other than those related to science.

While teaching eleventh- and twelfth-grade physics in a private high school, I came across a book that intensified my interest in and preoccupation with language. The associate director of the Harvard Smithsonian Institute, in *Inventing Reality: Physics as Language* (Gregory 1990), takes a pragmatic position in which we discard the languages that are no longer useful and develop new ones. I was so fascinated with it that I made the book an aspect of the twelfth-grade curriculum, reading and discussing it with my students. My analyses of students' ways of talking about the nature of science and the way these ways changed over an eighteen-month period became the starting point of a continued research interest (Roth and Lucas 1997). At the same time I became interested in and researched how students' own language in science changed. This book is fundamentally about what I have learned and where I have arrived at over the course of the past decade.

Projects such as this book—or, for that matter, Nobel awards, architectural designs, or political decisions—are most often associated just with the name of one author (team), leaving unnamed and forgotten all those people and things that made writing the books—or doing the Nobel-winning research, designing processes, and political decision making—possible in the first place. Because I was interested in language in use, my way of thinking about both aspects of language—talking physics and talking about physics—were increasingly influenced by pragmatic philosophers such as Ludwig Wittgenstein, Martin Heidegger, Richard Rorty, Donald Davidson, and Willard Van Orman Quine. Other important authors who influenced my thinking about language include Jacques Derrida and Martin Buber.

There are not only direct ways in which those surrounding us assist in making projects possible, but also important opportunities arising from the division of labor in society that allows professors like myself to dedicate their lives to research and writing. These contributions cannot ever be fully articulated, because they necessitate a description of human society and culture in general. However, I acknowledge those who were more closely associated with the different projects in which those data sources were collected on which I draw in this book.

The idea for this book came to me recently, while working on several chapters concerned with talking and writing science. This work occasioned me to look back over the past decade, and over the evolution of my ways of talking and writing about language in science. Although I have had previous interests in language and organized my teaching according to the metaphor of science as language, the direction taken in this book emerged as I was working on four articles published in 1995 and 1996 from which part of chapter 1 (Roth 1996b) and chapters 2 and 5 evolved (Roth 1995, 1996a; Roth, Woszczyna, and Smith 1996). Since then, my work increasingly has taken a linguistic turn, so much so that I began publishing in journals such as *Language in Society, Discourse Processes, Journal of Pragmatics, Pragmatics and Cognition,* and *Semiotica.* In these journals, I published pieces of data and initial analyses that have been developed further and used in this book (Roth 1999, 2000).

Three chapters are based on papers and articles that received international awards. Thus, chapters 3 and 4 are based on ideas that I developed while working with Reinders Duit and his doctoral students Michael Komorek and Jens Wilbers; together, we received, in 1998, an award for "Cognition during 'Hands-on' Physics: Toward a Theory of Knowing and Learning in Real Time" as the "paper with greatest significance and potential in the field of science education" from the National Association for Research in Science Teaching. The paper was eventually published in considerably different and abridged form with a different focus than the linguistic one I am taking here (Roth and Duit 2003). The coauthorship in both instances, however, reflects having worked together—my coauthors did not share my theoretical commitments with respect to language. Chapter 7, too, is based on an article (Roth, McGinn, Woszczyna, and Boutonné 1999) that received an award, this time from the European Association for Research on Learning and Instruction (2001) as the outstanding publication published by one of its members during 1999 and 2000. With these same authors, I published an article (McGinn, Roth, Boutonné, and Woszczyna 1995) that after many considerable transformations turned into chapter 6.

Part of the introduction was developed from an example I had used in a book review essay on a discourse perspective in mathematics and which appeared in *Linguistics and Education* (Roth 2001). Some of the ideas for chapter 1 arose while I was working on a series of studies concerned with the role of gestures in lectures and the learning of science. Several pieces were coauthored by my M.Ed. student at the time, Daniel Lawless, and appeared, among other journals, in *Semiotica* (Roth and Lawless 2002a) and *Language in Society* (Roth and Lawless 2002b).

I recognize the contributions of individuals who have assisted directly to the various studies on which this book is built and the financial resources that allowed me to conduct the research. In three chapters (1, 2, and 5), I draw on data collected while I was teaching twelfth-grade physics at Appleby College. I thank all those students who graciously agreed to participate, allowed me to videotape them, and gave me their time to participate in interviews. The administration considered the school a research site where teachers were invited to conduct their studies and, through the outcomes, to improve the teaching and learning environment. I am grateful to the school in general and the students in particular. Their permission gave me a start in my research career. Soon after collecting the data, I moved on to become a professor at Simon Fraser University. Two M.A. students at the time, Carolyn Woszczyna and Gillian Smith, supported by a grant by the Social Sciences and Humanities Council of Canada, assisted me in transcribing the videotapes and collaborated in writing a sociological study concerning the opportunities and constraints of computer-based learning environments (Roth, Woszczyna, and Smith 1996). Daniel Lawless worked with me on reanalyzing some of the videotapes with respect to the role that gestures play in the emergence of science talk.

The study on learning chaos theory (chapters 3 and 4) was planned and conducted together with Reinders Duit. His graduate students Michael Komorek and Jens Wilbers assisted in the data collection and Michael also taught the class, drawing on the expertise and materials that he had developed on the topic during his then ongoing dissertation research. The social organization of students into small groups investigating and discussing phenomena related to the chaotic pendulum was based on my research on the "diffusion of knowledge" in science classrooms. Together, we had many animated discussions in which conceptual change and language approaches came face to face. Sylvie Boutonné, Horst Bayrhuber, and Ralf Thomas also assisted in the data collection. Finally, my gratitude is extended to the directorate of the Wellingdorf Gymnasium (Kiel, Germany), which allowed us to do the study in its school, and to Mrs. Bobertz, who invited us into her classroom. Financial assistance for the project came from a grant by the Social Sciences and Humanities Research Council of Canada and from a study grant by the German Academic Exchange Service (Deutscher Akademischer Austausch Dienst).

The data for the studies in the split sixth- and seventh-grade classroom, where I taught a four-month unit on simple machines, were made possible by a grant from the Social Sciences and Humanities Research Council of Canada and by the administration and teachers of an elementary school in the greater Vancouver (British Columbia) area. I thank Ken Neale in particular, who invited my research team into his class, and his students, who accepted me as their teacher. Sylvie Boutonné, Michelle McGinn, and Carolyn Woszczyna assisted in the data collection, interviewing, and analyzing the data from a variety of perspectives and participated in the authoring of several articles.

Introduction

Toward a Nonrepresentational View of Language

Language is the central aspect of the human condition that enables cultural phenomena in the way we know them. Language as a formal system provides resources for conducting everyday affairs, including the *doing* of science. Writing science is only one aspect of doing science; talking science may in fact constitute a much larger part of accomplishing the various aspects that characterize science. Talking science is the medium through which we do science: it includes actions such as "observing, describing, comparing, classifying, analyzing, discussing, hypothesizing, theorizing, questioning, challenging, arguing, designing experiments, following procedures, judging, evaluating, deciding, concluding, generalizing, reporting, writing, lecturing, and teaching" (Lemke 1990, 1). However, characterizing talking science as a "medium" comes with a danger that Lemke surely wanted to avoid—making a difference between thinking, thoughts, or ideas, on the one hand, and the way these are made public to others, on the other. Certainly, there may be moments in life when we talk to others while harboring ideas that we then make explicit in our talk. Most talk in everyday situations, however, is not of that kind. Everyday talking is like walking in the sense that we simply walk without thinking about it; when walking, we certainly do not make plans and then implement them by placing our feet in the predetermined way. We simply talk and it is in talking that our ideas are constituted. There are no plans in an utterance or conversation for what we are going to say in the next sixty seconds or minutes. Even at the beginning of a turn at talk we do not know with any precision the shape our sentences will take and what their contents are (McNeill and Duncan 2000). Most talk therefore has an emergent characteristic, which contributes to the fact that social activities, like doing science at school, are contingent. Social events gain their definite character only after the fact. At any moment, there exist possibilities for different things to happen, for different things to be said, without the chance to engage several possibilities at once.

Theorizing language as a medium leads to a split between ideas, (mis-) conceptions, and so-called naive theories individuals are said to have, on the one hand, and the expression of these ideas, conceptions, and theories, on the other. This leads to a rationalist or intellectualist view of the individual who, in the manner of an information-processing computer program, assembles sentences based on ideas that are somehow behind the sentences. This leads to claims that students *have* one or another private alternative conception, misconception, or naive theory that they *expressed* in language. In this book I take a different perspective on language. I consider language as a resource that individuals rally in a situated manner—in this case, whatever people say is never their own, but always also part of some collective endeavor. This is so in more than one way. First, spoken language in use most frequently occurs in turn taking, one turn leading to the next, always in response to what has been said previously. Second, the moment we use language to express something, we draw on a social resource and therefore on something that is not our own; a completely private language cannot be used for communication. Thus, if a science educator interrogates children about the earth and the sun, they can provide responses although they have never considered the relation between the two entities before. In their everyday interactions with parents and other people, they have heard expressions such as "The sun is coming up behind the mountain," "What a beautiful sunrise!" or "The sun is setting." In all of these sentences, the sun is the agent. It is therefore not surprising when, pressed for an answer, the children articulate situations in which the sun is the agent and the earth the stable point of reference.

There is also a major difference between the ways in which language is used in scientific writing and in everyday conversation. In the former, all sense of agency is expelled and a disembodied, all-knowing author tells the story of discovery. In the statement "Diatom slides for microscopy were made following a procedure with no decanting or centrifuging . . . and 400 valves per level were counted," actions are described but the individuals who did them have disappeared. Any actor, even a robot, may have done what is described. In a similar way, the act and agent of observation is stripped so that only disembodied observations appear in scientific accounts. In the sentence "A striking feature of the diatom flora was the absence of planktonic diatoms, the only exception being an occurrence (8.7 percent) of *Cylotella kuetzingiana* at 100 cm sediment depth," the act of observation no longer figures, which thereby makes the "absence of planktonic diatoms" a fact.

As the following excerpt shows—I recorded it during the data collection phase in an advanced experimental biology laboratory—this language differs from laboratory talk where scientists do not efface their own agency. In this excerpt, a professor (Craig) and his research associate (Theo) are in the process of measuring light absorption in cone-shaped cells from the retina of a trout. Looking through the ocular of the optical microscope, Craig is responsible for aligning the slide-mounted cells with the beam of light. Theo operates the computer, which opens and closes the instrument that records the amounts of light. Theo comments upon the curve resulting from the last recording, describing it as looking pretty green. But he does not simply state some fact. Rather, he adds "to me" (line 01); he adds the same type of attributions in his next turns at talk, "if you ask me" (line 03) and "I think it is" (line 05).

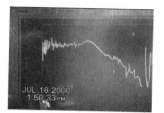

01	Theo:	Looks pretty green to me, but u::h, rather nice, actually.
02	Craig:	Okay, can be a double cone sideways.
03	Theo:	Looks pretty *pretty*, if you ask me.
04	Craig:	Okay.
05	Theo:	But I think it is in the green region.
06	Craig:	Okay, save that! Do you want me to bleach it?
07	Theo:	I think we don't need this one.

In the same way, Craig asks whether to "bleach" the photoreceptor that he currently has as target under the microscope. Craig personalizes his and Theo's agency by stating, "Okay, save that!" and by asking, "Do you want me to bleach it?" Here, both Theo, as the person deciding whether to save (usable) data to the hard drive ("Save that!" and "Do *you* want"), and Craig, as the person who would bleach the cell, are explicitly articulated in the utterance ("*me* to bleach it?").

This brief exchange shows us another peculiarity of laboratory conversations in science: it is highly indexical, that is, scientists refer to tools and entities in the laboratory using terms such as "it," "that," or "this." Furthermore, they do not name or describe the things that they are talking about, which, in the current situation are in fact different and the same simultaneously. Theo talks about the graph, which has, as the illustration shows, a discernible peak in the center of the display. This peak corresponds to the green region of the light spectrum— thus his comment, "Looks pretty green to me." Craig on the other hand talks about the photoreceptor on the microscopic slide, which he previously has described to be a single cone. Single cones absorb light in the blue or ultraviolet region. However, a double cone photoreceptor has both red- and green-absorbing members. By saying, "can be a double cone sideways," Craig revises what the entity under the microscope is, which make the two assessments consistent.

How then are the languages of laboratory talk and scientific reports related? A few anthropologists and sociologists, who have conducted studies of scientific laboratories since the 1970s, already reported such changes of language (Latour and Woolgar 1986). Such studies have shown that factual statements in scientific laboratories are initially unstable and ambiguous concerning what they are really about. This instability is especially notable very early in scientific work, before new discoveries are made. At this point, neither the objects and events subsequently being discovered nor the language describing them exist in a form that has been reified. Scientists therefore struggle without knowing that they are doing so, for

> someone like Galileo . . . is typically unable to make clear exactly what it is that he wants to do before developing the language in which he succeeds in doing it. His new vocabulary makes possible, for the first time, a formulation of its own purpose. It is a tool for doing something which could not be envisaged prior to the development of a particular set of descriptions, those which it itself helps to provide. (Rorty 1989, 12–13)

New knowledge (in other words, the stability of facts) arises as a consequence of (a) the convergence of sense and reference in conversations over and about inscriptions that exist in the form of electron micrographs, autoradiographs, or pulses on a computed axial tomography (CAT) scan; (b) the convergence of experiment and narratives reifying the distinctions between words and the world, while removing evidence of the work that allowed such a distinction to be drawn; (c) the stabilization of factual statements by progressive removal of qualifiers that point to the statements' contingent origins; and (d) the temporal succession of embodied scientific practices in the social-interactional settings of laboratories. In this respect, for example, one study reported that the "fact" of the first optical-pulsar-to-be emerged in the course of several hours of observation and talk as the detailed analysis of one night's (audiotaped) talk between astronomers showed (Garfinkel, Lynch, and Livingston 1981). In the course of the night, the astronomers constituted the first optical pulsar in talk over signals on a computer monitor rather than making a sudden discovery that they then named. That is, new phenomena are brought into the domain of discourse by

> a succession of construals, or tentative representations of possible outcomes. Construals are continually constructed and revised to describe and communicate *actual* outcomes. The process is actually more complex: there is a convergence of successive material arrangements (the apparatus) and successive construals (or tentative models) of and with apparatus, and of the outcomes of these manipulations. (Gooding 1992, 103, emphasis in the original)

Once such "discoveries" have been reported, others begin to see the same phenomena, although they had not previously seen them. Thus, "seeing" and "talking about" phenomena are in a reflexive relationship, constituting one another. If one views these new phenomena from the outside, or asks scientists in the field after a crucial investigation, the new facts seem to change the landscape of concepts more or less radically and instantaneously so that one can talk about a conceptual change. If, on the other hand, one follows the scientists responsible for the "discovery," the tentative emergence of new facts through convergence becomes evident. These two approaches to the study of scientists' work (and learning) have been characterized in the contrast of ready-made science and science in the making (Latour 1987). The languages of these two modes of science communication are strikingly different, a fact that has to be taken into account in science teaching if we aspire to allowing students both to learn along reasonable trajectories and to allow students to appreciate the process nature of science.

Research in the domain of science studies indicates that the objects and events under observation and the inscriptions made by scientists are initially very flexible; scientists' language shifts in the course of discovery work, and so do the objects and events that they attend to (Pickering 1995). More stable entities and talk emerge (a) as scientists converge in their ways of talking about objects and events or (b) as this talk increasingly fits the studied phenomena. In this sense, ways of talking appear to undergo evolutionary changes to become increasingly appropriate for describing and explaining phenomena. Here, I propose a view of learning in science classrooms that focuses in a similar way on the succession of students' talk until their language satisfactorily describes experiences.

WORLD, LANGUAGE, AND LEARNING

To foreshadow my way of looking at language use and evolution in science classrooms, I take in this section a look at language as it is used in everyday situations and how we learn to use language that we find as we engage in new pursuits. The analysis of episodes leads me to articulate a different way of framing the knowing and learning of a language such as those used in the sciences.

Language in Everyday Situations

Language pervades our everyday lives. Talk in particular is a central feature of most situations in which we find ourselves—unless one is taking an exam or writing a book. We do things with language; it allows us to get around. Knowing a language and knowing one's way around the world really are indistinguish-

able. Let us look at a few examples that I recorded in my field notebook while
sitting on a plane during on a trip from Eastern Canada.

01 Stewardess: ((Looks at passengers to the left and right of the aisles as she
                 walks backwards. She has a tray with stacked goblets and a
                 pitcher with water and ice cubes.)) Water!?
02 Passenger: ((Looks up, slightly nods.))
03 Stewardess: ((Pours water into a goblet, and offers it to the passenger.))
04 Passenger: ((As he is taking the goblet)) Thank you!

Our training (in fact, ideology) may lead us too quickly to assume that very
little or something very insignificant had occurred here, when in fact we wit-
nessed a complex event consisting of a series of verbal and physical gestures.
First, the stewardess oriented herself to the passenger, physically, by turning her
head, looking him straight in the face. We do not know whether he had heard
any of her previous utterances of "Water!?"; it doesn't really matter for the purposes of this analysis. Her utterance is a statement that there is presumably water
in the pitcher. If there was none, she might not say "Water!?" or if she did say it,
she would respond to a passenger's nod with a "Sorry, I just ran out." (In similar
instances with the request "chicken or beef?" her response to a passenger requesting beef was "I will come back.")
     The utterance is not only a statement that there was water in the pitcher but
also a request directed toward the passenger. His nod indicated that he understood the utterance to mean, "Would you like some water?" to which he silently
responded, "Yes, I would like some water." In fact, his hearing became apparent
in his response. In turn, the stewardess took his nod as a response to the implied
question. That is, this interpretation is consistent with his and her subsequent
utterances and gestures, which followed the offering and acceptance of the water-filled goblet. He marked his gratitude by uttering, "Thank you!" In this situation, the two interlocutors produced their turns in a way that is analyzable for
their possible completion not only by one another but also by anyone else overhearing them. That is, turn taking is achieved by the local analytic work of the
parties.
     In addition to the verbal gestures, there were physical gestures, too. Rather
than responding verbally to the request, the passenger slightly moved his head
downward, which Westerners understand as a sign of agreement, "Yes I would
like the water." (In other cultures, the movements of agreement and refusal may
be different.) Here, the nod moved the episode along by giving rise to the pouring of a goblet of iced water. That is, the stewardess understood the nod as a
positive response to her implied question, "Would you like some water?" Her
next two actions, the pouring and the offering of the goblet to the passenger
arose from this orientation to the customer and his nod. The passenger in turn
responded verbally to a nonverbal action, the hand holding the goblet toward

him, which he acknowledged as an offer by grabbing it and thereby accepting the offer. That is, the water-filled goblet in the stretched-out hand was accepted as an offer although there was no utterance that described it as such. Furthermore, the stewardess did not need to say that it was a water-filled goblet. This went without saying, for the passenger had seen the stewardess pour something from a plastic pitcher, which was therefore not coffee or tea, both being carried about in metal pots.

The utterance "Water!?" cannot be evaluated by itself but only as part of a larger context, constituted by the fact that we were on a plane and that the person here designated as a stewardess distinguished herself from others by wearing what we know or understand to be the uniform of the airline. There were several other similarly dressed individuals on the plane, who engaged in similar kinds of relations with the remainder of the people on the plane, clad formally and informally, but hardly ever two people in the same way. "Water!?" is then also heard in the context of an industry, where employees of some company engage in serving the clients. "Water!?" "Chicken or beef?" and "Anything to drink?" are integral parts of these situations and an orientation of the stewards and stewardesses. It is not so much that we (frequent) travelers understand these utterances but that we understand, are familiar with, the kinds of situations in which uniform-clad persons walk about with goblet-filled trays in one hand and an ice-water-filled pitcher in the other. The passenger did not have to interpret the utterances to understand what was going on, but being attuned to the situation, the passenger's response was immediate (without interpretation). It is when passengers are not attuned to the situation, for example, when they just woke up, that their response might be delayed or inappropriate.

Communication does not require words at all, as in the following example from my notes taken during the same flight.

05 Stewardess: ((Smiles, raises goblet-filled tray [or water-filled pitcher] slightly.))
06 Passenger: ((Smiles, almost unnoticeably.))
07 Stewardess: ((Pours a goblet of water, hands it to the passenger.))
08 Passenger: ((Slightly nods.))

In this situation, an exchange similar to the previous one occurred—the stewardess gave a passenger some water—without a similar exchange of words. Both passenger and stewardess were oriented toward a world, the voyage on a plane from Toronto to Vancouver, in which they found themselves without having to represent it or reflect about it.

In everyday conversations, people hear more than what an utterance literally says.

09 Passenger A: What time is it?

10 Passenger B: ((Looks at his watch.)) I think it is about forty-five minutes of
                   flight time.

In this situation, passenger A asked for the time, but the second passenger responded with an amount of time that he characterized as flight time. That is, rather than providing the current time—for whatever time zone—the second passenger heard the question to be about the amount of time since departure or to landing. His response made the question one about flight time rather than current time in Toronto or Vancouver. Thus, in another situation, for example, while waiting to cross a street on a red light for pedestrians, the second individual might have answered "ten to three." In this situation, we would take the second person to have heard the question differently, as a different kind of request. In his response, passenger B talked about forty-five minutes of flight time. Although he did not further elaborate, we can hear his response as "forty-five minutes of flight time left before landing in Vancouver," given that we had been on the Toronto–Vancouver flight for some time. Had we been in the air for only a short time, we might have heard the second passenger say something like "we left forty-five minutes ago."

We may hear the first passenger say other things, which would have become clear if B had responded, "It's getting long, isn't it?" or in the way a third passenger responded to my look when he returned from pacing up and down the aisles for a while, "I am in the bored stage." The utterance was heard as a question, that is, as a request that required a response, which would not have been necessary had the first passenger simply uttered, "This is a long flight!" or "I am starving for a smoke" (which she did as we walked out of the plane). The question "What time is it?" had been heard in a very particular way, more characteristic while traveling on a plane, train, or bus to some distant place. Again, what we understand is not the utterance but the situation as a whole, which includes the utterance as an integral and constitutive part. We are attuned to the situation rather than to the words, and therefore understand what is going on even if we only hear parts of what has been said. We, those who listened, responded, or overheard were equally attuned to the situation and responded to it rather than to the question by itself.

In this book, I take the position that much of students' talk in science is of that type, whether it is during laboratory work, presentation of an artifact, or argument over the winning design of a pulley system. The talk takes the form of articulating the world as the current activity unfolds, constituting gestures that move the events along to the next stage, rather than being *about* things, that is, being of representational type with intentions (underlying models) that precede the construction of sentences.

In these situations, the people on the plane found themselves in a familiar world. Students of science, however, are asked to attune themselves to worlds that they neither know nor have a language for. To explore what it means to open up new worlds, I elaborate the following example of my struggle to learn how to prune.

Pruning Book and Learning to Prune

In 1997, after moving to Victoria, I started gardening. This hobby has developed to the point that I now produce sufficient vegetables year-round to continuously supply my small household. One winter, I was supposed to prune the fruit trees and berry-bearing bushes. Never having pruned before, my wife bought me a book entirely dedicated to pruning, containing many photographs and diagrams of partially pruned pushes, showing where to cut and what to leave, similar to my example in figure I.1. Over a period of several weeks, I had repeatedly taken up the book, tried to read and make sense of it, and subsequently laid it aside. I was completely frustrated by the fact that I was unable to prune although there was not a single unfamiliar word and although there were drawings illustrating how to cut. I felt completely stifled and abandoned the idea of pruning. On the one hand, I had the text, composed of familiar words and drawings that did not appear to be overly complex. On the other hand, there were my bushes (figure I.2). The two did not seem to go together. They were not part of the same situation even on that day when I took the book outside and held it next to the bushes that the texts, photographs, and drawings were seemingly about.

In the winter, work methodically on each branch in turn.

Shorten the summer's growth from the tip of each main branch by half. Then cut back the side shoots to within one or two buds of the main stems. This encourages the production of fruiting spurs.

In time you will cut out old and unfruitful branches. Leave vigorous young side shoots to replace them.

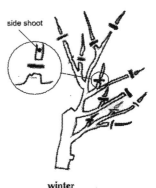

winter

MAIN TEXT: The following winter, shorten any crossing branches, and cut back *one* of the major branches to a bud just above ground level (this starts the cycle of regular renewal).

Figure I.1. Despite extensive instructions from a text on pruning and despite extensive photographs and diagrams, I found it difficult or impossible to prune, even when I took the book outside, holding it right next to the plants.

Figure I.2. In my initial attempts, I took the book outside to compare the photos, diagrams, and instructions with my own bushes. But however much I tried figuring out where I needed to make the cuts, I did not succeed. I was successful only after following around a twenty-five-year veteran of pruning and talking for about two hours.

Then, one week we read that there was a workshop organized by the owner of a tree nursery and fruit farm and run by his son. We decided to attend. The son of the owner who had pruned trees and bushes for about twenty-five years ran the workshop. Initially, he talked about growing fruit trees and pruning them. After about fifteen minutes, I turned around to my wife and said, "He is talking the talk! No better than the book!" But then he started pruning, talking while he was going along. He held up a branch, pointing to a place, saying that he wanted to encourage growth, and cutting in another place, where he wanted to stop growth. He cut and talked, sometimes interrupted by questions from the audience. He continued, explaining why to cut the branch he was about to cut and why he was leaving another one nearby, and pointed to a pruned tree that he wanted his tree to look like. Things seem to become clearer. I even started predicting which branches he would cut. Taking his actual cutting or not cutting as feedback, my predictions improved in accuracy. Two hours later, I was correct in about 90 percent of the cases.

I returned home and went straight into my garden. I looked at a bush and thought about where I would cut based on what I had seen and predicted to happen on the farm. I pruned one bush and a small tree. It all seemed so easy. Then, returning inside our home, I took out the pruning book. Lo and behold, everything was clear. The book was telling me exactly what I had to do, and it did so in a very clear way. It was a wonderful book—or rather, the book had *become* wonderful. But what had happened? How could the pruning expert's words, which had not been so different after all from those employed in the book, have made such a difference?

When I attended the workshop, I came to experience more than seeing the cutting of branches by the experienced horticulturist or hearing his descriptions and explanations. That afternoon, I participated in a world that was inherently shot through with meaning for the horticulturist, including (cherry, plum, apple, and pear) trees, (small and large) pruning shears, intentions and expectations, orientations, gestures, and language. That afternoon was different in that I had had the opportunity to participate in a different world, its particular orientations, and the language that goes *with* them. The language did not refer to things in this world but was copresent with them.

When I came home, I brought with me the experience of a different world, a world in which my own bushes and trees took on a new place, in which I took a new orientation, and on which I had a new perspective. In this new world, the formerly impenetrable manual also found its place. The text now accrued to a world that made sense in its entirety, that already was shot through with meaning. It was not the text that had become meaningful; rather, it had found its place in a meaningful world that had to exist so that I could recognize the book as a wonderful and exemplary manual. Now that I was familiar with the world of horticulture and pruning, the book made sense and I could see what its texts described and instructed me to see.

Students who frequent science classes mostly find themselves in much more disadvantageous situations, where they find much less similarity between the photographs and images of their textbooks and the phenomena that they encounter in the laboratory or the outside world. Further, unlike in my own situation, there are many words that students have never heard before, so they cannot draw on everyday ways of using them as initial resources for getting them started in using them in science too. In the following section, I will articulate how a world and a language coevolved as I struggled with a mathematical puzzle given to me.

EMERGING WORLDS

Texts are not always available when we learn something new, and in fact exploring and building a language may constitute a better way of building an experiential foundation for new worlds and new ways of talking to emerge. That is, as part of our practical actions, new worlds become salient and with them the language that describes them. More so, language itself is a resource to engage in practical activity and it is changed in use. I articulate this perspective—which I will subsequently use to analyze the emergence of language in the course of students' inquiries during science (physics) lessons—in the following example.

Several years ago, Daniel Lawless, then a graduate student of mine, used a text problem as part of his data collection on teaching and teacher knowledge in mathematics. After he had given the text problem to me, I not only attempted to solve it but also recorded the entire problem process during and immediately after I finished. The following account shows that by engaging in the practical activity of solving the problem, I constituted a new aspect of the world, which, together with the language I used to express myself *within* and *about* it, emerged from my embodied activity.

Daniel handed me a sheet containing the following text:

In a certain town there are two hospitals, a small one in which there are, on the average, about 15 births a day and a big one in which there are, on average, about 45 births a day. The likelihood of giving birth to a boy is about 50%. (Nevertheless, there were days on which more than 50% of the babies born were boys, and there were days when fewer than 50% were boys.) In the small hospital a record has been kept during the year of the days in which the total number of boys born was greater than 9, which represents more than 60% of the total births in the small hospital. In the big hospital, they have kept a record during the year of the days in which there were more than 27 boys born, which represents more than 60% of the births. In which of the two hospitals were there more such days? (a) In the big hospital there were more days recorded where more than 60% boys were born. (b) In the small town there were more days recorded where more than 60% boys were born. Or (c), the number of days for which more than 60% boys were born was equal in the two hospitals.

Upon seeing this puzzle, a vague image of two distributions emerged within me, which I immediately drew next to the text (figure I.3). The image of three children appeared to me, though I do not know why, each of them with a probability of 50 percent of being boy or girl. In an unfolding manner I envisioned the following series of rows composed of triplets of numbers, each individual number being a 0 or 1: 0 0 0, 0 0 1, 0 1 0, 1 0 0, and so on. In my mind, I ordered the triplets that had the same number of 0s and 1s into rows and counted that there were 1, 3, 3, and 1 of them resulting in four rows (figure I.4). This

Figure I.3. The first thing I was aware of thinking after reading the problem was the image of two bell-shaped distributions.

roughly gave me a shape resembling the distributions envisioned in figure I.3. I began to do another example, which would allow me to make a comparison with my three-children model, choosing a six-child case. But as the first sets of 0s and 1s formed in my mind's eye (i.e., 0 0 0 0 0 0, 1 0 0 0 0 0, . . . 1 1 0 0 0 0 0, . . .), the task of visualizing, enumerating, and counting the frequency of each seemed too complex without paper and pencil. But it was immediately evident that there was only one combination with six 0s and one combination with six 1s. I imagined the next combination, two 1s and four 0s as {1 1 0 0 0 0}, with the second 1 moving to the right, getting a total of five possibilities. Moving the first pair one step to the right and repeating, would give me four possibilities. Iterating this, would give me an additional 3, 2, and 1 possibility. There would therefore be a total of 5 + 4 + 3 + 2 + 1 = 15 combinations of two boys and four girls, and vice versa.

A seemingly forgotten image from my thirty-year-earlier high school experience emerged: it was a pair of parentheses enclosing two numbers, one on top of the other, without a line indicating fraction,

$$\binom{1}{3}. \tag{1}$$

But I did not know how to take this image any further.

At this time, I returned to my desk and started up MathCAD, a mathematical modeling program that I had previously used extensively with high school students for data analysis in a physics course and for engaging them in mathematics projects. I had also used the program with fourth- and fifth-grade students as a medium that "talked back" to them about their mathematical activities. I now began using it as a medium that would talk back to me. My previous experience had given me some competence in the kind of statements and queries it would accept—and for those it would not, the program would explicitly tell me that I had expressed something in an inappropriate way.

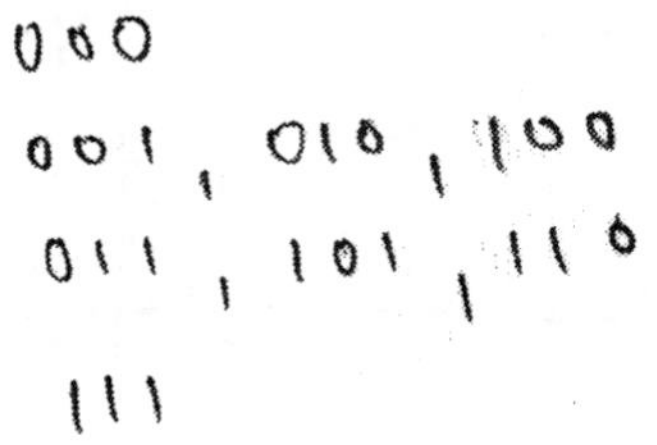

Figure I.4. I mentally ordered all possibilities of having boy-girl combinations in a three-child hospital, which yielded something of a bell-curve on its side.

I thought that I might find something similar to that last image, which I could subsequently use to get me further. But as I browsed through the manual of MathCAD, I could not find anything resembling the representation in equation (1). However, another image emerged from somewhere and took shape in my mind's eye,

$$\frac{1!}{1!\cdot(3-1)!},\qquad(2)$$

which I quickly typed into the computer. Without thinking about the keys or looking to the keyboard I held down the keys [⌘][=] (a command that tells the software to calculate the expression on the screen), which resulted in

$$\frac{1!}{1!\cdot(3-1)!}=0.5\qquad(3)$$

Without reflecting on what I was doing or the expressions that I manipulated, I first changed the numerator to 2, then to 3, each time pressing [⌘][=], which yielded

$$\frac{2!}{1!\cdot(3-1)!}=1 \text{ and } \frac{3!}{1!\cdot(3-1)!}=3.\qquad(4)$$

I then changed the 1s in the denominator of the second equation (4) into a 2, 3, and 0, yielding 3, 1, and 1 on the right-hand side. This sequence of 3, 3, 1, and 1 resurfaced the previous image of the 0s and 1s (figure I.4). From here, events unfolded rapidly. Again without explicitly reflecting on what I was doing, I defined x and y to cover the ranges from 0 to 15 and 0 to 45, respectively

$$x:=0..15 \quad y:=0..45$$
$$f(x)=\frac{15!}{x!\cdot(15-x)!} \quad g(y)=\frac{45!}{y!\cdot(45-y)!}\qquad(5)$$

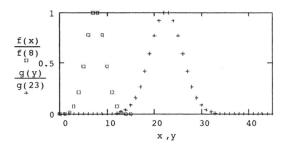

Figure I.5. Graphs of the two functions $f(x)$ and $g(y)$, representing the relative distributions of the number of (boy/girl) mixes in each hospital.

and then generated a box for making a graph. Putting the two functions $f(x)$ and $g(y)$ on the ordinate and x and y on the abscissa tells the software to plot each function: what the computer answered felt right (figure I.5).

Looking at the tail of each distribution, I went on to write an equation to represent the relevant area under each curve (i.e., above 9 and above 27).

$$\frac{\sum_{9} f(x)}{\sum_{x} f(x)} = \tag{6}$$

Without really thinking about what I was doing, I pressed [⌘][=] which did not yield a number but a different response (Figure I.6). Trouble! The talk back came in the form of a line, to which a box was attached that said, "Must be range." The line is like finger pointing to the number 9. The software seems to be telling me that instead of having this number I need to have a range of numbers at this particular place in my statement (at the bottom of the sigma). I re-

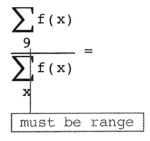

Figure I.6. The response was not in the form a number to the right of the equal sign, but something in the form of an error message.

spond to the "criticism" by making a change, replacing 9 by the variable z, and then telling the software that z should take all integer values from 9 to 15. Then I did an equivalent thing for the other variable (y) and function $g(y)$. I do not know why I replaced the 9 and x in the upper sum by z and defined z as going from 9 to 15; doing this simply emerged, all of a sudden. But the result of making this new statement was as follows.

$$z := 9..15 \quad w := 27..45$$

$$\frac{\sum_z f(z)}{\sum_x f(x)} = 0.304 \qquad \frac{\sum_w g(w)}{\sum_z g(z)} = 0.116 \tag{7}$$

This brought me back to the image of the town with its two hospitals and a sense that I had solved the puzzle. I envisioned a black-colored tail of the left curve that had a relative area of 0.304, which was larger than that of the right curve, 0.116 (figure I.7). I also thought that what I had done looked awfully complicated, like shooting flies with cannons. I had the strong sense that a mathematician would probably have a more elegant way of dealing with it, and I wondered how anyone could expect an ordinary teacher or student to deal with the task. Without further questioning myself, I remember having had a strong impression that this is too complicated for school mathematics and that what I had done was probably unacceptable in school mathematics.

The work on this puzzle shares a lot of similarities with students' everyday school activities, and allows us to work out some dimensions relevant to this book. When I started the puzzle, I had not thought in this way about hospitals or births or the relationship between the frequencies of births of boys and girls. I had never pursued the question about the likelihood of having three boys and

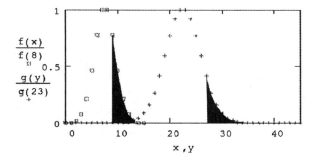

Figure I.7. Investigating the size of the tails shows that the smaller hospital contains a higher proportion of its area in the tail.

one girl (or vice versa) in a four-child family, though in casual conversation the topic of such distributions frequently comes up. Similarly, I had never calculated the likelihood of having seven boys out of seven children, such as in my brother-in-law's case. I am not certain that I would have been able to learn as much without the talk-back that the computer provided. I made statements or requested in its characteristic language and it provided me a response. Sometimes this response was about what I had "said," in which case I went about changing the statement I had made and requesting further feedback. In the process of my activity, both an aspect of the world and a language to articulate and talk about it emerged. That is, a new world and a new language coevolved not by pondering but by acting. Sometimes the language was inconsistent with my sense of what the world should be like or with how I expected the software to respond. I then had to change, evolve another way of articulating entities in and communicating with the software.

Such experiences, however, may actually provide a horizon, though not explicitly present, and may tune us to pursue something as an "interesting" problem. Working out its problem and searching for a solution opened up a new world, new ways of thinking not only about hospitals but also about chance more generally. I had never thought about probabilities in this way and therefore was treading new and unfamiliar terrain. But as with all travels in new and unfamiliar terrain, I could not know whether what was salient to me was actually relevant to the ultimate solution of the puzzle; at any part of my engagement, I could not know whether I had to step and take another look. The fact that something appeared compelling or that I ultimately arrived at a reasonable solution acceptable to mathematicians does not make my own trajectory more or less treacherous.

When we do not know a domain, we cannot know which past experiences are relevant, which language is appropriate for describing salient elements, which stance to take, and which aspects to make salient. Furthermore, when the problem is sketched in a text, we have no way of establishing its deep structure but have to go by what lies at its surface, at least to begin with. This becomes an orientation. In my own situation, I remembered vaguely having heard that the frequencies of male and female births change during war times—I was unable to assess if there was anything to these statements or whether they were merely unfounded folk wisdom. My second image was that of the two distributions, which are inherently mathematical and oriented me to a mathematical approach. In fact, my graduate student was doing a study on the mathematical knowledge of teachers, which was another framing condition that oriented me to take such an approach. Finally, the text is about probabilities, those of boy and girl births (about 50 percent each) and those of having days in which the frequency of boys was greater than 60 percent of the total number of births.

In my learning the (mathematical) language of modeling the hospital cases, a second issue is important. To succeed, of course, I needed to be willing and eager to engage with this puzzle the way I did. We cannot assume that all students automatically engage with the puzzles that they face at school on a daily basis. There is research that shows differences in engagement along the lines of gender, socioeconomic status, and culture.

As I continued, new images began to emerge over which I had no control. That is, my orientation became a horizon and new ideas emerged within it. But I had no control over the nature of these images. Nevertheless, they became resources for me to engage in further activity. For example, I did not know why I chose to look at a three-child hospital, or, for that matter, whether thinking about the puzzle in terms of a three-child hospital situation would be fruitful, especially given the fact that the very problem hinged on the question of whether the 60-percent-boy rate scaled up from the fifteen-child hospital to give the same number of days in the forty-five-child hospital. But once this image had emerged, I "played" with it, working out and ordering all combinations. It is clear that working out and ordering *all* combinations is something not easily done with the two hospitals because the number of possibilities involved are tremendous.

As part of the activity, a trajectory of activity *emerged,* leading to some solution. The particular language was *contingent,* the computer having provided certain cultural resources, much like an author of a novel draws on standard English and yet produces a language that is unmistakably hers, or much in the way a composer uses musical language and yet produces that everybody recognizes as his. Although Gustav Mahler and Richard Strauss both composed at the end of the nineteenth century, drawing on the same musical resources that were available to them at the time, they expressed themselves in highly personal language entirely their own.

The nature of the resources that emerge was out of my control. Thus, I do not know why and how the 0s and 1s emerged into my conscious thought. But once they were there, they became another resource, a language with which to continue. I never played out the entire six-children hospital situation, perhaps because of the large number of cases to consider. A new image emerged: equation (1), again beyond my control. I pursued it for a while, searching for something in the MathCAD manual that resembled it. Although I had forgotten how to use it, I remembered equation (1) to be part of a mathematician's language to deal with possibilities. This search did not yield any results, but, and perhaps associated with my original encounter of equation (1), another image surfaced: equation (2). It turned out that this new image could easily be implemented in the language of the mathematical modeling program that I had at hand.

When I began, I did not know what equation (2) "meant." It was a fragment of a language, the implications of using I did not know at the moment. With MathCAD, I had a medium at my hand that "talked back." I said something like equation (2) and the software responded with equation (3). I changed my expressions and received new responses such as equation (4). That is, in these situations I tried a forgotten language and received responses, from which I could gauge the effect using the language I had. In a sense, because there was no equivalent in MathCAD for equation (1), I could not receive feedback and therefore could not gauge the responses from my environment that this bit of language would evoke.

After I had made the two statements in equation (4) and received the responses from the environment, it was again an emergent thought to continue with the second of the two statements and to replace the 1s with 2, 3, and 0. The responses to the four statements as a whole, the set {1, 3, 3, 1} was identical to the set of counts that resulted when I iterated all possibilities of boy–girl combinations in a three-child hospital. The language I had evolved, its grammar and semantics, was appropriate for articulating and describing the "natural situation" that I attempted to model. From here on, things unfolded rapidly, an indication that I was on familiar terrain. I could not explain *why* I replaced the 1s in equation (4) with an x and why I chose to use a function notation $f(x)$. But I already had made an association between figures I.3 and I.4, a "continuous" distribution histogram and a histogram; equation (4) gave me the histogram in figure I.4, so the function would give me a distribution for any hospital. The distribution of days in the two hospitals in question would then be modeled by the two functions in equation (5).

Until now, I have not addressed why I would write the definition of x (or any other variable) in the form "$x := 0 \, . . \, 15$." I wrote this definition down without reflecting in the same way I might say to my neighbor, "What a nice day!" when there is blue sky and sunshine. Yet it allowed x to take integer values, so that all x's would form the set {0, 1 . . . 15}. The values of x would be integers; it did not vary continuously or in steps of 0.1, 0.01, or any other step value. Although I did not think, "I have to use integer values," my statement was such as to select integer values only. I did not perceive any inconsistencies when the two distributions (figure I.4) appeared on the monitor. In my final steps, there was one moment where the results of making an inappropriate statement became salient. After typing equation (6) and receiving a response that I knew to be an error message, although I was not thinking, "This is an error message," I made some more rapid changes in my expression. Although this appears "natural," I could not know at that point whether these changes would give me a reasonable result. That they did should not lead us to take a rationalist approach to the emergence and reification of language. Both language and world emerged as a consequence of my actions that did not yet know what the world looks like and whether the language would be an appropriate way of dealing with it.

MathCAD responded with a statement of its own, "Must be range," and a line that linked the statement to the number "9." When I wrote my notes fixing the account provided here, I did not recall having pondered the question, "What does the statement, 'must be range' mean?" My changing the "9" to a "z" was as quick as my neighbor's response to my earlier statement about the nice day,

"But a little on the cool side." Then I added the statement "z:= 9 . . 15"; it allowed the upper statement to calculate a sum—counting all days when the number of boys was greater or equal to nine.

Although there was an error message, a more detailed analysis of this moment reveals a particular logic in equation (6). In the lower sum, the x could be read as covering the entire range of its definition, from the lowest to the largest value. Read in this way, my statement for the upper sum could then be glossed as "add up all $f(x)$ for which x is 9 to the largest value." However, the moment I wrote "9," it did not appear "wrong," inconsistent with the grammar of the language I was using at the moment. It was through the feedback that I noticed that I had made an inappropriate statement. The program told me—though not in the form of a "correction" that many language teachers would choose—that I had made a statement that did not make sense to it in this context. (In contrast to human beings, computer programs are very inflexible when it comes to "understanding" statements and actions that do not exactly correspond to what the programs expect.)

In this situation, the solution as process and product were contingent results of my actions. In the previous example of trying to prune my trees and bushes, I initially had abandoned the activity, unable to engage with the issues and thereby unable to evolve a language to interact with the world. In the present example, MathCAD provided an interface that allowed interaction to occur, and, through feedback, for me to develop a new stance and attitude to the world. In this, MathCAD was both a material and a sociocultural tool—and despite its structure, there were ways of talking to it that were not permissible in its world.

I earlier quoted the philosopher Richard Rorty saying that the world does not tell us what language to speak. Here, MathCAD is also a world, but a very special one. It is a cultural artifact that is the result of the entire human culture preceding it. In its structure, we have cultural structures, so that I interacted with my culture rather than with nature in its raw state. MathCAD talked back because it is the product of human culture, and I could talk to it, because I am the product of the same culture.

In this situation, language appeared in two ways. First, it was the medium *in* and *with* which I explored. In this medium, I tried out statements the repercussions of which I did or could not know prior to trying them out and seeing what the responses from the relevant part of the setting (MathCAD) would be. I made different statements, such as in equations (2)–(4), but only pursued the implications of one of them rather than those made possible by the others. Second, the language I explored was *about* something else, about hospitals and the frequency of days when more than 60 percent of the children born were boys. But the two ways in which language appeared cannot be separated. Navigating the world of the distribution is inextricably bound up with the language of distribution, so that navigating the world has become indistinguishable from knowing language more generally.

TOWARD A DIFFERENT VIEW OF LANGUAGE IN SCIENCE

In the previous sections, I articulated a view of language that differs from the way science educators generally think about it. Knowing language, in this view, is no longer distinct from knowing one's way around a particular section of the world. It is a nonrepresentational view of language, which precedes its representational use in written circumstances. I drew on personal examples from my everyday world, because my readers can associate with these and their own similar experiences.

In this book, I elaborate this approach to look at school science, which I understand as an attempt to get students to talk and write particular languages in particular ways. My approach dispenses with language as a third thing that intervenes between the individual subject and the world it knows in pragmatic and theoretical terms. This means that once we have learned new ways of articulating a world and talking about it, we also have learned to handle this world more easily. This, then, allows us to judge as inappropriate our previous ways of articulating things from their tacit backgrounds and talking about them. Simultaneously, I treat language as something that is both heterogeneous and continuously undergoing change. There are many ways in which language is deployed, and none can be reduced to theoretical propositions without destroying what people mean with and through them.

> There are many interim stages between interpretation which is quite enveloped in heedful understanding and the extreme opposite case of a theoretical statement about objectively present things: statements about events in the surrounding world, descriptions of what is at hand, "reports on situations," noting and ascertaining a "factual situation," describing a state of affairs, telling about what has happened. These "sentences" cannot be reduced to theoretical propositional statements without essentially distorting their meaning. (Heidegger 1977, 148)

In the view presented here, language is not a medium for expression (of mental content) or representation. In taking this approach, we set aside the idea that both individual self and its material surroundings have intrinsic natures, which can be described and known in some absolute sense. Because language and the situations in which we encounter it always already exist in patterned ways when we come to this world, they are resources in and to our actions. There is therefore a dialectic relation between individual talk and collective language, individual ideas and collective, social representations. The relations are dialectic because I concretely realize an utterance, use language *in order to* orient myself and do something, but what a particular language element can do and what it implies always already exist in a generalized way, as ways of orienting and doing things at a collective level. The purpose of this book is to articulate this perspective in its relevance to the evolution of new ways of talking in science classrooms more broadly, though all of the examples used come from my own teaching and research experience in physics.

The examples used in this book derive from three physics courses that I had either taught or centrally participated in making possible. These include a split sixth- and seventh-grade unit on the physics of simple machines in which students spent large chunks of time designing and prototyping machines and presenting them in whole-class meetings to their peers, who functioned as a critical audience. I also taught a twelfth-grade qualitative physics course in a private high school, which included the use of a computer-based Newtonian microworld as an important component. Finally, together with my colleague Reinders Duit and two of his doctoral students (Michael Komorek and Jens Wilbers), I planned a unit on chaotic system that provided extensive opportunities for academically streamed tenth-grade students to explore and make sense in small-group explorations; I also had served as observer, cameraman, and person of first contact to one student group.

In chapter 1, I show how language is part of a more general, "emotional" gesture by means of which students superpose a world according to humans onto a given world, or, in other words, I show how language and the corresponding world coevolve. By means of language, hand gestures, and body positions, students take a particular orientation or stance, which frames what and how they learn. Importantly, taking a stance is consistent with the observation that new descriptive languages are speaker centered or, as some describe it, "anthropomorphic." I describe how observation sentences emerge first from students' actions in science classrooms and how these sentences make possible new, more general "observation categoricals." Because language is the medium for talking and the medium that is being changed by talk, "talking science" may no longer be a fortunate expression—unless we abandon the position that the term *science* denotes what scientists do or what we can find in textbooks. My notion of articulating a world intends to blur the boundary of knowing language and knowing the world more generally, allowing me to reserve "talking science" to those situations where talk bears a family resemblance with the language and registers of formal science.

Once we accept the supposition that there is no difference between knowing a language and knowing our way around the world generally, there are consequences for how we understand language in classroom science. For example, new linguistic and worldly elements emerge in the course of individual courses of action (as my earlier hospital example shows) and, more so, in collective activity. In chapter 2, I describe how, by using activity structures to combine the opportunities of an interactive software program and new conversational structures (student–student talk rather than lectures), I had hoped to support a variety of student actions on scientific inscriptions, conversations about them and their meaning, and the development of competence in canonical forms of talking science. During free explorations of and in the computer-based microworld, students' learning could be described as a coevolution of world and language. The possibility for the changes in both arose from the ontological ambiguity of objects and events that allowed for their *interpretive flexibility*. Over time, students' talk not only *converged* so that they shared a descriptive language in their groups, but this talk also *converged* with accepted ways of talking about Newtonian microworlds; thus, accepted ways of talking science *emerged* from the inconclusive muddle of earlier forms. The changes in the students' science talk were achieved collaboratively and cumulatively through minute adjustments of their descriptions. Much group work had to be expended in order to stabilize the emerging, new forms of talking science. The physical presence of the computer-based microworld provided a situation that allowed students to take new orientations in a collective manner; in this way, some of their work consisted of finding common orientations, common ways of seeing and talking. Working together allowed them to come to understand one another not by means of acts of intellectual interpretation but by giving themselves to the same spectacle, something that resembles an unconscious recognition that precedes all definition and intellectual elaboration of sense. Their communication was not just grounded in common experience, but the latter was also the precondition for communication: Common experience and communication form a dialectical unit and they coemerge. Gestures that rendered objects or events and the pointing to or touching of objects facilitated the evolution of a shared orientation, and therefore of common experience and intercommunication.

Drawing on a second case study from a different classroom, I articulate in chapter 3 the contingent emergence of world and language. Central to this case is the observation that the world does not tell us how to articulate the world in our actions and tells us even less which language to choose. That is, whatever we perceive as structure is interpretively flexible. But once we view a circular object as a ball and a particular figure as a basket, the possibility emerges that we conceive of something like "reverse gravity" in the same way that the study of a pendulum more likely provides the conditions for "Foucault's pendulum" to become an explanation than if the same situation were framed as a "swing." Chapters 2 and 3 provide examples of how observational and theoretical languages emerge in contingent ways from student activities. Although emergence is a contingent process, it does not have an unlimited degree of freedom. Other events in the classroom, the language emerging from the actions of other student groups, and the language that a teacher articulates, all provide resources and orientations and therefore constraints on the evolution of language within a particular group.

In the subsequent two chapters, I describe the possibilities and constraints associated with the existence of other groups and teacher as additional resources for the evolution of a new language in activity. In chapter 4, I describe aspects of this interaction between local forms of language and the global developments within a class, drawing on exemplary episodes and interviews from the tenth-grade unit on chaos theory. At the heart of chapter 5 are opportunities that investigations of Newtonian microworlds provide to a teacher. By engaging my students in conversations, I model taking an orientation and thereby mediate students' ways of seeing and talking. This chapter shows how I used the context of Interactive Physics to identify students' ways of seeing and talking science. I then implemented a series of strategies to make forces "visible" to students. The conclusion focuses on Interactive Physics as a tool that does not embed meaning as such but becomes an integral part of a situation in which particular orientations, including perceptions, gestures, and talks, are especially fruitful and coherent. I focus on the potential of the microworld to serve as a mediational tool during teacher–student interactions that permits a teacher to elicit and evaluate student understanding, the teacher's role during the activity, and the relationship between assessment and intervention in support of changes in students' science talk toward more canonical forms.

In the consideration of whether a group of people would adopt a new language or new language elements, two kinds of arguments are often provided as reasons why contributions from insiders and outside experts may or may not be readily adopted. Concerning outside experts, if their language is too different from that of the group, the latter may not be able integrate the language into its own repertoires. At the same time, the status of expertise or the potential benefits of mastering the language may be sufficient incentive for adopting new ways of talking—for example, many educators subscribing to chaos theory have very little understanding of the mathematics of complex systems. Finally, new language that emerges within a group more likely bears family resemblances with existing language so that one could assume its uptake to occur more easily and rapidly. In chapter 6, I investigate an earlier hypothesis that teacher-introduced theoretical language is less likely to be taken up than student-introduced theoretical language. I draw on an extensive ethnographic study in a split sixth- and seventh-grade classroom where I taught a unit on simple machines.

Chapter 7 cuts across all previous chapters, showing how orientation to some artifact, group size, and physical configuration of people and artifacts changes the structure and content of conversations in science classrooms. In this chapter, I draw again on the study in the split sixth- and seventh-grade unit on simple machines. Four activity structures were used, which differed in terms of the social configuration (whole class, small group) and the origin of the central, activity-organizing artifact (teacher designed, student designed). The study describes how different artifacts, social configurations, and physical arrangements led to different interactional spaces, participant roles, and levels of participation in classroom conversations and, concomitantly, to different discursive forms and content. The artifacts had important functions in maintaining and sequencing conversations. Depending on the situation and the role of participants, artifacts served as resources for students' sense making. Each of the different activity structures supported different dimensions of participating in conversations.

1

Taking Position and Orienting in the World

The languages we use are not something that is somehow stored somewhere in our minds, used as a medium to get our ideas (sometimes assumed to exist independent of language) outside ourselves and to make them thereby available to others. We have to abandon this idea that language is a tool and medium of expression. In the everyday world, we neither represent the world in our mind nor use language to represent it to others. We always already find ourselves in a world, orienting toward some project. The languages we use are part of orienting ourselves, taking a position, and moving the situation along by transforming it through our verbal and material actions. The language we use is therefore always relative to some situation, always tied to a particular way of being and orienting in the world. Knowing a language and knowing one's way around the world are indistinguishable. This has immediate consequences: words in and by themselves are not meaningful. Anyone who has played the game of "word destruction" knows that words do not have meaning. To play the game, one picks any word and says it over and over again. It will not be long until the word has emptied itself of all sense, that is, all of the connections that it might have with other words and situations.

Language, therefore, has to be considered as an integral part of a situation. In its capacity to be part of taking up a position in and toward the world, language closely interfaces with gestures, particularly those that we produce unconsciously as part of communicating. In fact, an utterance itself is a gesture, an act in speech, being part of the meaningful whole that is communication in situation (Merleau-Ponty 1945). To understand the utterances of others, it is self-evident that I have to know the words and grammar. But this does not mean that the words create within me associated representations so that the speaker's original representations are reconstructed in my, the hearer's, mind. We do not primarily communicate with representations or ideas but with other human beings, their particular ways of being, and the worlds to which they are oriented. Rather, we use words in the same way we use gestures, to orient one another to and in the present situation. That is, we live in a world into which utterances are already inscribed; the situations we live every day and the words we use there make an integral part. It is for this reason that in everyday conversation, we do not have to expend any effort to "understand," for we are already in a world that in its entirety constitutes the background to our sense-making actions. As background, it is the very thing that allows us to experience a thing as something meaningful. The moment we hear another's utterances (or see her bodily gestures and orientations), our own mode of being, our orientation to the world, is modulated by an intention that we recognize as present in the situation.

When we do not know a domain, that is, when we tread unfamiliar terrain as I had done in the pruning and hospital examples of the introduction, we have to structure the setting and concurrently develop a language that allows us to articulate (tell) the structure for coparticipants during situated activity. Our utterances (verbal gestures) realize a particular structuring of the present experience, a modulation of our way of being in the situation. This language subsequently may be used to talk *about* the situation. The telling allows us to take an initial stance, to take a position in the world and orient within it. It constitutes a form of exploration. As I will show in this chapter, neither talking nor even telling is a privileged mode in the early parts of exploration, when the world, body position, and hand gestures are equally part of the efforts of seeking an orientation. The privileged status of language in communication, especially its character of *about-ness*, develops only subsequent to exploratory phases during which we constitute the world and our articulations of it.

Such a theoretical position on language has implications for the way we think about meaning. Frequently, scholars talk about "the meaning of words" or about students who "make meaning" of words and sentences that they encounter in science classes. However, when language is part of an orientation to and integral part of a world, words in themselves cannot "have" meaning, nor can they receive meaning through whatever intellectual activity on the part of the students. Rather, meaning has to be thought of as immanent in our living bodies, as extending over the entire sensible world—as my examples in the introduction from the conversations between passengers and stewardesses showed.

In everyday activity, particularly in explorations of unfamiliar terrain, utterances are part of more general attempts to take up a position in the world. Utterances and therefore language constitute a form of finding and defining one's orientation with respect to the things that we come to recognize as surrounding us. These things appear to us in ways that depend on our orientation. From this theoretical position it therefore does not come as a surprise that students—as people more generally—use person-centered descriptions of the objects that they first encounter. A person-centered perspective imbues objects with the place of another, taking a stance similar to my own, in the world that encompasses the objects in the situation, including my own body. Some research associates so-called anthropomorphic descriptions with the reasoning of naive physicists and children. But I show that because it is more associated with the naturally unre-flective, everyday ways of being in the world, it may be a good starting point for exploring terrain that we do not yet know. Even competent scientists (including Nobel laureates) talk in anthropomorphic ways such that they take the perspec-tive of the system that is the topic of their talk (Fox-Keller 1983). Gestures are an integral part of taking and making one's position available to others. This chapter therefore associates language and gestures. In a subsequent chapter (chapter 7), I will also consider body position and orientation with respect to the setting as a whole and discuss how this mediates the ways in which conversation participants use language.

BACKGROUND: PHYSICS OF MOTION

The episodes on which I draw in this book come from three science classrooms: sixth- and seventh-grade students studying simple machines, tenth-grade stu-dents learning about chaotic systems, and twelfth-grade students exploring mo-tion phenomena. For better understanding the background situations, descrip-tions of the different courses are provided before substantive aspects of the lan-guage in the respective classrooms are analyzed. In this chapter, readers encoun-ter some of the twelfth and sixth/seventh graders that I had taught. Here I begin with a description of the twelfth-grade, qualitative physics course.

The course was organized to reflect the findings of science studies research, which had attributed a social function to inscriptions—representations other than text, including photographs, naturalistic drawings, diagrams, tables, graphs, and formulas. In the early 1990s, while teaching physics and heading a science de-partment in a private school, I had come to realize that inscriptions could be conversational artifacts and social objects that enable learning and facilitate in-teractions in the classroom community. Shoptalk over and about inscriptions (functions, equations, tables, concept maps, drawings) played a central role in my classroom organization. By changing their shoptalk to adapt it better to their experiences (which included interactions with me, the teacher), students trans-formed this talk for dealing with new phenomena: This transformation of a (dis-cursive) practice in the course of activity is synonymous with learning. By fore-grounding the social function of inscriptions, my teaching accounted for (a) the situated, local, and distributed nature of knowing; (b) the recognition that tools and computational media in important ways support, extend, and reorganize knowing and learning; and (c) the potential of computational media to radically and dramatically reshape the landscape of individual and social action by changing basic patterns of communication and knowledge.

The course I taught was based on the assumption that learning means to achieve a certain level of competence in talking physics. Thus, I planned many activities that got students to use physics language with one another. These activities included (a) open investigations of motion phenomena chosen by students according to their own interests, (b) explorations of phenomena in a computer-based microworld (Interactive Physics), and (c) collaborative concept mapping with the main concept labels of a unit. Students were asked to read relevant chapters in one of the available textbooks on their own and to complete six word problems per week. The open investigations of natural phenomena constituted the core of the curriculum, the microworld activities occurred once every other week, and the collaborative concept mapping took place once a month. Microworld activities and concept mapping were contexts that allowed students to focus more on the verbal aspects of the physics of motion than on the mechanical aspects of implementing their practical research.

Interactive Physics is a computer-based Newtonian microworld in which users conduct experiments related to motion (with or without friction, pendulums, spring oscillators, or collisions). The microworld allows different representations of observable entities (measurable quantities). For example, force, velocity, or acceleration can be represented by means of instruments such as strip chart recorders and digital and analog meters. I planned the computer activities because Interactive Physics superposes arrows (vectors) representing these quantities and the objects, which look like drawings of things in the natural world (e.g., figure 1.1). This superposition creates hybrid objects bridging phenomenal and conceptual worlds. Students therefore have concurrent access to phenomenal and conceptual representations, which they do not have with real-world experiments. By alternating between real-world and computer activities, I hoped to assist students in developing a stable language of and about motion phenomena independent of particular situations (labs, concept mapping, and microworld).

All student activities with Interactive Physics included, at a minimum, one circular object (figure 1.1). A force (full arrow) could be attached to this object by highlighting and moving it with the mouse. The object's velocity was always displayed as a vector (an arrow that has magnitude [length] and direction) and students could modify its initial value by highlighting the object, grabbing the tip of the vector, and manipulating its magnitude and direction. Students were instructed to find out more about the microworld, especially the meaning of the arrows, that is, the vectors representing force and velocity. Although students concurrently conducted real-world experiments on motion in which they analyzed distance–time, velocity–time, and acceleration–time graphs, they were not

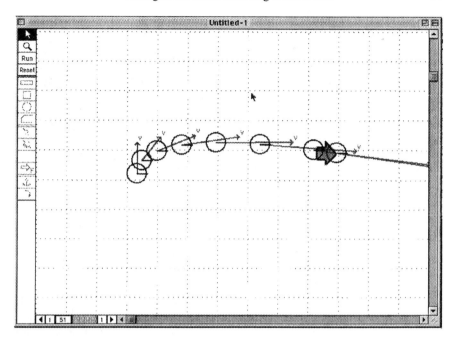

Figure 1.1. Interactive Physics provides an interface that layers phenomenal objects, such as "balls," and conceptual objects, such as velocity and force vectors (arrows). The object in the particular task was to find out how the different arrows affect the motion of the circular object.

told the scientific names of the arrows. In part, I did this because as a teacher who believed in inquiry-based learning, I wanted to know whether students would eventually use these terms without being instructed to do so. As shown in chapter 2, this can lead to a situation in which students use many different names to denote the same two arrows. I therefore enclose the words *velocity* and *force* with French quotation marks (i.e., «velocity» and «force») when I refer to the arrows as material objects independent of the terms students used to denote them.

Some of the prepared activities displayed nothing more than the circular object (including its velocity) and a force. A constant force that continuously acts on an object will cause it to change its velocity—unless there is another force like friction compensating for it, which is not the case in the modeling activities featured here. In figure 1.1, for example, the force points from left to right and a little downward. As a consequence, the velocity of the object, which initially pointed straight up not only becomes longer (increases in speed) but also points

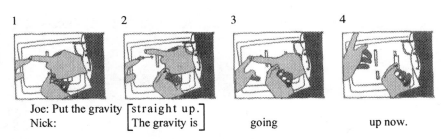

Joe: Put the gravity ⎡straight up.⎤
Nick: ⎣The gravity is⎦   going   up now.

Figure 1.2. Using their hands as part of communication, the students orient themselves and one another to salient elements. (For transcription conventions, see the appendix.)

increasingly in the direction of the force (changes in direction) until velocity and force are nearly aligned in the last freeze frame.

Other activities required students to manipulate the arrows (force and velocity) to hit a small rectangle and knock it off its pedestal. After setting «force» and «initial velocity», students could run the simulation (experiment). A tracking feature froze the motion as if the moving object had been photographed multiple times on the same plate. While a simulation was running, the cursor took the form of a stop sign, and a simple mouse click would stop the motion. The replay feature allowed the inspection of individual states in the motion of the sphere.

The episodes used in this book come from four groups that I videotaped repeatedly over the course of six weeks working with Interactive Physics to complete a variety of tasks I had designed as part of the physics course. The participating students were in many ways representative of the students I had taught in various public and private schools throughout my career as a high school teacher. These students were not typical science students and most did not enroll in science or a science-related field at the university level. They distinguished themselves from students in the public school only in the fact that most of them were from well-to-do families with sufficient financial resources to afford the fees charged by the institution. The students worked together rather well and, although they did not know each other initially, they stayed together in their groups for the entire school year.

PICKING OUT ENTITIES (SALIENCE, GESTURE, MOTION)

A crucial element in the evolution of a common language about scientific phenomena is a shared orientation toward some aspect of the world, that is, the situation currently of interest. My longtime experience as both a teacher and a researcher shows that we cannot assume that students automatically see the same entities as each other, even when the situation they are looking at is rather simple, as with the present events on the computer screen (see chapter 2). The greatest challenge for students is to structure the perceptual field and come to some agreement that their respective perceptual structuring can be taken as the same, for the practical purpose of their collective work. In this situation, point- ing to and gesturing provide important resources to align a coparticipant to something one has identified, even if a descriptive language for navigating the world does not yet exist. Pointing to and gesturing are crucial to enhancing sali- ence, picking out and communicating entities from the scene to which copartici- pants are oriented. Therefore, it is not surprising to see students use gestures as a central feature of their communication, especially in the early stages of their investigations. In this, the episode in figure 1.2 is typical, showing the hands of three students in front of the screen, each taking its part in the conversation, even if the third person did not talk here. (For the transcription conventions used in this books see the appendix.) Joe (the hand to the right) gesturally enacts "straight up" (frames 1 and 2). The latter part of his (gestural and verbal) propo- sition is overlaid by Nick's (the hand to the left) contribution (as the other per- son is vying for a speaking turn), which also consists of verbal and gestural con- tributions. Giving up his turn, Joe stopped talking and then removed his index finger (frames 3 and 4), which was already in position for a subsequent proposi- tion. Here, we can see turn taking enacted not only in the verbal modality (a much studied phenomenon in the domain of conversation analysis) but also in the gestural modality.

Gestures are, at this stage of learning science, not just ancillary and provid- ing redundant information as some claim (e.g., Crowder 1996), but are central to successful communication, and, therefore, to the emergence of understanding. Thoughts for the speaking subject are not a form of representation; the subject does not explicitly posit objects and relations. "The orator does not think before talking, not even when he is talking; his utterances are his thoughts" (Merleau- Ponty 1945, 209, my translation). That is, particularly in this situation where students are unfamiliar with the nature of the objects and a language that de- scribes it, the working together of the three modes of communication discussed here (perceptual entities, words, and gestures) is crucial. For example, in the following episode (figure 1.3), Glen asked his partner Ryan to modify the ex- periment in a particular way. Without the perceptual and gestural resources available in the situation, Ryan would have been hard pressed to know what Glen was talking about. However, when the three modes of communication are taken together, we can understand his communication as a request to attach «force» (which Ryan currently held by means of the cursor) and orient it in ver- tical direction upward and then turn «velocity» so that it was also oriented up- ward.

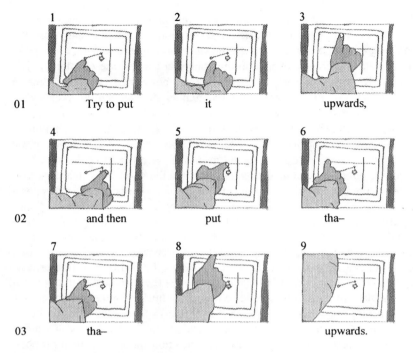

Figure 1.3. Using their hands as part of communication, the students orient themselves and one another to salient elements.

In the first instance, Glen moved his index finger from touching the ball upward and parallel to the screen (frames 1–3). Although Glen had not specified in this episode what "it" is that was to be directed upward, the situation was made less ambiguous to a certain extent. «Force» had been the object that the conversation was about and Ryan currently held it with the cursor—there was a historical precedent of talk about an entity that was held by Ryan and therefore salient in an additional way. Glen began the second part of his utterance with "and then" (line 02, frame 4), which suggested a second request, this one concerning the second object clearly identified here by the gesture. Although Glen had difficulties expressing himself in words, his gesture (line 02, frames 4–6) enacted what one has to do with the cursor to move «velocity» into an upward position: his index finger touched the tip of the arrow (frame 4), the hand then turned until the index finger pointed upward (frames 5–6). Here, the gesture simulated an action that was not communicated in words: the hand "rotates" «velocity» whereas the utterance simply suggested to "put . . . upward." Finally, in line 03, the entire hand moved upward with the index finger continuing to point into the same direction. Because the index finger already showed the direction in which «velocity» was to be turned, line 03 can then be seen as a gesture that projected what would happen if the experiment is set up the way lines 01 and 02 suggested: the circular object would move vertically upward.

In this situation, the words were insufficient to communicate on their own. Glen had said, "Try to put it upwards, and then put tha–, tha– upwards." Without further information, we do not know what was to be put upward or what the referent of "upwards" was. It would be difficult to understand even with visual access to the scene. There still existed multiple possibilities for which entity the talk was about and what form of the "putting upward" action should take. However, together with deictic (pointing) and iconic gestures, the three communicative modalities (perceptual structures, gestures, and words) taken together provided these students with important resources for orienting to the situation, making entities salient, and arriving at a common orientation to situation and entities. All of these orientations are required in bootstrapping the process that leads them to a common language.

There was a further interesting aspect in this episode relating verbal and gestural modes of communication. Research shows that during learning phases, there is a delay between gestures and corresponding words such that the latter precede the former (Roth 2003). Here, Glen suggested to "put [«velocity»] upwards." Although there are suggestions that the agreement between verb and gesture has to be analyzed (McNeill 1992), "put" in itself did not specify what to do (with the arrow). Rather, viewing the episode on video gives the impression that the utterance "upwards" was delayed in forthcoming. I therefore view the gesture, intimating a turning of «velocity» in the upward position, as being completed considerably before the utterance that provides a meaningful description of the action.

When students do not have a common language for picking out entities or when it is not certain they are attending the same entities, pointing (deictic reference in the gestural modality) becomes a central resource in coordinating the three modalities. This is exemplified in the next episode (figure 1.4) that represented one exchange between the two students Joe and Mike. A third student, Bryan, had the mouse with which the on-screen entities are modified. Joe suggested that Bryan had to click on the tip of the "big arrow" (achieved by grabbing the "handle" which allows an arrow to be changed in magnitude and direction) to change "its direction." But from Joe's suggestion it was not clear exactly what he wanted to be done. The longer «velocity» arrow can be changed (in magnitude and direction) by "grabbing" the black dot at its tip. The shorter but wider «force» can be changed in magnitude and direction by grabbing and moving the black dot at either end. Furthermore, the utterance "its direction" may actually have referred to the direction of the circular object's motion, which can be changed by changing either arrow. Mike's response revealed to his peers what he had heard Joe saying and thereby also revealed his understanding to us.

01 Joe: If you wanna change its direction, click on
              the tip of the big arrow.

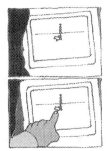

02 Mike: No, if you want to change the direction, you
              click here.

Figure 1.4. Using their hands as part of communication, the students orient themselves and one another to salient elements.

Mike responded that, to change the direction, Bryan had to click "here," while he simultaneously touched the screen at the back end of «force». This pointing (deictic) gesture constituted «force» as the signifying figure that was to be salient against a more diffuse ground—more specifically, the black dot at the end of «force». He therefore indicated that a change in the direction of «force» is accomplished by manipulating the arrow with the handle salient as a black dot. Mike did not just point out a particular spot. Rather, the black dot motivated the utterance "here" and the pointing gesture as much as the verbal and gestural deixis motivated the perceptual salience of the black dot. In essence, then, Mike heard Joe talk about «force» and, in providing a different description of the action for changing the direction, both corrected Joe and displayed what he understood the "big" arrow to be by unambiguously pointing to one of the two arrows («force»). This episode is therefore an example how people deal with the ambiguity of deixis in praxis. Given that there were two arrows in this situation, there was a potential for alternate entities being pointed to (referents). Mike therefore engaged in a sort of conversational repair, because it was not clear which object was being referred to and where the action was to take place.

As we will see in the next chapter, there was considerable variation in the words and phrases for the different elements in the microworld, and in understanding how these elements (object, arrows) interact. In this group, students referred to the outline arrow («force») using twelve different terms (little arrow, big arrow, time-set, time, direction, time-and-direction, velocity, redirection, gravity, force, reverse-gravity, gravity). Similarly, they referred to the other arrow in eleven different ways (little arrow, big arrow, initial speed, velocity, force, effort, strength, speed, direction, speed-and-direction, velocity). In this seeming chaos, deictic and iconic gestures were crucial for establishing a common orientation, which in turn established a common ground for finding appropriate descriptions and, ultimately, for arriving at a shared theoretical discourse. Thus, in the following episode (figure 1.5), Glen's gestures already provided

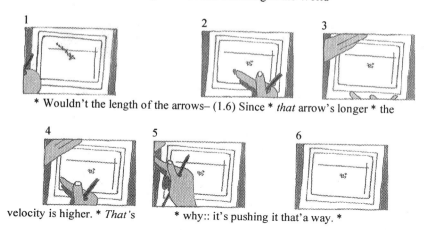

* Wouldn't the length of the arrows– (1.6) Since * *that* arrow's longer * the

velocity is higher. * *That's*   * why:: it's pushing it that'a way. *

Figure 1.5. The students orient themselves and one another to elements in the situation, which thereby become salient for everybody present.

descriptions and explanations that were more appropriate than his verbal descriptions. Here then, his gestures considerably preceded his verbal representation of Newtonian physics. In this situation, gestural (and verbal) deixis was crucial in coordinating utterances, gestures, and the phenomena in the microworld. Let us take a closer look at the episode.

In this episode, the indexical term "that" appeared three times. An analysis of the situation as a whole reveals that each time not only the referent but also the function was different. In the first instance, "that" had a deictic function designating a particular arrow standing in opposition to the speaker (distal use). Coinciding with the utterance, the right hand that had moved to the right, came to a sudden stop. As can be seen from the second frame, the fingers of the right hand stood parallel to the outline arrow («force»). This finger position, the noticeable (abrupt) stop of motion, and the coincident utterance "*that* arrow" led to a convergent interpretation that the referent of the right hand is the force arrow («force»). The listener could draw further confirmation for this interpretation from the causal connection between "that arrow" and the force arrow because it was the one that they had previously manipulated, whereas the other arrow had changed only as a function of their action.

In the second instance, "that" introduced the causal consequence ("*that's* why") of the hand arrangement he had set up and described in the previous part of the utterance; "that" falls at the beginning of gestural trajectory which iconically re-represents the earlier visible trajectory (frame 1). Finally, in the third instance, "that" was linked to "way," the immediately preceding trajectory ("way") enacted by the gesture. In vernacular, "that'a way" most frequently expresses a specific direction. Here, however, when read against the ground of the earlier curvilinear motion of the object and the corresponding positioning of the arrows, "that'a way" together with the curved motion of the hand (frames 3–5) highlighted not only the existence of the trajectory but in particular its curvilinear shape.

The utterance "it" was used twice, but gesture and perceptual ground helped disambiguate the two referents ("it's pushing it"). The utterance occurred while the right hand followed the left, fingers pointing to the left; taken together with "it's pushing it," the right can be understood as literally pushing the left hand (frames 3–6). Here, the first use had as referent the hand and arrow that was pushing (enacted by the hand) and the second occurrence had as referent something that was pushed—which, in this case, could have been the second arrow and left hand, or the object.

At the time of this episode, Glen (like his two peers) did not yet describe the arrows in scientific terms, that is, as force and velocity. He used the appropriate scientific (verbal) language only two weeks later during the subsequent lesson with the microworld. However, in the present episode, his hand gestures correctly articulated and described the relationship between the concepts of velocity (left hand) and force (right hand) in the way that the arrows represented them. He characterized the action of the outline arrow as "pushing," which is a vernacular form of describing forces (often used by teachers during the first teaching of the force concept). Finally, he associated the longer pushing arrow with a resulting higher velocity. Here, the referent of "velocity" was not completely clear and two readings are possible. Because the utterance coincided with the positioning of the left hand, "velocity" can be heard as the referent to the left hand: therefore, the longer force (right) arrow pushed more and therefore led to a longer velocity (left) arrow. But the fragment "Since *that* arrow's longer the velocity is higher" can also be heard such that the longer right arrow was equivalent to a higher velocity, in which case "velocity" would have found its equivalent in the right arrow (incorrectly so from a scientific perspective). However, the nature of the referent for each of the two hands was made less ambiguous by their position in space in the course of the motion. The fingers of the right hand kept a constant direction just like «force», whereas the left hand changed direction, though less rapid so, in the way the single-line arrow did previously. Thus, Glen's gestural description and explanation of the events was scientifically correct long before he gave his first verbal explanation of the events.

FIRST EMERGENCE OF SCIENCE TALK

Finding an orientation to and in the world, articulating the present setting in physical activity, and using words to name what has been articulated are the foundations of a mature scientific language (Quine 1995). When a formal and consistent language to describe experience does not yet exist, perceptions, body movements, and first utterances together articulate a sensible world in its material articulations. This articulation is a double process in that only what we already know as distinct entity (e.g., what has been perceptually articulated) can also be named and thereby verbally articulated (Heidegger 1977). The intelligibility of the world, as a network of material articulations, is also articulated in words. Here, intelligibility precedes words that have a quality of being about the world to which we already relate (Buber 1970); words therefore always accrue to existing significations. Meaning, rather than being provided with signification, already exists as a background that accepts new words and language. It is by taking up a position and by acting in the world that it becomes articulated, allowing significations to be expressed in observation sentences and observation categoricals, the building stones of theoretical (scientific) language *about* the present situation in particular and the world in general.

Observation Sentences

Students' first viable observation sentences are highly context sensitive in the sense that interlocutors have access to the setting as a whole, which allows them to orient to all of its aspects. Speakers make available their positions and the salient things that they are oriented to in a variety of ways, including their utterances, gestures, and body positions. Attending to the speaker's orientation, gestures, and utterances, and the objects that the former make salient, allows listeners to take a stance corresponding to that of the speaker, which is coextensive with understanding what is being communicated. The next episode (figure 1.6) exemplifies the nature of students' observation sentences.

At this point, in their exploration of the Newtonian microworld embodied by Interactive Physics, different students still used the same words to denote different entities. In this episode, Glen uttered, "The little arrow always stays straight, whenever we get it– Like when we are doing it, it goes in that straight direction." While he was speaking, his right hand, holding a pencil, moved from left to right twice. When taken together, perceptual ground, gesture and pen, and talk limited the interpretive flexibility of the communicative act. Any one of these communicative resources on its own would leave a lot of leeway as to what was being communicated, whereas together, the three modes constrain one

another and clarify the orientation taken by the current speaker. Thus, the pen motivates our noticing of the "little arrow" and is, at the same time, itself motivated by the shape and direction of the arrow. That is, the object perceptually available to the coparticipants and the shape and direction of the pen mutually constitute each other as referents. In the first five frames, Glen held the pen parallel to the two arrows. As the hand moved from left to right, the pen, consistent with the words, "always stay[ed] straight." In the second part of the transcript (frames 5–8), Glen appeared to talk about the circular object that "goes in that straight direction." Here, somewhat confusing the matters, the hand moved through a curvilinear trajectory and away from the screen, the pen no longer in an orientation that "always stays straight." The pen can be seen as another elaboration of the "little arrow." In this case, however, the pen was a motivated elaboration, because its shape and direction paralleled that of the arrow—the two entities stood in an iconic relationship to one another. This is not always the case. There are other situations in my database where students used pens to stand in for entities that were very different in shape and orientation, or referred to entities only in metaphoric ways. Thus, in one instance, a young woman used a fountain pen to stand for an atom. She used the uncapping of the fountain pen to illustrate how electrons could become separated from the remainder of the entity to create a positively charged ion. That is, the particular function of the pen depended on *this* situation as a whole, providing a particular expression of orientation. On their own, gestures and objects do not mean anything; there are no gestures or body language that have meaning on their own.

Reading across the three expressive modalities—perceptually available microworld entities, gestures, and utterances—we can understand this episode as consisting of two observation sentences. The first observation concerned one of the two arrows that "always stay[ed] straight." Here, the expression in the perceptual modality was inconsistent with that of the verbal modality, for it only showed a single state rather than a series of states that would motivate the descriptor "always." The orientation of the pen, which stayed constant across the three frames of the utterance (frames 1–3), recalled an observation made immediately before this instance, made the observation present again, *re*-presented it. In the second part of the utterance, Glen made a verbal assertion about something ("it") going in a straight direction, which can be heard as an assertion about the object. At the same time, the gesture seemed to be inconsistent with this reading, for frames 6–8 show that pen and hand do not remain parallel to «force» and trajectory. However, given that Glen sat to the left of the computer, his arm is actually extended to its maximum so that any motion would be curvilinear unless he had bent forward or gotten out of his seat.

Observation Categoricals

As students continue to explore the focal situations, they begin to formulate relationships, particularly causal relationships. Once again, these formulations do not appear at first in the verbal modality, but as an assemblage of the three modalities. Here, we return to an episode already encountered repeatedly and presented in figure 1.5. It exemplifies the nature of initial observation categoricals. Glen had linked two observation sentences into a general statement that turned out to be valid not only for this but also for other situations: «velocity» gets longer and changes its direction in response to «force», which is pushing the object. Taken against the things displayed on the monitor, his words and gestures express a certain orientation not only against the background but also to the setting as a whole.

In this episode, Glen's gestures already provided descriptions and explanations, which were more consistent with standard physics language (and therefore more viable in the ecology of the school context) than his verbal descriptions. Here then, his gestures considerably preceded his verbal representation of Newtonian physics. In this situation, gestural (and verbal) deixis was crucial in coordinating utterances, gestures, and the phenomena in the microworld. At the time of this episode, Glen and his classmates had not evolved a language to describe the circular object and arrows in internally consistent (and even less in scientific) terms. That is, although the words "force" and "velocity" may have appeared in their conversations, these terms were not used in a manner consistent with the language of physics textbooks. This consistent and appropriate scientific (verbal) language would emerge only two weeks later during a subsequent lesson with the microworld. When we look at the gestural modality in the present episode, however, we can interpret the relations as correctly describing the relationship between the velocity and force as the corresponding arrows («velocity» and «force») represented them. In figure 1.5, we see that the fingers of the right hand parallel to «force» (frames 2–5) always stayed parallel. In contrast, the fingers of the left hand (frames 3–5) that were initially parallel to «velocity», changed their direction in the way «velocity» could be seen to change on an earlier screen during the immediately prior experiment. That is, the hands—as signs standing in a reflexive, motivating relationship with what was visually available to all group members (perceptual signs)—described the situation in a correct scientific way, although the words on their own were still inappropriate.

My analysis and the events immediately following this episode also highlight another aspect related to gesturing as a way of orienting in and structuring of the world. Although we may be temped to attribute a particular meaning to communication, interlocutors may not understand some utterances (communicative acts) in practice. Here, neither Ryan nor Eliza appeared to understand the relationship between the arrows on the screen and those in Glen's utterance; his utterances did not help *them* to structure the events and therefore to orient themselves in a particular way to the setting. Consequently, both engaged Glen in a (conversational) repair, which itself drew on multiple modalities.

01   Ryan: *What?*
02   Eliza: Which arrow is longer?
03   Glen: Do you know how we had this ((Points to «force»)) one bigger than
               that ((Points to «velocity»)) one.

Ryan's utterance ("*What?*") was a generic indicator for not having understood. In uttering "*What?*" he indicated interest; he indicated that he was oriented toward the setting. But he also indicated that he was unable to identify what Glen wanted to orient him to specifically. In fact, the utterance "*What?*" constituted itself an action to orient Glen to an aspect of the setting, that is, the absence of a common orientation to the same entity. Here, Ryan communicated that he was unable to orient toward and pick out that aspect of the microworld to which Glen was oriented, here the arrows. Interestingly enough, although one might assume the mutual, perceptual availability of the objects, Eliza asked which of the two arrows was longer. In response, Glen used verbal and gestural pointing to isolate the two objects involved in the comparison "this one bigger than that one."

BODY AND ARTICULATION

In the previous episodes, we saw students who were physically oriented toward some aspect of the world before them, a microworld, a world within a world. With their pointing gestures, they made direct contact with the entities that appeared before them, allowing them to make distinctions that their words alone did not or could not make. It is the physical act of pointing that distinguished one "handle" for turning an arrow among all the handles perceptually salient. Furthermore, students mimicked the shape and movement of entities with their whole bodies, but particularly with hand gestures and arm movements. These gestures are referred to as "iconic," because of the similarity relation with some aspects in the world. The similarity relation is not natural, but its recognition a cultural-historical accomplishment that comes to be shared across specific cultures (Eco 1976). With and as living bodies, the students produce configurations that articulate a similarity relation with the world around them. These bodily actions are accompanied by utterances, themselves productions of a living body. That is, in these episodes, we see entire student bodies situated in and being constitutive part of the world become expression for another part. The entire body, including position, gesture, and utterance articulates an intentional object, which is immediately understood (rather than interpreted) by the respective audience, who in their own bodily orientation reflect the stance. The episode represented in figure 1.2 shows that at this stage, there was an intermingling of bodies, hands, and utterances seeking to orient themselves toward different aspects of the microworld and toward one another. The students engaged in this world with their whole bodies, physical entities among entities, and this "life among the things has nothing to do with the construction of scientific objects" (Merleau-Ponty 1945, 216, my translation).

Living among things, we engage *with* them, even if we do not think *about* them. In fact, the objects do not appear *as* objects of thought but as useful things that we encounter in use, to which we relate. For example, when we eat, we use a spoon or knife and fork. Yet we do not think about them, they come in hand: they are at hand. We eat and we converse. Yet although we do not think about these eating tools, we use them in particular ways, which makes them different from other things in our surroundings. In this way, we *pick* things *out* of the surrounding, which gives them their signification. We can, if necessary, point out these significations, using gestures together with original, basic words, "Take this!" while pointing to the fork. But we can also articulate the things and what to do with them such as when we tell our children, "Eat your pudding with the spoon; don't eat it with the fork!" All of these are different levels of telling things apart, but not all of them require language. The signification of spoon, knife, and fork precede any words that our children can use. The words come to be used in situations already articulated, structured in some rather than in other ways. Before the words "spoon," "knife," and "fork" can have any salience to the child, eating, food of different consistency and size, family gatherings, and so on already have been experienced in structured ways.

The language embodied in students' utterances is an integral part of their search for an orientation, identification of things and events. At the point of the episodes I discussed here, the students did not comprehend the events in a scientific way; they did not have a semantic model somewhere on the inside that could have generated their utterances. The words were but noises that had not found their place. At this point students sought to articulate the world in their actions and perceptions, and articulating the world is an integral part of this search of a practical understanding of how the Newtonian microworld works. Because the students did not yet know how this world works, there could not have existed an internal mechanism—idea, naive theory, (alternative) concept, or semantic model—that generated their utterances. Any such mechanism, if there ever was one, was the outcome of experiences such as those shown. If the students could make sense of one another's orientations, it was because they were copresent to one another, the situation, the surroundings, and the circumstantial milieu of the activity.

My analysis highlighted three planes at which communication minimally needs to be studied: the world that is perceptually available to the coparticipants, their gestures, and their utterances. The relationship between gestures and the perceptually available world is transactional, that is, the shape of things and events motivates the shape of the gestures, and the gestures motivate the articulation of the perceptual ground in particular ways. I return to the discussion of this relation below.

So far, only implicit in my analysis is the fact that language implies a collective situation. The individual does not require language, for he or she can get along by making relevant distinctions without having to use words for pointing them out or even describing and explaining them. But in the collective situation, words transcend the individual. In coming to a shared language, individuals in a group transcend themselves and become other—at the very moment they communicate, signify something, they have to draw on a resource that is no longer their own but also of and for the other. "Since it returns to the other, it exists asymmetrically, always for the other, from the other, kept by the other. Coming from the other, remaining with the other, and returning to the other" (Derrida 1998, 40). To this topic, too, I will return when taking a look at the evolution of language in small groups and entire classrooms.

Until now, I have used brief snippets from conversations to show how students orient in and toward the world, perceptually isolate and gesturally articulate features, and evolve first observation sentences and then observation categoricals. In our daily lives, whether in school or elsewhere, however, we do not just physically orient ourselves to the world, things, and other beings, but we

Figure 1.7. The physical demeanor—body movement, hand gestures, physical positioning toward the artifact and one another—expresses the opposition between Shamir and myself. The three plates correspond, from left to right, to lines 08, 10, and 21, respec-

also engage in projects that give directionality to intentions. Toward the accomplishment of these projects, we rally all the resources at hand—material, gestural, and linguistic. The project nature is evident in the following episode, which features a student in the process of articulating the design of a pulley-mediated tug-of-war that would have given him and his peers an advantage over me, his teacher, who had previously won such a competition facing him and twenty peers. The entire sequence exhibits an oppositional intention, rallied to convince others that his design was a winning one. In this endeavor, the student took an orientation: he wanted to beat me in a hypothetical tug-of-war that was the topic of our talk. He drew diagrams on the chalkboard and took up a position in a double sense, both to the hypothetical tug-of-war presented there and toward me, his opponent in the argument. Figure 1.7 shows this double orientation, as the student moved from constructing the battlefield in a diagrammatic way, and then, turning toward me, animating the drawn elements using not only hand gestures but also his entire body.

TAKING AN ORIENTATION

The episode occurred in a split sixth- and seventh-grade science class where students argued over scientific models (drawn on the chalkboard) of a tug-of-war mediated by a pulley system. (Ethnographic details of the particular science unit in question are provided in chapter 6.) I show that in the early stages of understanding physics, orientation together with hand gestures and body position play an important role in communication and, therefore, in the emergence of scientific ideas. I had previously beat about twenty students in a tug-of-war, but had "cheated" by using a block and tackle that had given me an advantage. It was a way of setting up a situation whose unexpected outcome could then be discussed. Students now attempted to propose alternative pulley designs that would not have given me an advantage, or rather would have given them an advantage. With this, they took up position, a project; they wanted to win both the debate and the hypothetical tug-of-war.

In the initial part of the conversation, students and I drew different pulley systems on the chalkboard to describe the situation. But then, students began to construct models for situations in which the teacher would not have benefited despite the use of a pulley system. At the end of the seventeen-minute conversation, there were eight different designs students and I had drawn on the chalkboard; these designs served as topic and background to the ongoing talk. The present excerpt is from the second part of the conversation featuring one student (Shamir) who, in the course of his presentation, constructed one alternative configuration. He had initially tried to explain his model verbally from the seat; a classmate then attempted to construct a drawing according to Shamir's instructions but failed. Because neither his classmates nor I understood what he attempted to say, Shamir then went to the chalkboard facing me, also standing next to the chalkboard (figure 1.7). The three images in the figure articulate the intentionality implicit in the interaction: There is an orientation toward the diagram, the entity to be elaborated and representing the contest, and toward one another, the opponent in the tug-of-war and in argument. The other students watched, listened, and reacted (applause, moaning) to the interaction.

The episode began when I asked Shamir where in the diagram the different parties would pull (line 01) because, up to this point, Shamir's drawing and talk had not provided this information. My question, "Where do I pull? Which end do I pull?" indicated to Shamir—as his next turn showed—that I did not understand where the string was attached or who was pulling at what end. Until then, Shamir had only attributed one rope, the one for the teacher. If the class had been at the other end, it would leave one end of the rope loose. In a sweeping gesture (line 02), Shamir then attributed to me the rope that attached the pulley to the banister.

01   Teacher: Where do I pull? Which end do I pull?

02   Shamir: You can pull on here. *

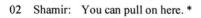

03   With the– okay (3.8 s) *this* * is a banister.

04   Teacher: But we have the banister * here.
05   Aslam: Oh God!

Visibly disconcerted that I did not understand, Shamir started a new diagram without talking for the moment (line 03); but I stopped him short by pointing out that there already was a banister drawn on the chalkboard (line 04). Again, the utterance as situated action not only indicated that there was already a drawing with a banister, but also suggested that the speaker should make his argument by referring to it rather than producing a new one. That is, I had held Shamir accountable to the earlier drawing which already included a banister. By means of theatrical emphases, Shamir aligned me (and his peers in the audience) to the key elements of his design and their placement (lines 06–19). Through his emphases in the uttered words and the accompanying deictic gestures, he rendered unequivocal the placements of exactly those elements that had been ambiguous during his earlier verbal presentations (though some of his peers apparently understood him even then).

06   Shamir: (5.2 s)
07   ((Erases diagram, begins new one.))
08   *BAnister.* *
09   Teacher: Okay.

10   Shamir: *Long string* *
11   Teacher: Okay, pulley.

12   Shamir: *Roth* *

13   pull *here.* *
14   Teacher: OK.

15   Shamir: ((Draws circle.)) Then * *there* is a pulley.

     Apart from the utterances that articulated my attention to his presentation (lines 09, 11, 14), I did not interrupt Shamir. The diagram and his articulation of its element unfolded until I asked him where the place of the class was in his model (line 16). Perhaps I expected the diagram to be completed; perhaps I was a little unsettled about the amount of time it took Shamir, who liked to argue with all of his (eight) teachers, to articulate his alternative design. Despite my question, Shamir continued at his pace, drawing and pointing out element after element, relevant entities and thereby articulating an orientation to the hypothetical tug-of-war.

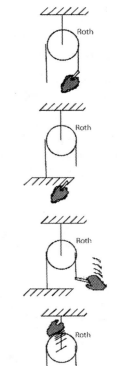

16   Teacher: And where do you pull?

17   (1.7 s)
18   Shamir: And then * *there* is another banister

19   and then we pull (.) * here.
20   ((Several students applaud, one "Yeah" can be heard.))

21   Shamir: You, [(ye [j'st?)–] *
                  [((Shakes head.))

Eventually, Shamir completed his drawing. He turned his body, facing me completely, while his hand points back to what he thought was a winning configuration (figure 1.7). Unlike his earlier verbal presentation from the back of the classroom (which was difficult and even incomprehensible to his peers and teacher alike), his description in the form of a drawing was much less ambiguous. Furthermore, his design now existed in material form and was available for critique: taking up and communicating a position provided others with the opportunity to hold him accountable; his communicative actions had made him accountable. Such a critique was immediately instantiated. It came both in the form of Aslam's observation that the teacher did not have to pull at all and in my subsequent applause, which not only acknowledged but also celebrated this critique. Aslam's comment had furthermore underscored a concern that had been voiced earlier in the conversation. Sharon had pointed out that the pulley was attached in such a way that the class was pulling on the banister rather than competing against me, their opponent.

In this episode Shamir did not merely produce utterances to mean something but his entire body engaged in the interaction to produce the argument, giving an expression to the intention of winning the argument and, therefore, a potential tug-of-war that he, his peers, and I could potentially enact. That is, the argument cannot be reduced to the words alone, but involves the physical orientation, gestures, and utterances. In this whole, he evolves and gives expression to an argument even before he intellectually grasped and correctly talked *about* pulley systems. His utterances took part in the making of differences; they constituted a form of telling in activity. He drew not just a line representing a banister; in this situation, he drew a banister. And just as he completed the line, he uttered what linguists might transcribe as "'bænistə" and what participants heard as "banister." Just as his arm and hand were drawing a «long string», his vocal apparatus produced the sound that we heard as "long string." Because he was not just drawing and verbally articulating something but also arguing with me, his head and body reoriented from the diagram toward me with a slight turn. With this movement, however slight, he launched each piece like a weapon against me, his body continuously engaged in producing a new weapon and then throwing it into my direction.

At the heart of the ongoing debate was the exact placement that the different elements in the pulley system (i.e., support/banister, rope, pulley) should take. Deictic gestures therefore played the important role of identifying elements and their location in the system. Here then, deictic gestures isolated and articulated individual elements. Drawing an element did double duty in (a) individuating the element itself and (b) indicating its placement in the situation as a whole. For example, I argued, "But we have a banister here," while touching the top part of the drawing (line 04). My orientation to the diagram and my verbal and gestural actions contributed to making this element (and the fact that it already existed) salient, bringing it to the foreground against everything else in the room and on

Y*ou can   p*ull   on here *

Figure 1.8. Shamir used his whole body to enact where I would be pulling on the system that he had designed.

the chalkboard. Whereas I pointed to an existing element, Shamir made the elements, he talked about salient by drawing them. Thus, he drew some lines on the chalkboard and uttered "banister" (lines 03, 07–08). Here, because he drew the element, it and its location with respect to the other features on the chalkboard stood out; simply drawing this element in this way articulated it as significant. This is even more evident in the case of the elements following the "banister," for each new element was placed in respect to other already existing ones.

Following line 08, Shamir therefore established the entire domain under consideration by drawing each element, attributing the actors to pull on particular ropes, and uttering the verbal expression associated with each element. In this case, the nature of the elements was especially salient because Shamir drew them on the chalkboard that served as ground against which the diagram stood out. Furthermore, for each new element, not only the chalkboard but also those already existing parts of the emerging diagram functioned as ground. Articulating an element by pointing to it and by drawing it were therefore slightly different actions. In the first instance (e.g., line 04), the deictic gesture pointed to part of the drawing. However, much of the work of delineating the extension of the element, and thereby isolating it from the remainder of the drawing had to be done by the listener (observer). When Shamir drew an element such as "long string," the gesture actually pointed to and thereby picked out the element in its entirety.

In addition to the deictic gestures, Shamir used gestures where his hands moved along a particular string. These gestures did double duty, as they were both deictic and iconic. While Shamir indicated that someone (teacher, students) "pull[s] (on) here" (lines 02, 13, 19, [21]), the gesture made salient both where the agent was to hold on (deixis) and in which direction to pull (iconic gesture). These gestures, which enacted pulling in an iconic way, are further elaborated in the drawings of line 02 (figure 1.8). As Shamir uttered "you," his hand was already in upward motion; it reached the rope above the pulley while pronouncing "pull on," and then continued the motion along the rope until the completion of "here." Thus, in this case, "here" is not a simple deictic device to point out the element on which someone pulls (e.g., "long string"). But "pulling here" is enacted together such that the gesture makes salient both the element pulled as well as the direction of the pull. While his hand moved up, his upper body moved slightly backward, as if counterbalancing a force on his hand (also and even more visible in the rightmost photograph in figure 1.7). Thus, he was not just indicating some element where there is some force, but the forces appeared in his gesture and in his body that iconically enacted pulling. At this point, the sweeping gesture not only pointed out where I, his opponent, would be pulling, but also the direction of the forces. His entire body therefore "animated" aspects of the hypothetical tug-of-war over and about the diagram and exhibited the dynamic of the system part in addition to declarative aspects of the drawings at hand. Thus, talking in the presence of the diagram allowed him (as well as others when they were at the chalkboard defending their designs) to express important topological features of the situation, including forces and their direction, which the typological nature of talk could not easily express. It is noted that in the absence of any feedback from the diagram, in the way that MathCAD had given me in my mathematical explorations of the hospital task in the introduction or that the twelfth-grade students had received from Interactive Physics, Shamir could not know whether the system actually operated and mediated forces in the way he argued. Thus, whereas he enacted the individual forces accurately, I knew that his setup would not give him the advantage that he hoped to be getting from it. That is, his presentation was at variance with the standard ways of science.

The episode is interesting in terms of the changing origin from which the pointing and referring occurs, that is, the origin of deixis. When Shamir enumerated the elements, he always placed them "there," in front of me (his opponent in argument), the class as audience, and himself. But when he suggested where the different parties pulled, he always indicated them with the verbal deictic "here," taking the perspective of the agent pulling at the place indicated. He not only animated the diagram, he became part of the system and took the position where pulling occurred. In addition, the sweeping movement of the hand also indicated the direction, and in fact, enacted the pulling. He therefore took a first-person perspective of the event. The shift occurred depending on who he presently talked about. The inside observer perspective added flexibility to distance by bringing the listener into the space of the narrative, which heightens both the narrative and its rhetorical effects (McNeill 1992). There is the opposition in "you," and the shift in perspective to "here." Phenomenologically, "you" designates the other opposite to the self; simultaneously, objects and others are placed "there," whereas the self is placed "here." Both articulate a self–other orientation implicit in the competition that we enacted in our talk. In this, there is a blending of the animate (student) and the abstract (inanimate) physical event; Shamir made interpretive journeys from the intertwined constructed realms of (a) the world of physical events and (b) the world of the visual representation of the objects and events.

HOLISTIC NATURE OF COMMUNICATION

Domains such as semiotics and linguistics have focused predominantly on language as the *primary* modeling system, often considering nonverbal means as secondary, derivative, or partial translations of the primary system. Educators have followed suit—much of schooling is an exercise in the mastery of words, an exercise in which particularly white middle-class students excel. In contrast, my videotapes show that to beginners, relevant structure in visual, gestural, and verbal modes are different even though they are highly underdetermined and variable. Thus, the twelfth-grade students did not structure the computer or experimental displays in the way a physicist or physics teacher might do. Furthermore, students also differed among each other in terms of what they determine to be salient. For example, despite the relatively simple configuration in the figure, it was not notable to students at first that the outline arrow («force») did not change in magnitude or direction, that the line arrow changed both magnitude and direction, or that the trajectory of the object was parabolic. The figure-ground ensemble has to be taken as variable, because in the perceptual processes of the individuals, they are variable. In the next chapter, I will show that the utterances also were variable. Students used many different words and word combinations to refer to each of the arrows before they settled on a particular one. It is in the context of particular utterances, or the background, that a denotation takes shape in the same way that some aspect of the ground takes shape and becomes figure. For example, if there is an arrow pointing upward behind the hand, the sign function relates the direction of the finger and that of the arrow. (In a different context, the same configuration may indicate testing for wind striking the finger horizontally.)

Observation and theory expressions made concurrently across all the three modalities are more complex than in individual modes of communication. However, over time, and with increasing familiarity, the verbal modality assumes the function of primary representational mode. (At that point, students can write about some scientific investigation even though they are absent from the setting and materials where they conducted it.) I had moved to the consideration of the three modes (verbal, gestural, and perceptual) motivated by Eco's (1984) description of signing as a process in which some "lumps" from the dynamic continuum of the physical world come to stand for other "lumps." As a result, the relationship between the different lumps is symmetrical: ink on paper in the form of "tree," the sound transcribed as "[tri:]" (International Phonetics Association), a «tree» in the garden, or its rendering in a line drawing each may stand for one another during communication. Therefore, we can think of students' communication as running in any one or more of the three modalities. There is the world not only before but also encompassing them from which particular entities are made salient by means of utterances, different types of gestures, and body orientations. There are the gestures that tell part of the story, and there are the words. The difficulty arises in part from the fact that the three modalities can be shifted with respect to one another during periods of transition (that is, learning in a new domain). What my videotapes of students learning science language reveal is a multilevel process. First, there are the processes of shaping the content and expression (gesture, language) continua. Second, there are the processes by means of which expression continua are correlated with their possible content, which is an aspect of the material situation that includes human beings. Finally, there are the processes by means of which signs become associated to the segmentations of the content continuum.

Nonverbal signs have to be considered in a theory of communication because of their prevalence in face-to-face conversation and particularly in those interactions when the conversational topic is a feature within the setting itself. These nonverbal aspects of a situation are in fact central to what constitutes meaning and understanding. Certainly, language is the most powerful semiotic device, but there are semantic spaces that it does not cover as effectively as other devices (Lemke 1998). In other words, the indexical ground is intimately tied to basic processes of human interaction and participant frameworks. I show here that leaving it out of the analysis of communication means omitting one of the resources of semiotic processes. This observation parallels the suggestion that the indexical ground shapes the interaction (Hanks 1992), which in turn shapes the indexical ground.

Both gestural and verbal modes have a deictic feature that can be used to foreground the perceptual mode within the interaction. Some readers may assume gestures to be somehow unambiguous and therefore sufficient to ground some utterance, that they are indexes or signs that ground utterances, or expressive media. But this is not so. The shape and direction of the pointing is itself ambiguous so that what is being communicated arises from the interplay of percept, utterance, and gesture. In this, gestures are no different from the pencil that Glen had used—it, too, can be used to signify different things, sometimes bearing an iconic relation with the thing signified, at other times merely bearing an arbitrary relation. Each mode, however, constrains the flexibility of the other through their co-occurrence. From this triangulation of potentially different meanings, a lower number of specific senses and references arise.

PERCEPTUAL SIMILARITY BETWEEN SETTING AND GESTURE

In the foregoing episodes, the perceptual similarity between gestures and the objects and events of the world at hand played an important role. Perceptual similarity or "iconicity" (Roth and Lawless 2002a) is an important resource for orienting others to an aspect in the setting. That is, when gestures look like some other thing in the setting and if there are other indications that the two should be related (such as body orientation), then there are opportunities for both gesture and the other thing to become salient.

Research on the nature of iconic reference and the level of perceptual similarity is of considerable practical interest in at least two domains. First, developmental researchers who attempt to infer children's understandings from their utterances and gestures have to take into account the research that showed that during change in understanding there is a discrepancy between gesture and utterance (Goldin-Meadow, Alibali, and Church 1993). To make appropriate inferences about what a gesture means, we need to know the relationship between the gesture and the situation as a whole. This has to be done from the perspective of the learner who does not yet know the ultimate meaning relations that will exist for him or her. Second, teachers who want to assist students need to make appropriate inferences from gesture and situation to provide appropriate resources that will allow students to evolve verbal expressions associated with some concept being gestured. In these instances, individuals are said to rely on the perceptual similarity between gestures and worldly entities to read what their interlocutors do not and cannot make available in the verbal modality. This puts enormous emphasis on the interpretation of iconicity. To extend our discussion of iconicity and its problems, I elaborate the following examples.

The gestures such as those in figure 1.2 appear unambiguous and nonproblematic. The index finger pointing upward (line 01), an image of an arrow aligned in this direction, the turning of «velocity» (line 02), and the moving hand (with index finger pointing upward) predicting a particular motion (line 03) are all forms of gestures that can be categorized as iconic. This iconic nature is particularly recognizable because there were possibilities of comparing the gesture with what was perceptually available immediately before or after. These perceptually available things are signs in their own right, telling those who are copresent in the situation what the current state of affairs is. In the episodes depicted in figures 1.5 and 1.8, the gestures were iconic with respect to the previ-

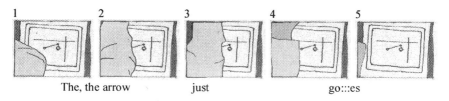

Figure 1.9. Glen's arm moves forcefully upward without having a perceptual equivalent elsewhere in the setting.

ously seen trajectory of the circular object and with the rope in the diagram of the hypothetical tug-of-war, respectively. However, categorizing the gestures as iconic is much more problematic in figure 1.6, where Glen's utterance, "It goes in that straight direction" was accompanied by a gesture in which the hand holding a pen moved from left to right across the screen (frames 6–8). In this motion, the pen did not remain parallel to «force» as previously suggested and the trajectory of the hand (articulation of perceptual object) did not move straight—as the object had done earlier—or parallel to the earlier displayed trajectory. Thus, the trajectory and orientation of the gesture and pencil differed from the trajectory and orientation of the object on the screen. However, trajectory and orientation are the critical issues in the motion phenomenon explored. And yet, in its structure, we recognize the gesture not only as iconic but also as an aspect of the orientation that the student took with respect to the events. In figure 1.9, the contradictory nature of iconicity is further accentuated.

On the surface, the episode constituted an observation sentence about some arrow that Glen suggested "just goes." With his performance, he oriented his peers to something. The question is whether this attempted orientation drew on perceptual similarity, or whether the gesture, evidently in the class of iconic gestures, bore perceptual similarity with something else not immediately available in the setting. Here, given that the previous experiment involved only «velocity», we can understand it as the sense of "arrow." Furthermore, the previous image on the screen showed—to the outside observer—constant «velocity» (magnitude and direction), in which case "just goes" could be heard as "unchangingly." However, the gesture did not seem to bear any relation to the events on screen. The hand moved such that the arm rotated around the elbow (frames 1–3) and, in the end, descended (frames 4–5). The hand, therefore, described a curvilinear trajectory away from the screen. As such, it was not iconic to anything perceptually available in the setting that could have served as the motivating counterpart of the gesture. The gesture evoked a curvilinear trajectory while the verbal modality provides the description "the arrow just goes."

Interlocutors likely operate under the assumption that the three modes are consistent with each other. The interpretive flexibility associated with what is made available in each modality is therefore constrained. On the other hand, in periods of conceptual transition, the different modalities may express different entities and processes. At these moments, the nature of the entities and processes in the world are different; what is salient is a matter of the historic constitution of individual perceptual processes. Much research remains to be done to find out how coparticipants in a situation align one another in and to some situation and the project that they collectively conduct where they are.

ANTHROPOCENTRIC LANGUAGE

Here at the end of this chapter, it is opportune to address the question of anthropocentric language, because it is related to the issue of taking up a position and orienting oneself in a particular setting. The case studies presented here illustrate how students use language, gestures, and salient elements in the perceptual ground to orient one another to aspects of the setting and thereby to move some collective project ahead. When Shamir argued with me, he not only showed where different parties were to pull in the diagram but also threw his whole body into the battle to enact the pulling motion and forces. My analysis brought out how, as a designer of the representation, he placed each item of the system in front of us, like a series of gauntlets thrown at the floor in front of me, followed by his challenging regard. Then, when he positioned himself to articulate the forces in and actions of the system, he became part of the system itself, from the position of which the events are expressed.

The other episodes in this chapter, too, show how students take up a position with respect to (an aspect of) the world at hand, how they orient themselves to it physically, intellectually, and emotionally as part of a more general project. In Shamir's case, his project was to win the argument and the imaginary or potential tug-of-war. This orientation expresses itself visibly in the position of students' bodies and gestures relative to the setting. In this, language constitutes but another gesture that is integral to the situation as a whole. This is sometimes difficult for us to understand, because historically we have privileged language as something special that is *about* the world rather than as a part of orienting in the world, an action at the same level of other action. Here, I found this suggestion helpful: think about language not in terms of words but in terms of sounds (Mikhailov 1980). Sounds are material elements in our environments, just as traffic lights, knives and forks, or gestures are. They are also patterned, some recurring in particular settings together with other material things, including foods, tools, gestures, human bodies, and so forth. They obtain significance because of their correlation with these other things, that is, all of these things form a network of signification that we are familiar with even if we do not talk or reflect *about* it or some aspect of it.

Now, we always find ourselves in some situation, where we take up position and orient ourselves, even in novel and strange situations. The self is the center of the experience and the lived world is relative to the person. It is therefore not surprising that what we say, especially in novel situations and settings, is relative to our current position and orientation. This *thrownness* in situation is our primary relation to the world; it is centered on our way of being. Language is just one aspect of this person-centered position with respect to the world, which is very different than the disembodied, third-person perspective inherent in scientific language, which has evacuated all first-person experience, the direct and unconditioned participation in the world. The world *as* experience, populated with objects and events that we name, talk, and reason about requires a radical shift in orientation from an unmediated participation in the world to a sign-mediated orientation to things and events in the past (Buber 1970). In the beginning is the relation to and participation in the setting. On the other hand, objects and events are the *result* of our experience in setting, emerge as separate entities from the tacit and indistinct background from active engagement in and with the world. Once objects and events have become figure before the ground, we can name, talk about, and describe them. We form observation sentences and observation categoricals. Scientific language can only emerge when I, as a perceiver, can become separate from what I perceive.

Who we are in everyday experience is something like the blind spot. To discover this spot and to engage in self-analysis require a radical shift, a distancing characteristic of writing and a writing culture. Self-analysis requires the "isolation of the self, around which the entire live world swirls for each individual person, removal of the center of every situation from that situation enough to allow the center, the self, to be examined and described" (Ong 1982, 54). My ongoing ethnographic research in scientific laboratories shows that this isolation is not characteristic of most everyday experiences, and even scientists do not reflect and engage in self-analysis while they collect data and do science—this again is something that they do in particular data analysis sessions and during the process of writing. That is, scientists too use language to take position and to articulate their orientation before they write *about* their experiences in a disembodied way.

Many students and teachers talk about physical objects as if these had intentions, much like human beings whom they encounter in the same ways as material bodies among other materials. Such expressions may not literally mean that students imbue human-like characteristics such as decision making to the balls and pendulums. It is not a new sort of animism or simplistic form of reasoning but, in fact, a very experience-centered approach to cognition (Ochs, Gonzales, and Jacoby 1996). Anthropocentric language may have a deeper root in situating knowledge in bodily experience, an approach that led to the notion of embodied knowledge. It may be one form of situated knowing, or a form of analyzing situations in terms of one's own actions. Thus, video game players do not think about figures that they manipulate. Rather, they take the place of these figures. Similarly, more experienced instruction givers in a videogame situation do not talk about how the figures are to be moved, but in terms of a command as if the player was in the action itself (Chapman 1991). Thus, anthropocentric language can be seen as a language grounded in physical and perceptual experience. Intersubjectivity (that we understand others and know that we understand) is fundamentally grounded in the dialectic of self and other, and the reciprocity of intentionality. Communication and comprehension are possible because of the reciprocity inherent in my intentions and the actions of others, and, equivalently, the intentions of others and my actions. Here, the other is first and foremost other than self, so that intentionality is grounded in reciprocity rather than in primitive forms of thinking.

2

Coevolution of World and Language

Talking is part of taking position in and toward a world that not only surrounds but also encompasses us as one of its constitutive elements. The utterances we use to articulate the world as it appears to us in our perception are only part of a more general attitude that we take toward this world, and one of several forms of gesture that allows us to orient ourselves and communicate this orientation to others. When we are in a familiar setting, our comportment (utterances, hand gestures, body position) is recognizably appropriate to the situation. In other words, we understand the world that is so familiar to us and in which we are literally at home. However, it is equally self-evident that when we are in unfamiliar terrain, our movements, gestures, and language cannot be certain. Because perception is inseparably tied to action (Churchland and Sejnowski 1992), being in unfamiliar terrain with unfamiliar entities and events, we often do not perceive what is evidently available to those who have inhabited the terrain for a long time. To understand this, all we have to do is think about expert chess players, who have come to see the board and its figures in terms of patterned configurations, whereas beginners see individual figures on specific positions. We learn to perceive the world in its relevant detail only by interacting with it. Think about being thrust into a completely darkened room. To know what your new world is like, you have to move about, using those senses that work under these conditions, for example touch, sound, and smell. In moving about, salient structures emerge, that is, the world emerges together with its characteristic joints (articulations) where objects border and thereby distinguish themselves as being different from one another. Your primary relation from which the world emerges is one of participation; only subsequently can you detach objects, others, and yourself and provide, based on your experience, cause and effect relations between them. That is, the structure of this world, its objects and events emerge as you move about and interact with this world. It is obvious that you can verbally articulate only those entities and events that have become apparent in and as result of your actions. New patterns constitute new ways of articulating the world, which is a prerequisite for telling it apart verbally.

Our actions in the world are constrained by the way we are built; the nature of the physical world, including human beings, therefore limits the ways in which we can articulate it in action and subsequently in words. Our language is the upshot of our experience in the world, directly or by metaphorical extension (Lakoff and Johnson 1999). That is, although the world does not tell us which language is appropriate for its descriptions, there are structural limits to how it can be articulated, which has consequences for how we can experience and know it (Decety and Grèzes 1999) and therefore how we can describe it. The range of actions available to us at any moment is a function of our past history. Different individuals will have different ranges of actions. The language an individual has at hand is therefore also a function of his or her history. Available actions and language constitute something of a ground, a surface of emergence for new perceptions and language. As my pruning and hospital examples showed, the particular perceptions at any one point was out of my control, although I could always aspire to looking at and perceiving the situation in a different way. This has as a consequence that new perceptual patterns and new ways of telling emerge contingently and beyond our control. Because the world does not tell us how to perceive it and which language to use to tell others what we perceive, there is an inherent flexibility in how the world comes to be articulated, that is, how it takes on the particular joints it does and thereby how it provides us with resources for further actions.

The account of my engaging with the hospital problem showed that there was a coevolution of the form and content of the language I used to communicate with the software, on the one hand, and the world I encountered in action and perception, on the other. The more I explored, the more fine-grained and articulated the mathematical world describing the hospital became, which I could then articulate (describe) in words. In this chapter, I suggest that for students in science classrooms, too, the world available to them in action and perception, on the one hand, and their language for talking about, describing, and explaining it, on the other hand, coevolve. In the following, I present case materials that show how students attempt to take up a position in an unknown world, which comes to be structured (articulated) through their physical and verbal actions. The episodes take us back to the twelfth-grade physics course where students investigated motion in a Newtonian microworld (Interactive Physics).

The students sat around computers (figure 2.1a); in the course of the lessons, I visited each group repeatedly, asking what they were doing and what they had found out (figure 2.1b). I had hoped to support a variety of student ac-

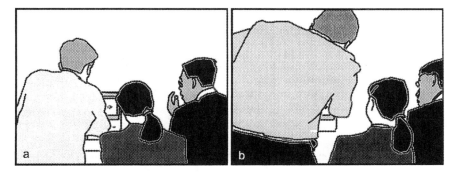

Figure 2.1a. The students sat in around the computer sufficiently close to touch the monitor. **b.** I made the rounds to visit with each group, interacting with the students, asking about progress, and engaging them in conversations.

tions on scientific representations (the vectors attached to the objects), conversations about scientific representations and their meaning, and competencies in talking physics in forms compatible with the curriculum. Perhaps a little naively I had assumed at the time that the rather limited number of entities in this world would constrain students' perceptions and talk and therefore allow them to evolve rather rapidly a language consistent with Newtonian physics. Initially, there was a great variability in the ways students used particular words to make salient to one another different aspects of their world, that is, to articulate these aspects; we might also say that there was a great interpretive flexibility pertaining to the objects and events of the microworld despite the limited number of entities it contained. Over time, following the interactions of students with the world and their interactions with one another, the number of ways in which they looked at, acted toward, and talked about began to decrease. (In part, this occurred in interactions with me, their teacher, who curtailed ways of seeing; but this story is to be told in chapter 5.) Important to the present chapter is the fact that the students converged on common ways of talking and thereby stabilized the ways in which entities could be perceived, told apart, talked about, described, and, ultimately, explained in stable and consistent ways. In the following section, I provide an account of how students came to articulate the Newtonian microworld in actions and words.

ARTICULATING A (MICRO-) WORLD

Student learning can be described as an adaptive change along a trajectory from initial articulations of the world that eventually becomes talk *about* the objects and events in the computer-based microworld. Possibilities for change arose from the ambiguity of these objects and events that allowed for their interpretive flexibility. Over time, students' talk not only converged so that they shared a descriptive language in their groups but also converged with normative ways of talking about Newtonian microworlds; thus, appropriate forms of science talk emerged from the inconclusive muddle of earlier forms. Changes in students' science talk were achieved collaboratively and cumulatively through minute adjustments of their descriptions. Much group work had to be expended in order to stabilize the emerging, new forms of talking science. The microworld also facilitated students' sense-making activities as it provided (a) a backdrop against which they could develop shared ways of talking and (b) an immediately available referent for grounding their arguments; thus, it functioned as an anchor for achieving topical cohesion in the science talk.

Interpretive Flexibility

Educators implicitly (and sometimes explicitly) assume that the resources for learning they make available to students are perceived in the intended way. However, this assumption is generally not fulfilled even for adolescent and adult students (Roth, McRobbie, Lucas, and Boutonné 1997a). It is not simply that students who do not yet know what they are supposed to learn interpret given things and events in different ways. Rather, they perceive and act in worlds different from that of the teacher, and these worlds are also dissimilar for different students. Thus, I have been able to document that not only did students observing some teacher demonstrations produce very different explanations for what happened but their descriptions of what they had seen differed: where some saw motion, others did not see any motion at all. That is, these students perceived different events: their articulations of what happened were very different. Before we can expect a common language of explanation, we need to have common articulations and observational descriptions, which are based on common ways of perceptually structuring the setting, or at least the relevant part. This may require work of aligning others so that some degree of certainty exists that everyone is looking at the same object. We can therefore think of the microworld as being perceptually and interpretively flexible—the nature of its objects and events and the words used to move around within it are not necessarily the same for coparticipants. At the same time, interpretive flexibility has to be a fundamental aspect of knowing, for otherwise there would not be possibilities for learning and development. That is, the indeterminate nature of objects and language that describes them is an inherent feature in human knowing (Derrida 1988).

Interpretive flexibility is an important resource in the evolution of student activity, and therefore in the world as it is available to students through percep-

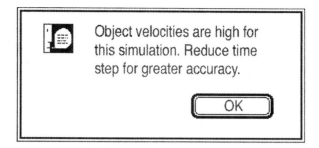

Figure 2.2. This software message popped up on the screen immediately after Ryan had lengthened «force» and, upon the instruction of Glen, had run the experiment.

tion and in action. The following episode begins a little into the first lesson when the students worked on their microworld tasks. (In the transcript, only the circular object and arrows are reproduced; they are only reproduced when they had changed.)

55	Glen:	* Oh yeah the big arrow's time, 'kay (1.2) the big arrow's time.
56	Ryan:	Okay, we'll make it shorter.
57	Eliza:	So then the little arrow is direction. (1.0)
58	Glen:	Yeah the big arrow is direction. No I mean the big arrow is velocity–
59	Eliza:	=No, time–
60	Ryan:	=No, it's time but it also directs, though.
61	Eliza:	Yeah and then the little arrow, no the little, isn't the little arrow. (2.3)
62	Ryan:	We don't know yet. What did I do?

Glen picked up on Eliza's earlier description of «force» as denoting time (line 55). Why might she have correlated the utterance "time" with «force»? Immediately prior to the moment presented here, the three had decided to do an experiment where the force vector was longer than the velocity vector. Glen instructed Ryan to run the simulation. The ball and its arrows quickly disappeared, followed by a software message displayed in a box: "Object velocities are high for this simulation. Reduce time step for greater accuracy" (figure 2.2). Ryan read this message aloud by following the text with the cursor. Eliza then asked what a "time step" was. It is at this time that Glen responded, "Oh yeah, the big arrow is time–" (line 55).

In this situation, the software message in figure 2.2 appeared just after one of the three students had acted in the world, that is, lengthened «force». As he ran the simulation, a text-filled box popped up that had not popped up previously. The only change they had made was lengthening the force arrow. That is, their action articulated a structural feature, the length of the arrow, which had been changed. The text in the box provided a description "object velocities are high," followed by an instruction to do something, "reduce time step," followed by an implication, "for greater accuracy." Here, what became salient was the instruction "reduce time step," which the software presented immediately after the students had lengthened «force». They had articulated the length of the arrow by increasing it, and the software talked back, indicating to them to "reduce time step." Here, at least temporarily, the relation between a malleable arrow (an aspect of the world) and an aspect of language ("time step") emerged. The verb "emerge" indicates that something had not been there before, that is, the relationship between «force» and "time" has evolved from a situation where it did not exist. Furthermore, the relation expresses a togetherness of at least two things, which is expressed by the particle "co," which becomes the prefix "co-." Here, then, «force», an aspect of the world as it was experienced by the students, and "time" *coevolved* in their mutually constitutive relation. The relation between other perceptual entities and words similarly coevolved. Let us now return to the episode.

Ryan suggested testing this idea of «force» as "time" by running a new experiment with a smaller «force» (line 56). Continuing with the task of finding terms for the arrows, Eliza suggested that «velocity» denoted "direction" (line 57). However, Glen made clear that he denoted and viewed the two arrows differently; he first used "direction" to denote «force», but then changed it to "velocity." In this, he disagreed with Eliza who reiterated the denotation "time" for «force». Ryan modified an earlier description, now describing «force» as "time [that] also directs." His description described «force» as the agent that changed length and direction of «velocity» (line 60). This left Eliza confused, and Ryan, rather than risking yet another term for «force» suggested that they, collectively, still did not know.

Glen shifted to a new description and proposed that the "little arrow" always stayed the same (line 63); he held his pencil parallel to «velocity» to indicate direction, thus suggesting to Eliza, as we know from the previous chapter, to orient to «velocity».

63	Glen:	So the little arrow, the little arrow always stays straight, whenever * we get it.

64	Ryan:	You can turn it. * ((Turns «force» by grabbing it at its tail and moving it around.))
65	Eliza:	Yeah, you can turn it.
66	Glen:	Yeah like when we're doing it, it goes in that straight direction anyways. ((Follows earlier displayed trajectory of object.)) *
67	Eliza:	Yeah but I think that little arrow might also be direction (1.3)

68 Glen: But the big arrow is also direction.
69 Eliza: =I know, (0.9) can we look, can we now move the little arrow?

In the present context, "the little arrow" was more likely about «force» because Ryan and Eliza considered the possibility of changing the direction of "it," while Ryan demonstrated how to change the direction of «force» by "grabbing" «force» at its tail and pivoting it around its tip (lines 64–65). Glen viewed his response as a contrast ("Yeah, but when we are doing it, it goes in that straight direction anyways") for he accompanied his statement by a gesture in which the pencil showed the change in the direction of «velocity», while his hand described the trajectory of the object (line 66). Here, he clearly demonstrated a change in the direction of «velocity», suggesting that it was «force» and not «velocity» that stayed constant. While this constituted a contradiction to his earlier statement, it was in agreement with the position of Eliza and Glen. Eliza then proposed that "the little arrow" indicated direction (line 67), but Glen countered, "the big arrow is also direction" (line 68). Eliza used "the little arrow" as a way to tell «velocity» apart from other things. This is consistent with her statement in (line 69), their collective action of changing the direction of «velocity», and what appeared to be a common orientation prior to the present excerpt; but this was inconsistent with the use of the same term in lines 64–65. Glen in turn used "the big arrow" to make «force» salient, consistent with Eliza's label, but inconsistent with his prior use of a different label for the same referent.

In this episode, the verbal articulation of «force» changed and the things "little arrow" and "big arrow" were associated with alternated repeatedly. "Little arrow" and "big arrow" each constitute conjunctions of two observations, one articulating an object (here, arrow), the other size. Such conjunctions describe any science in which little or big and arrow are not only both salient but also situated together, expressing a compact clustering of visual qualities characteristic of some body (Quine 1995). Prior cultural experience allowed the participants to pick out particular entities from the display, the arrows. However, although the predications "little" and "big" had the function of making distinctions between the two arrows, they did not unambiguously achieve this. Both were used in everyday situations as observation descriptions for short and skinny and tall and fat, respectively. Thus, a longer but skinnier «velocity» can be "little" and "big" simultaneously, likely not for the same person but for different persons. This is what happened in the present situation and without the students' awareness of it.

These students used other terms as well in association with «force», including "time," "direction," "velocity," and something that "directs" motion. Similarly, "little arrow" indexed «velocity» (line 57), «force» (lines 63–65), and again «velocity» (lines 67, 69). This suggests an interpretive flexibility of the objects and events in the microworld and of the terms used by the students. In their conversations, the particular linguistic (and therefore cultural) resources

Table 2.1. Interpretive flexibility of the vectors «force» and «velocity»

Glen, Eliza, Ryan		Bryan, Fran, Joe, Mike	
«force»	«velocity»	«force»	«velocity»
little arrow	little arrow	big arrow	skinny arrow
big arrow	big arrow	velocity	velocity
time-set	initial speed	force	kinetic energy
time	velocity	transfers kinetic	motion going on a
direction	initial speed	energy	path
time-and-direction	velocity	moves [ball] for-	direction and time
velocity	force	ward	velocity
redirection	effort	force, kinetic en-	speed
gravity	strength	ergy	velocity
force	speed	kinetic energy	
gravity	strength	force and energy	
gravity	speed	direction	
	direction	some kind of force	
	speed-and-direction	pressure	
	velocity	kind of force	
		force	

used and the terms for specific objects changed, implying a change in their mutual orientation. This flexibility is apparent from table 2.1, which lists the different terms these three students used in the course of their interactions. I contrasted their list with that of another group working on the same tasks but on another computer. It shows a similar range of variations, though the particular terms differed.

In this part of the conversation, the students converged on "direction" as a critical, descriptive term for both «velocity» and «force». This consensus emerged in spite of the changing nature of objects, events, and terms to describe them. These common ways of talking emerged as students contributed different descriptions. For Eliza, the "little arrow" showed the direction of the object's motion (lines 57, 67), while Glen and Ryan suggested that the "big arrow" also contributed to the direction of the object's motion (lines 60, 68). This episode illustrated a shift in their conversation (from the discussion of «force» as time) and a corresponding change in the experiments students decided to conduct; in these new experiments, they changed the direction of «force» and «velocity» both with respect to the coordinate system and relative to each other.

Hand in hand with the interpretive flexibility frequently went the occasioned (situation-dependent) character of students' investigations. They explored the microworld phenomena in what is an ineffective search from the perspective of the person who already knows both Newtonian physics and the software package. Most of the students' experiments developed out of specific situations on the screen and in conversation rather than from some structured approach. For example, while trying to increase «force», a student disconnected it from the circular object which occasioned a test of motion without «force». From a teacher and analyst's perspective, students explored critical cases and varied parameters in haphazard ways. But to come back to my analogy of the darkened room: if you do not know where you are and what the world is like, you have to explore it first without knowing where you should begin. Any structure only emerges from the exploration. Although a physicist might explore the cases of both vectors lined up in the same, opposite, and orthogonal orientations, she would do so because of her existing familiarity with Newtonian physics. My own research among scientists shows that as long as they find themselves in familiar worlds, they often act in the rational ways they usually claim for themselves. As soon as they are in an unfamiliar context, whether this is in the laboratory or on some graphing task, their behavior is strikingly similar to that of the students here. They are groping in the dark (Roth 2004a); structures slowly emerge from and as a consequence of their groping. All of this evidence suggests that activities when people do not know some aspect of the world nor have a language for describing it are explorations in the course of which both world and language coevolve. But of course, school classrooms are not settings dealing with completely novel entities; teachers know what they want students to perceive and how they want students to talk about they see. Teachers therefore constitute constraints to the evolution of world and language, though, as I will show in subsequent chapters, they cannot uniquely determine outcomes.

From an interactionist and pragmatic viewpoint, talk is a form of action. In this view, students' learning is expressed in the modification of existing language and associating it with entities that become salient among others by telling them apart from the ground and other entities. Through such modifications, current ways of talking are situationally adjusted to optimize actions for the task at hand. Because in their actions, students treated objects, events, and the labels in a flexible manner, the latter had ambiguous status; the intrinsic nature of phenomena was not fixed, but shifted as students adapted their ways of talking about the situation at hand. Some may consider this interpretive flexibility a barrier to learning. However, it was considered here an important resource. Interpretive flexibility allowed students' significations to change so that they came to share ways of using words within a group.

Curtailment of Interpretive Flexibility

In the following episode, Eliza, Glen, and Ryan had their first conversation (about the microworld) with me, their teacher. The episode shows how, from my perspective, this interaction curtailed the interpretive flexibility of microworld phenomena in specific ways such as to channel the students' explorations and talk. Here, I listened to the students as they elaborated their talk while being oriented to «force». Eliza returned to an earlier observation sentence, "The big arrow is time," but now qualified it to include direction (lines 80, 82). Ryan provided a different description, new to this conversation, according to which «force» "increases velocity the longest" (line 83).

78	Teacher:	What did you find out so far? *
79	Glen:	We found out that– (1.0)
80	Eliza:	The big arrow is time.
81	Ryan:	Yeah it's well– (1.2)
82	Eliza:	Time and direction.
83	Ryan:	It increases velocity the longest.

The orientation of this interaction and therefore the nature of the talk were considerably different from what it has been. These students were no longer trying to do things in the world and use language as one of the ways in which they aligned one another to the task, what has to be done, and what can be seen on the display. My question *explicitly* referred them to the past, "What did you find out so far?" (line 78). It was by reflecting on the past that objects and events were referred to; the talk now was *about* these entities rather than being *with* them. The students' relationship to the microworld in general and its objects and events in particular had changed from an involvement with them to talking about them—which not only required the orientation to the past but also was a prerequisite for the emergence of objects in themselves as separate from their involvement with them (Buber 1970). Their utterances were observation sentences about objects that had been objects of and were known through experiences. But our talk also had the quality of exploring an issue *in* talk itself: talk was not only about something else but also a way of exploring ways of talking. This comes with the double nature of talk: it is both an activity in itself *and* an activity that makes other activities its topic—though in practice, the lines between the two are never clear.

After the students had completed their utterances with respect to time, direction, and the effect of "the big arrow" on velocity, I provided a different reading of the screen display (lines 84, 86, and 88). I asked them to run the simulation again and then, stopping the simulation, likened the display to a time-lapse photograph produced through multiple exposures at equal time intervals (line 88). This reading allowed the three students to develop a new way of talking about the display (lines 89–92).

84	Teacher:	It increases velocity but see that um::: (3.5) that the time is sort of given by the ah, spacing, what the computer (2.8) can you run it? (3.0)
85	Ryan:	Yeah.

86   Teacher: * STOP IT! STOP IT! (2.3) Now look, you see these are like pictures, like a multiple flash picture (2.2) so you see the object at different. (2.0)

87   Ryan: Places–
88   Teacher: =But at constant time intervals see the time, between the first and the second picture is the same as between the fifth and the seventh– sixth picture.
89   Ryan: It's just that it was moving faster.
90   Glen: Faster, yeah.
91   Teacher: Yeah so?
92   Eliza: That shows acceleration? (1.9)
93   Teacher: So if you say *that*, you should now test it. What kind of test can you do to see that it's acceleration?
94   Eliza: A different direction, like an up and down?
95   Teacher: Why don't you try that?!

Ryan, supported by Glen, elaborated his earlier utterance and now included that the description that the object "was moving faster" (lines 89–90). My comment "Yeah, so?" (line 91) is a *continuer*, that is, a renouncement of my turn at talk, and at the same time an invitation and encouragement for the students to continue in the elaboration of the topic. Furthermore, the questioning tone of my utterance implied that students were to draw a conclusion. Eliza wondered if Ryan's observation could be seen as an instance of acceleration (line 92). Although my response looks like a question (lines 93 and 95), associated with my walking away, it was heard by students as an encouragement to explicitly test this new conjecture.

In this episode, the students' talk about the display changed from an association of «force» with time to one with change in motion. For example, Eliza, who first explained that «force» represented time and direction (line 80), later conjectured that the display featured an instances of acceleration (line 92). Ryan, who first said that «force» "increases velocity the longest," changed his description (supported by Glen) to "it was moving faster" (lines 83, 89). These new descriptions and conjectures emerged after the students had heard my description of the screen display—the flash pictures were taken at equal time intervals. That is, students responded to my utterances in changing their talk about the phenomenon, and with it, saw something different than what they had earlier seen. My utterances had been resources that enabled new ways of seeing and talking to emerge. These new ways were not by necessity more or less scientific—they never can be because every resource embodies both its reproduction and new, varying production. But in the present situation, the new way of talking had gotten them off associating «force» and "time," an association that had emerged following an interaction with and feedback from the microworld. That is, although both resources (computer feedback and my articulation) were consistent with cultural practices, it led students to forms of talking that were more consistent with the standard language that I was to teach them in one instance, but inconsistent in another. Some readers might be tempted to think that there was an asymmetry between the teacher and the software, associated with authority on the subject in this classroom. But this is not so, as I show in chapter 6, where the question is whether there is an asymmetry between student-produced language and that imported to the classroom by the teacher.

In the present situation, the students changed their description. However, I did not ratify this new way of talking about the microworld phenomenon but walked away and left them to their explorations. I encouraged students to take their current way of talking as a resource for designing new investigations. This new description seemed acceptable to Ryan who had struggled earlier trying to integrate Eliza's talk with his own. In the previous episode, rather than contradicting her suggestion of «force» representing time, Ryan had suggested that «force» was also associated with the direction of motion (line 60). Similarly, without contradicting Eliza, he offered a different reading in the present episode (line 83). The modified statement "It's just that it was moving faster" (line 89) was then acceptable to his peers. However, his use of "increasing velocity" as a descriptor of what physicists would call accelerated motion did not mean he talked in ways compatible with Newtonian physics. For it is not evident from this episode that he used "velocity" to talk about «velocity». Rather, he may have referred to «velocity» as an "effort" that had been imparted to the moving object (he did so later in the conversation), an indication that he spoke about velocity without seeing in «velocity» another description of the phenomenon.

In this episode, the students established a new way of talking about the screen display. This new talk was achieved collaboratively such that their contributions in (lines 89, 90, and 92) read, when joined together, "It's just that it was moving, yeah faster, that shows acceleration." This collective way of talking becomes evident when the latter part of the episode is compared with the earlier part where Eliza and Ryan talked in different ways. Ryan's way of talking did not present a contrast, but rather an addition, to Eliza's way of talking. This was an indication of their preference for agreement to achieve shared ways of talking rather than for adversarial moves (which are indicated by utterance openings stating contrast).

The new way of talking emerged from the interaction between the task (finding appropriate descriptions and explanations for the events in the microworld), my description of the microworld, the students' own ways of talking, and the microworld. The students integrated my utterances into their conversation such that it now allowed them to talk about and consistently tell apart different things in the display. Culture entered the students' conversation in the form of constraints constituted by the microworld (which limited the range of user actions) and my specific ways of talking about some aspects of it. Such constraints, though, are themselves subject to interpretive flexibility, which is why students will not by necessity discover Newtonian physics for themselves by using software such as Interactive Physics. However, additional conversations with me, if viewed as authoritative ways to be emulated, limited the possible ways in which the screen display could be articulated. That is, they curtailed the interpretive flexibility of microworld objects, events, and language that articulated them and that can be used to talk about them. These interactions can thus be viewed as part of a learning process that introduced students to the standard ways of talking physics, that is, to the practice of physics. It has to be underscored that the purpose of these conversations was not to transmit definitions, because these cannot in principle capture concepts and objects, that is, uniquely designate and denote them. Rather, the conversations in the context of the microcomputer worlds had the effect of constraining the range of ways of talking that students could use the words "velocity" and "force" and thus to curtail the flexibility with which they could be associated with particular microworld objects and events. (I provide a more detailed analysis of teacher–student interactions in chapter 5.) Together with the moments when I used the microworld to illustrate some specific effect, students could experience the computer microworld as part of my (discursive and physical) actions. Suffice it to say that I first identified students' ways of seeing and talking about the microworld phenomena. I achieved this by engaging them in a conversation in the course of which they explicated their present understandings. Second, if the students' science talk was situationally more appropriate from a disciplinary perspective, I moved on to another group; if not, as it was in this episode, I took some action to help students see and talk about the microworld in new ways.

Emergence of Newtonian Talk

In the course of their talk over and about the objects and events on the computer screen, the students did not instantly change from telling things apart to the standard forms of talking Newtonian physics. In fact, as I will show in the next chapter, the emergence of the standard and legitimized ways of talking is as much an outcome of contingent processes as nonstandard ways of talking. The emergence and subsequent stabilization of standard ways of talking is just a special case of a more general process that also provides opportunities for nonstandard ways to emerge. Here, standard Newtonian ways of talking about the events on the computer monitor emerged slowly and tentatively from the muddle of their earlier talk in the face of the inherently ambiguous nature of the microworld objects and events and the expressions used to articulate and denote them. At times, the students seemed to have it; but then they lost it again and saw and talked in ways that were inappropriate from a physicist's perspective.

As table 2.1 shows, the normal scientific terms for «velocity» and «force» appeared, disappeared, and then reappeared in the conversations. But it was this flexibility that also allowed the emergence of the standard Newtonian language. If language was not flexible in nature, scientists would never be able to move from their current ways of understanding through scientific revolutions to new ways of talking; if there was no flexibility in language, students would never be able to move from their everyday talk through the muddled, exploring articulations to the culturally acknowledged now standard ways of talking physics.

In the present situation, not only language but also the ontology (nature) of the displayed objects changed. The arrow, seen in one instance as a sign denoting time, had become an agent that forced objects at another point in time. From a standard physics perspective, the developments in this episode were significant: Students began to perceive what a physicist would see. At the same time, their language in setting and actions began to change and with it, the language that they used to describe what they saw and did. This is a necessary condition for being able to participate in physicists' language about the events in the microworld. We should expect that for those whose learning trajectory includes graduate studies in physics, the seeing and talking will take on more and more of the features shared within the community of physicists.

The following episode illustrates how the three students evolved their ways of articulating the microworld to include features critical for a standard and therefore by the curriculum-legitimized view of the observed events. Here the three students agreed for the first time that they could articulate the smaller arrow as "velocity" and «force» as something that changes the direction of motion. Such features in the students' talk emerged and sometimes disappeared again because the nature of these features was still ambiguous. They were still used to get around in the microworld rather than being about getting around. These features had not yet been abstracted from the situation—they constituted a form of *telling things apart* rather than *talking science*, which is *about* objects and entities.

Just before this episode, Ryan (who still had difficulties manipulating the system) had accidentally set «velocity» in a vertical direction and «force» in a horizontal position. All three students showed interest in this configuration and decided to run the simulation rather than pursuing a previous idea. Eliza's talk in the current situation made salient two aspects of the motion. The object first moved in the direction indicated by the initial position of «velocity» and then shifted increasingly into the direction of «force» (line 111).

111 Eliza: * Well, it starts out in the direction of the arrow and then it goes into the direction of the big arrow.
112 Ryan: Yeah, the big arrow, so maybe the little arrow is in the initial direction.

113 Glen: Let's stretch, no let's put the big one underneath and stretch it really
                    long.

Eliza's statement was an exploration of language in situation; it was also an observation sentence describing the behavior of the onscreen entities in *this* situation. The exploratory nature of the talk can be seen from Ryan's elaboration of the immediately preceding utterance. He added the predicate "initial" to "direction" and thereby clustered the visual qualities of the display on the left-hand side (line 112). Such predication is a first, primitive grammatical construction, a first but significant step toward the reification of bodies and the language that goes with them (Quine 1995). Here, «velocity» is "little" early on in the simulation; the direction of the "little arrow" and the object's motion early on are hypothesized ("maybe") to be the same. The statement therefore was an observation of part of the events, and therefore highly situated. However, we can see in the utterance a first intimation of an observation categorical that generalized the direction of «velocity» with the direction of the motion.

Glen then suggested to do a new simulation in which «force» and «velocity» pointed in the same, upward direction (line 113). This would test or clarify the effect of «force» on the motion of the object. Here, the language had the purpose of articulating «force» and aligning the coparticipants toward a next action; the language here was less *about* the situation than it was to bring about change. To implement such a change, the movement of the activity into the future, coparticipants articulated the things and indicated what was to be done. Ryan, however, had difficulties in preparing «force» so that it pointed upward. They students therefore did not implement the test and ended up with an experiment similar to the previous one: the initial velocity was larger in magnitude and pointed more to the right. At the point where the transcript continues, they had run the simulation three times. Eliza described an observation in which the object "starts out really fast" (lines 140). Ryan and Eliza utter a few more words orienting them to the early part of the motion (line 141) and to a possible next action (line 142). Glen then uttered the beginning of a focal observation categorical, which constituted the reification of an object, "The longer the smaller arrow, it goes–." Here, the pronoun "it" was essential, a vital link between "the smaller arrow" and the (motion of) the object; such essential pronouns strengthen the link between simple observations and lead to the reification of entities described in observation categoricals such as "Whenever. . . it . . ." (Quine 1995, 27).

140 Eliza: * It starts out really fast.
141 Ryan: =It starts out–
142 Eliza: So do I–?
143 Glen: =The longer the smaller arrow,
                    [it goes–]

144 Ryan: [Initial] speed–
145 Glen: =Yeah, velocity.
146 Ryan: Velocity.

Ryan also contributed a few terms, "it starts out," "initial speed," and "velocity" (lines 141, 144, 146), the last one following the same utterance by Glen (lines 145). It is evident here that the students did not so much articulate an observation as try words in the context. Thus, Ryan first used "initial speed" but changed immediately after Glen had uttered velocity. None of the utterances actually constituted a complete sentence, articulating an observation or something else. The students explored the suitability of words in this setting as much as they explored the setting itself.

In the following manipulation, Ryan disconnected «force» from the circular object. They decided to test this new configuration. In the context of the screen display resulting from the simulation, Glen produced an utterance that had the structure of a focal observation categorical, "when[ever]. . . it . . ." (line 157). We do not need to worry for the moment that it was an incorrect statement from a physicist's perspective, because replacing "in" with "with" in the second part of the sentence would make it correct. These students were in their exploration of language as much as they were in the exploration of the microworld—the purpose of their activity was to structure both, which required exploration. Glen's gesture in the second part of his production, which traced the trajectory at a constant rate, suggested both a constant direction and constant speed (which contrasted the gesture analyzed at the end of the previous chapter, where he accelerated the motion while uttering "it goes–").

157 Glen: So when you don't run it with the arrow ((Touches circular object))
             ⎡it goes in the same velocity   ⎤
             ⎢((* Traces trajectory))   ⎥
158 Ryan: ⎣It just goes in the same direction⎦ ((Traces trajec-
             tory.)) this arrow like is initial– (2.3)
             ⎡the later direction   ⎤
159 Eliza: ⎣That means it's a constant–⎦
160 Glen: So like (2.8) this arrow ((Touches screen at
             «force»)) forces it ((Gestures horizontally)) to a certain ⎡extent.⎤
161 Ryan: ⎣ It   ⎦
             changes direction after the start.

Ryan articulated the notion of a constant direction, suggested that «velocity» determines motion initially, and began to describe the effect of «force» on the later part of the motion (line 158). The following two utterances further elaborated Ryan's statement. Attempting to clarify the first part of Ryan's observation, Eliza commented that «velocity» was constant in the absence of «force» (line 159). Glen added by observing that «force» "forced" the object;

this comment was further elaborated by Ryan who said that «force» had changed the direction.

Earlier (lines 111–112) Eliza and Ryan had provided, for the first time, utterances that articulated those details of the display that are important for standard explanations of the on-screen events. Their observation sentence stated that the object moved first in the initial direction of «velocity» and then changed its direction toward that of «force». The three students' articulation of the initial conditions ("it starts out in the direction" and "initial") suggested that they did not attend to the changing direction of «velocity» along the trajectory. To a physicist, «velocity» is, by definition, always tangent to the trajectory. At this point, however, the students were not at a point of articulating events such that they made salient the character of «velocity» shared within the physics community. In the second part of the episode, all three students used "speed" to talk in the context of «velocity» (lines 140, 144–146). Although Glen and Ryan used the word "velocity," their utterances "it starts out" and "initial" suggested that the initial part of the motion was articulated. But here, for the first time, students considered «velocity» as speed or velocity. If one regards Newtonian ways of talking as the goal of the students' learning trajectory, this part episode constitutes an advance over previous ones. The third part of the episode documented the students' increased focus on the direction of motion, which changed only when «force» acted on the object ("forces it to a certain extent" and "it changes direction after the start"). At this point, the students' talk included speed (lines 140–146), direction (lines 157–161), and the effect of «force» on the direction of the object's motion (lines 157–161). The third part also illustrated the important function of the computer display as a mediational tool in student conversations. Glen and Ryan touched the screen at the location of the object they talked about (circular object, «force» vector), and gestured or traced the trajectory described by the circular object. These actions greatly reduced the possibility of misalignments within their group.

The episode is evidence for the three students' collective achievements. They each contributed to the emerging descriptions that not only reflected what they "saw" but also what they "knew" about the system. For example, the use of "velocity" to denote «velocity» was jointly evolved as all three added to the description (lines 140–146). Furthermore, the episode provides evidence that the students converged on a shared language. First, Eliza mentioned "high speed" as a contrast to speed in an earlier experiment. Then, Glen attempted to articulate the same contrast in a generalization ("the longer the smaller arrow"). Finally, Ryan and Glen agreed that "velocity" was a useful way for talking about the phenomenon they observed («velocity»). In the same way, their talk in lines 157–161 can be understood as a collectively elaborated and therefore shared description. Sameness of the motion in the absence of «force» was expressed by each student ("same velocity," "same direction," and "its a constant"). Furthermore, Glen and Ryan used similar talk when making statements about the consequences of earlier observations. If motion remains constant in the absence of «force», then it must be «force» which "forces" the change (lines 160–161).

Convergence and Stabilization

The students arrived in this episode, for the first time, at a description that later became their preferred mode not only for articulating entities and simulations in context but also for talking *about* the microworld. That is, they began to first converge on ways of talking among themselves and this way of talking was consistent with the standard language of the physics community. This way of talking emerged from their previous, muddled articulation in activity and was made possible by the flexibility of objects, events, and talk. From a more traditional approach to the history of scientific and technological products, the present episode constitutes the moment of so-called invention or discovery, the moment of what other scholars describe as a new conception. The presented episode allowed a glimpse of *how* this new form of talk evolved in the face of the interpretive flexibility of the microworld phenomena and the constraints set by the range of possible phenomena. Reconfirmations and repetitions in students' talk not only served to arrive at common ways of talking, but also contributed to stabilization of specific ways of talking about the microworld.

This episode illustrates how students began to converge toward a way of talking that had family resemblance with standard language, that is, they began using linguistic resources consistent with Newtonian physics to describe the objects and events in the microworld and to explain their relation. This achievement was largely collaborative and emerged from students' own prior tentative expressions across the three modes perception, gesture, and speech. Glen and Ryan uttered an observation categorical (based on the contrast between the present and previous experiments) according to which «velocity» was "stronger" when «force» was longer (lines 191–193).

191 Glen: So when the big arrow, the big arrow, the big arrow is bigger–
              ((Points to «force»)) (0.9) No the length–
192 Ryan: Is longer
193 Glen: =is longer, than that ((Points to «velocity»)) one, it's more stronger.
197 Eliza: Like, you mean whichever arrow's longer?
198 Ryan: Yeah, like you see if (0.8) this one, watch, see if this ((Points to «ve-
              locity»)) is the initial speed. ((Runs simulation)) (1.3) What did it
              say? ((Reads software message, "The object velocities are higher
              from the simulation.")) The object velocities are higher from the
              simulation.

Between the first two parts of the episode, the three students had run another experiment. Eliza then asked Glen for a clarification of his earlier statement (line 197). Ryan began to illustrate their common orientation by pointing to «velocity» and running a simulation. He interrupted his talk to read the software message about object velocities that were too high (line 198). It was at this point that Glen uttered the previously analyzed statement relating the two arrows and the corresponding trajectory of the object (see figure 1.5).

199 * Wouldn't the length of the arrows– (1.6) Since * *that* arrow's longer * the

velocity is higher. * *That's*   * why:: it's pushing it that'a way. *

Here, Glen took over and elaborated his earlier statements into a focal observation categorical, "Since that arrow's longer, the velocity is higher" (line 199). The length of a specific arrow was correlated with the velocity of the object—this constituted a first explanation. That is, he stated that the greater «force» (which he gestured by holding his fingers parallel) pushed the object to increase the velocity along a trajectory that he indicated with a sweeping motion of his hand. After running another simulation, Eliza, too, stated a focal observation categorical: the higher velocity, the longer the arrow (line 207).

207 Eliza: The higher the velocity is, the longer the arrow is
208 Glen: Yes, so that would push since that velocity is higher, then that one,
            [it carries it faster   ]
209 Ryan: [Yeah, it carries it up] and we'll make this one long now.
            ((Lengthens «velocity»))
210 Glen: So the *longer* the arrow, the *longer* the arrow, the higher the velocity.

Glen agreed and pointed out that the object was "carried faster" by «force» (line 208). Ryan simultaneously expressed the same idea and suggested a new experiment with a greater «velocity» (line 209). As he began to increase the velocity of the object, Glen commented that the longer «velocity» signified a higher velocity (line 210).

In this episode, the three students drew on the elements of standard Newtonian language to explore talking about their experiments in the microworld. They linked a larger «force» to a larger «velocity» (lines 191–193) and used "it's pushing" and "speed/velocity" to refer to «force» and «velocity», respectively (lines 198–199). Glen's gesture, by means of iconic resemblance, indexed «force» and, by means of the resemblance of its motion with the object's trajectory, made salient which of the two arrows did the pushing and which quantity was affected by that push. Finally, all three linked a longer «velocity» to a larger "velocity" (lines 198, 207, 208).

All three parts of the episode provide evidence for collaboratively achieved observation sentences and observation categoricals and for their collective way of using them. In the course of lines 191–193, Glen and Ryan jointly achieved the description that a bigger «force» was related to a "stronger" «velocity». While Glen articulated most of this observation categorical, Ryan provided a key word that allowed Glen to complete his sentence. This is not to say that either Glen or Ryan had something in their mind but that the sentences first emerged *in* and *from* these interactions as ways of telling things apart and orienting others, and only then became sensible ways of talking *about* the microworld in front of them. In fact, it is the formation of focal observation categoricals that made an utterance useful across and therefore independent of specific situations on the screen. Because observation sentences were independent of the specific on-screen situations, they also allowed a detachment of the students from the particulars of any on-screen situation and their involvement (through manipulation) with them.

The appropriateness of Ryan's contribution was an indication that he had an orientation to the events in common with Glen. In the second part, Eliza asked for an elaboration of Glen's earlier comment (line 197). "Like you mean . . . ?" was a way of seeking confirmation that her orientation toward the entities and language was compatible with that Glen had taken. Ryan and Glen produced the answer collaboratively (lines 198–199). The conversationalists now drew on "speed" or "velocity" as resources to name the object «velocity». Eliza also used "velocity" in a way that was consistent with theirs (line 207). The third part of the episode then brought together an observation categorical ("the *higher* the velocity is, the *longer* the arrow is") with a possible causal antecedent in the form of a "since . . . then" pattern ("since that velocity is higher, then that one carries it faster"). Again, Glen and Ryan simultaneously articulated the effect of force on the motion of the object ("carrying it . . ."), indicating common ways of being attuned to the setting. In the end, they reconfirmed Eliza's earlier statement (line 210).

On the surface, the three students seemed to have arrived at a way of talking that was consistent with standard Newtonian description. Later evidence showed that the students' way of talking was not yet firmly established and entrenched, an indication that the description they had achieved here was still brittle. But this evidence also showed that in the end, Eliza, Glen, and Ryan evolved a language appropriate for the task at hand. Furthermore, the transcript of the present episode permits an interpretation that highlights possible features of the students' talk that were inconsistent with Newtonian language. According to this interpretation, a stronger force may still have been responsible for a larger velocity rather than acceleration ("since «force» is longer, the velocity is higher" and "since that velocity is higher, then that one carries it faster"). However, after a brief conversation with me, these ways of students' talk stabilized. In chapter 5, I will provide a more fine-grained analysis of these interactions between students and myself, which provided resources for the present talk to converge with Newtonian physics. Evidence from the following class period showed that the three students' ways of talking had become solidly entrenched so that they, without further interacting with me, came to consistently talk in Newtonian ways about the microworld phenomena and the scientific representations (vectors) that appear in the display.

SCIENTIFIC LANGUAGE EMERGES FROM ARTICULATING WORLD

Talking is part of an expression of the articulation of the world; the utterance does not translate an idea already fixed, but accomplishes it. And if the students' language in the present case studies was more akin to muddle than coherent scientific language, it was because theories or concepts did not and could not yet exist. Because students were already familiar with certain ways of talking, there was a ground upon which new ways of talking could emerge and evolve. In the previous section, I described students in the process of constituting and navigating a Newtonian microworld. In the process they articulated entities in actions and talk, but their talk was not so much *about* something as an aspect of getting around, taking position, telling one another what to make salient, and so forth. These students did not have a semantic model, conception, or even naive theory. They saw certain things for the first time and differed at times as to just what could be seen on the monitor. They also used language as part of structuring their experiences and the world given to them in their perception. At this point, we should not overinterpret the situation and conclude that students actually *meant* something by what they said. If anything, meaning existed in the situation insofar they found themselves in a physics classroom where they were asked to engage with things and entities that they did not know and that they could not yet integrate with what was already a meaningful world. Whatever they encountered was new, and to have the experience of meaning, these new things had to accrue to their already existing, familiar world. These things, as words, accrue to meaning rather than meaning coming to them. Thus,

> that one uses familiar words in unfamiliar ways—rather than slaps, kisses, pictures, gestures, or grimaces—does not show that what one said must have meaning. An attempt to state that meaning would be an attempt to find some

familiar (that is, literal) use of words—some sentence which already had a place in the language game—and, to claim that one might just as well have *that*. (Rorty 1989, 18)

Initially students did not talk *about* the microworld because they did not yet have the necessary reflexive distance required for talking about some world theoretically. This world, while existing materially, did not exist for these students in the sense that they knew how entities behaved, related to one another, and so forth. However, in the course of the events described here, the particular language useful in the context of the microworld emerged and evolved from a myriad of possible starting points. The students drew on their existing familiar individual linguistic resources in this novel situation. As the events unfolded, the students came to orient, perceive, and speak in increasingly similar ways during their microworld adventures. That is, the practical actions provided the conditions for the emergence and evolution of the language simultaneous with the emergence of the perceivable patterns in the material world. The language coevolved with the world articulated in students' physical actions and hand gestures; it coevolved with students' room to maneuver in a world opened up through their practical exploration.

In this unfolding, the students' coevolving language and world had much in common with the coevolution of the world relating to the distribution of boy and girl births and (mathematical) language I described in the introduction. Through my actions, the world became articulated, but my actions were interdependent with the linguistic resources that I had at hand or that resurfaced into my consciousness in rather vague ways. The problem and therefore the hospital world took shape in the exploration, which already required a particular stance and orientation and which was irreducibly connected to the language at hand. It was as if a clearing were opening up as I explored, but I had no control over what was revealed in this clearing—which of the linguistic resources would come to bear, or even which linguistic resources became salient and relevant. Of the different articulations and resources, only some were pursued, just as the students came to use some words and left others by the wayside. In my example, I interacted with MathCAD, itself a microworld that responded to my actions. In the case of the students (here Eliza, Glen, and Ryan), both the microworld and the peers responded to an action (verbal, gestural, material).

In this situation where students enter new and unknown worlds, learning can be described as the emergence of new aspects in their lifeworld. These new aspects involve the coevolution of ways of talking and reified entities that become resources in the actions of the students. New forms of descriptive language emerged from the muddled telling that they did in the setting to orient one another and get around while they were still very much groping in the dark. That is, the present setting allowed students to move from their own everyday language to a new language useful for navigating the microworld, but also useful for getting around in the scientific community. The new vocabulary emerged from their interactions within small groups. This development of common ways of talking, thus, led to distributed and collective rather than individual achievements. The very possibility for change resided in the flexibility of objects and events. Of course, the different objects and entities also exist in a material sense, as dots on a screen, and in this sense, they are not flexible. However, we can conceive of these objects and events in a dialectic way, so that they are relevant in human activity in more than one way—simultaneously in their material form, as (variously) perceived entities, and as outcomes of actions currently envisioned by the acting subject (Leont'ev 1978). What changed was the way students structured the material world, the actions that became available, and what they could envision as results of their action. Paralleling this development, they also drew on (existing) language as a resource to be structured and reconstituted in ways that were consistent with the structures of the world that emerged. Language is useful for representing things only then when its structures are compatible with and map onto the structures of the domain that it models—here the material world. As my research among scientists showed, in professional research, too, these two types of structures and their relation coemerge (Roth 2004b).

Learning therefore was a process of evolutionary change of language that took place in a setting including students, computer software, and computer displays. The language eventually converged with Newtonian language. Both the microworld—as a resource enabling and constraining the actions of the students—and teacher talk provided constraints that curtailed some of the ambiguity and therefore constrained the development of students' telling in activity to talking science in specific ways. This view of the coevolution of language and world may appear strange when we look at it from the perspective of someone who knows. To us teachers, the things and events in this microworld often appear so self-evident and simple. The world seems to be given. All the students have to do is look and apply language. But this is not so! We know this as soon as we (carefully) analyze our own first attempts of exploring and navigating new terrain. It is as if the world was revealed over time rather than being there in its fullness: we come to see certain aspects for the first time, as we clear away the veils of innocent ignorance and increasingly bring light to the clearing. The following example further shows that we do not perceive the world as a whole with all its articulation the first time we lay our eyes on it.

A few years ago during a fellowship stay in Germany, I undertook an experiment. I decided to ride my bicycle repeatedly along an initially unfamiliar route and, one I had returned, to rigorously record anything that I could remember and particularly that had become salient. For twenty-one days, I took the same route. My field notes provide ample evidence of new salient entities and practices over this period of time. For example, on the fifth day, I noted for the first time white posts on the side of the road. Almost simultaneously, I noted that they appeared to be, with some exceptions, equally spaced. Then, all of a sudden, I also noticed that there were numbers on these posts, 10.2, 10.3, and so on. Although I was not aware of such marked posts existing at my home in Canada, I began to suppose that these were distance markers. Using the stopwatch function of my watch, I clocked the amount of time it took to ride ten intervals, for example, from 10.5 to 11.5: It took me around two minutes. If the posts indicated distance in 100-meter intervals, then I had covered 1,000 meters, which, multiplied by 30, would give me 30 kilometers per hour (30 x 2 minutes). Because this appeared reasonable, I began to use the posts as distance indicators to calculate how far I had gone and also to measure and calculate the speed with which I was going.

The world in this example was not given to me once and for all, but new features became salient every time I took the route anew. That is, new entities in this world arose from my activity of navigating it; in fact, the world was not the same but continuously expanded. I had not noted any posts until the fifth trip. For all purposes, they did not exist in my world; I lived in a world without white posts and without the numbers marked on them. Therefore, my actions during and my descriptions of the first four trips did not and could not include them. But as soon as I noted them, they became resources in my actions, themselves the result of my previous history. I drew on instruments and the (mathematical) language at hand to evolve new possibilities for action, such as measuring distance and speed.

When we start exploring new phenomena, we are typically unable to make clear exactly what it is that we want to do before developing the language in which we succeed in doing it (Rorty 1989). In part, we cannot make clear what we want to do because we do not have sufficient practical understanding of the world into which our investigation projected us and what this world allows us to do. Our practical understanding may not have developed to the point of allowing phenomena to emerge that we subsequently understand to be interesting. It is only when our actions and perceptions lift certain aspects from the ground of our experience that language can point to these and thereby can articulate the intelligibility of this world. Our new vocabularies then make possible formulations of their own purposes. The vocabularies become new tools for doing new things that we could not have envisaged prior to the development of our actions and perceptions, and prior to a particular set of observation descriptions.

It is important to note that I had no control over the sudden presence of the posts in my world or, for that matter, over their absence during the first four trips. There is no theory (that I am aware of) that would predict at what point the posts as an invariant feature in the environment should become salient, but we know that movement with respect to the environment provokes invariants to emerge (Noë 2002). Furthermore, I had no control over the idea that the numbers indicated distances from some origin—which in fact I went to find for my experimental route—or that I could use these numbers to measure total trip distances or speed of travel. It appears to be a fundamental aspect of the human condition that someone who makes something new "is typically unable to make clear exactly what it is that he wants to do before developing the language in which he succeeds in doing it" (Rorty 1989, 13), poet, scientist, philosopher, and every ordinary person alike. The new vocabulary—or old vocabulary associated with a new situation (e.g., "atom" was used differently by the Greeks than it is used by a physicist of the twenty-first century)—makes new actions possible, including a formulation of its own purpose. It is a resource that allows us to do things that we had not and could not envisage before—things that the resource had created and helped to provide. Thus, the mathematical vocabulary at my hand constituted the hospital world that I explained using the same vocabulary. The mathematical vocabulary that constituted the posts as equidistant markers constituted the world of distances and distance measurements. In the same way, the students in this chapter evolved a vocabulary and a world together. Drawing on linguistic resources, which emerged out of their control, they developed a particular set of descriptions that allowed them to do things that the descriptions helped to create.

This chapter shows that there were many changes in the way students (perceptually, linguistically) articulated aspects in this microworld. New ways of articulating the world emerged rather then revealing themselves upon first sight. This is what the discovery approaches of the 1960s to 1980s got wrong, for they assumed that students would find theory by interacting with the world. The episodes in this chapter show that the microworld did not tell the students how it wanted be spoken about. The microworld cannot propose students a language to speak. Only the students and other human beings (e.g., the teacher) can. That is, notions of criteria and choice cannot explain the changes in vocabulary. The changes are better explained as the loss of habits and the gradual acquisition of new ones. This is the case for the students in the same way as it is for scientific revolutions.

> After a hundred years of inconclusive muddle, the Europeans found themselves speaking in a way which took these interlocked theses [that constituted the Copernican revolution] for granted. Cultural change of this magnitude does not result from applying criteria (or from "arbitrary decision") any more than individuals become theists or atheists, or shift from one spouse or circle of friends to another, as a result of either of applying criteria or of *actes gratuits*. (Rorty 1989, 6)

From this perspective, there cannot ever exist criteria within human beings or in the world to ground decisions about the choice of vocabulary. There are, nevertheless, constraints to the way in which we can perceive and act in the worlds partly of our making. Our existing vocabularies constitute resources that we use and reuse as part of the attempt to bring structure to our world, a world of which language is a constitutive part. Thus, it is not surprising to observe students talking the same kind of inconclusive muddle that early people found themselves in while evolving new languages for talking about the sun, stars, and the universe.

It should be quite clear by now that I consider language not to be a medium for expressing something other than itself, meaning, or representing something other than itself, facts about this world (Wittgenstein 1974). Language is but an aspect of the structures that surround us in the social (as words) and material world (as physical sounds). Language cannot express something deep within us, because whatever we make to constitute the inside is itself the result of language. Together with body orientation and bodily gestures, language is a way of making and taking a position in the world. This erases the distinction between knowing a (microworld) language and knowing the (micro-) world more generally.

INTERPRETIVE FLEXIBILITY AND CONVERGENCE

The pragmatic view of language espoused here supports an evolutionary metaphor for learning. The notion of interpretive flexibility of phenomena provides for multiple (but not always a priori available) ways of talking from which selections are made. The drift I described appears to be a fundamental condition of situations where written language does not play the dominant role that it takes in a culture of writing. In the absence of writing, "there is nothing outside the thinker, no text, to enable him or her to produce the same line of thought again or even to verify whether he or she has done so or not" (Ong 1982, 34). At the same time, this lack of stability provides exactly the possibility for change that we need to allow students to evolve ways of talking that eventually are deemed suitable to the world at hand, whereby the experienced world itself is not independent of the language that has evolved. Because of this, new ways of talking need to be recurrent, emerge, and come into use as individuals, small groups, and larger collectives find the ways of orienting and positioning along with particular ways of telling things apart. It is therefore not surprising to observe new phenomena and talk emerging from and adapting to the contingencies of particular learning settings.

In their groups, students adapted ways of articulating and talking in a triple sense. First, their collaborative work provided opportunities for convergence of material phenomena and ways of articulating until focal observation categoricals had emerged that not only provided a fit between the two but also was independent of the situation. Second, students converged in their respective ways of employing linguistic resources, which thereby established a common language. Third, the emergent way of talking within student groups converged with Newtonian language *about* the microworld. Rather than being a problem, the inherent ambiguity in worldly events and the flexible way of articulating them was a resource for the evolutionary and adaptive changes of descriptions and thus for learning. This process of making convergences was part of the stabilization work needed for new descriptive language to survive the immediate setting.

A pragmatic view of learning as evolutionary change of language comes with an advantage: it allows teachers to deal with classroom phenomena directly, a point that I elaborate in much greater detail in chapter 5. That is, teachers hear students talk and they can then talk with the students. Teachers do not have to try to get into the heads of students to find out their conceptions. Depending on what they see, teachers can then design on-the-spot interventions to mediate this talk in particular ways that might favor the emergence of some linguistic forms over others. Because of the flexibility of phenomena and talk, convergence toward standard forms of language is not a necessary and inevitable outcome but depends to a large extent on other constraints in the setting. From this perspective, learning can then be conceptualized as a process by which members of a community help newcomers to open up new parts of the world and to evolve language suitable to get around in it. Much of the literature on learning from a cultural perspective can be read in the same way. To master a professional language such as physics means to be able to act and interact with others who know physics. As with any other community, physicists evolved language practices that are distinctly different from those of other communities. Learning to use so-called concepts and conceptual tools, then, is a process of curtailing interpretive flexibility and multiple ways of talking according to the specific context of their application.

Interactive Physics makes use of vectors that are important representation devices in the physics community. In this way, the animated diagrams were not only instructional tools but also in important ways reflected the practices in which physicists engage. In this chapter, I showed that objects in the world are not consistently perceived; they were not and cannot be inherently meaningful. They were part of a meaningful whole of specific projects, characterized by the specificity of relevant situations, tools, ways of talking, and social relations. Thus, for those fluent in physics, Interactive Physics is a Newtonian microworld with a clear structure (it functions according to the Newtonian laws of physics). However, this structure was not available to the students, to whom microworld objects and events were inherently ambiguous. Any structure could only emerge from their interactions with and in the world—it makes little sense for science educators to decry that students do not see the existing regularities in the course of physics instruction. These regularities (structures) will only become self-evident once students have in common with the physics community explicit language, implicit assumptions (common sense), and embodied experience in the world.

Interactive Physics (as any other inscription) is both a cultural terrain and a cultural tool. However, it does not embed meaning, unambiguously or ambiguously. Tools do not have meaning even in their use in the patterned actions of practitioners; they have a place in a meaningful whole. Resources have not only an enabling but also a constraining quality on the activities of which they are part. The hope we can have by providing microworlds such as Interactive Physics lies in their provision of a limited number of objects, properties, and measurable quantities. One can only hope that these constraints allow the evolutionary adaptation of students' articulations of worlds in activity that allow them to move toward standard ways of talking, and therefore to the possible observation sentences and observation categoricals that are consistent with the curriculum a teacher espouses.

EVOLUTIONARY TRENDS: FROM STRUCTURING THE WORLD TO EXPLANATIONS

When I reanalyzed students' laboratory conversations, I was struck by the extent to which the development of language competence mapped onto some aspects of an existing typology of sign production (Eco 1976). Instead of the production of signs (signifying resources), we can also think of learning in terms of an increasing structuring of perception and action, including gestures and speech. Here, I retain from Umberto Eco's (1976) classification only those aspects that are relevant to the analysis of communication from my database, and I modify individual categories to make them consistent with the evidence in our database. The remaining categories are mapped in figure 2.3. I begin by introducing each category and then proceed to articulate the changes in modes of sign production and modalities of expression as students become increasingly familiar with some perceptual field (e.g., produced during investigation).

Eco classifies the modes of sign production according to the physical labor required to produce an expression ranging from simple recognition, to ostension, replica, and invention of previously nonexistent expressions. "Recognition occurs when a given object or event, produced by nature or human action (intentionally or unintentionally), and existing in a world of facts as a fact among facts, comes to be viewed . . . as the expression of a given content" (Eco 1976, 221). This category describes those instances in my database where students attempt to produce some phenomenon, simply looking at it (often without words) and sometimes commenting (i.e., "it doesn't work," "we can't get it to work," etc.). In this case, students are simply concerned with producing the phenomenon rather than developing theory.

| Modality | Modes of Sign Production | | | | | |
| | Recognition | Ostension | | Replica | | Inventions |
	Unstructured Events	Examples	Samples	Stylizations	Combinational Units	Structured Events
Percept	xxxxxxx	xxxxxxx	xxx	xx	x (arbitrary object)	
Gesture			xxx	xxxx	xxx	x
Speech		x	xx	xx	xxxx	xxxxxxx

Figure 2.3. In the evolution of students' communication, which occurs in the figure from left to right, the weight each modality carries changes from percepts to speech. Gestures seem to take an intermediate role.

Eco notes, "Ostension occurs when a given object or event produced by nature or human action . . . is picked up by someone and *shown* as the expression of the class of which it is a member" (1976, 225). He goes on to argue that ostension constitutes the most elementary form of active signification and uses the example of holding up one's shoes not to say "shoes," but rather "my shoes are dirty" so that the object is both sign and referent. In this case, it is as if the speaker said "«shoes (ostension) + these (mention) + shoes (referent)»" (225). In my research I have observed many instances when students, asked about what they have found out, simply utter something like "look, I'll show you" and redo the entire investigation (silently, or simply naming some objects). Because the selected object (investigation) is selected as a whole to express its class, I categorize this as an *example*. When students show only part of the investigation to stand for the entire investigation (and gesture and describe omitted parts), we classify the situation as "sample."

Replicas constitute a class of production modes that govern the most usual elements of sign production. Here, one takes account only of "replicable objects intentionally produced in order to signify" (228). This definition covers all those expression units that use a continuum more or less alien to their possible referents and are correlated to content units in an arbitrary way. These expression units include (in addition to verbal devices), ideograms, coded kinesic features (gestures meaning no, yes, that way, etc.), musical notes, traffic signs, symbols in logic and mathematics, and so on. In my database there are numerous instances where students use arbitrary objects to stand for the entities that they talk about. For example, a student picks up three pens, then identifies two as transparency films that are rubbed; she then identifies the third pen as standing for atoms that can be separated into nucleus and electrons (she pulls the body from the cap). Subsequently, the entities (films, atomic nucleus, and electrons) are no longer referred to in gesture or speech, but signified by means of the pens. Here, the objects used to signify have an arbitrary relation to their referents and therefore function in communication in the same way abstract words or gestures do. They are combinational units. When these objects are taken from the equipment of the investigation, they signify the objects and events to be explained in a stylized form. Finally, I categorize as "structured events" those instances when students have arrived at a new way of perceiving and explaining some aspect of the world, which, in investigations, they often produce and see for the first time.

As students become increasingly familiar with some phenomenon, from initial recognition to the point of evolving an adequate and viable language for describing and explaining the phenomenon, there is a change in the modality of expression. Figure 2.3 shows that the emergence of scientific language begins with a ("raw") stimulus at the level of perception. Students start by manipulating objects and watching events, frequently without commentary. When they are subsequently asked to account for what they observed, they often redo ("We'll show you") the investigation and thereby provide an example (near-copy) of the event. As they continue in their attempts to account for observations and start to provide theoretical descriptions, students begin to enact parts of the investigation by means of gesture including possible observations (samples). In subsequent attempts, gestures are increasingly used against the equipment (no longer enacted manipulations) and a large number of deictic expressions (gestural, verbal) develop. As their inquiry continues, arbitrary objects (e.g., pens, rulers, and notebooks) are used as placeholders for objects involved in the experiment or conceptual objects (e.g., electrons). Finally, students provide observational and theoretical descriptions with a minimum of gestures and in the absence of the experiment. In the ultimate stage (e.g., during exams), students provide complete verbal descriptions for the manipulations, events, and explanations.

Running parallel to this development is a second developmental sequence in which students move from simply "naming" objects (gestural and verbal deixis, words, and arbitrary objects) to constructing observational descriptions of specific events, to constructing observation categoricals, and finally to providing complete explanations. In this second sequence, gestures often precede the verbal modality in each of the four categories (naming, specific observation, observation categorical, and full explanation).

While reliance on the phenomenon steadily decreases (moves from the phenomenal toward abstract representations of the phenomenal), there is an increasing involvement of the gestural and verbal modalities. However, near the end of the sequence, reliance upon gestures as an expressive modality also decreases; consequently, communication has shifted almost completely into the verbal modality. Students describe in words (and sometimes use gesture or diagram) the phenomenon and provide a scientific explanation (including writing and diagrams) for it.

In the present chapter, I have provided a global account of the emergence and evolution of language. In chapter 3, I will draw on the research in a different classroom in a different country to show that explanatory talk (theories) evolves in contingent ways and may turn out to be inappropriate or incorrect (from the teacher's perspective) although there is no single point where one could blame students for irrational behavior. In chapter 4, then, I will provide a case study that contextualizes the developments within groups in the developments of language at the classroom level, highlighting particularly the mutual constraints of language development at the individual, group, and whole-class levels.

3

Contingency of Explanations

> Two roads diverged in a yellow wood . . . and both that morning equally lay in
> leaves no step had trodden black. Oh, I kept the first for another day! . . . Then
> took the other, as just as fair. . . . I took the one less traveled by, and that has
> made all the difference. (Frost 1915/1966)

In his poem "The Road Not Taken," Robert Frost makes thematic the contingency of not merely a voyage that has no particular endpoint but life in general.
Each moment in our lives is a branching point, where we move in one direction
without being able to see too much ahead to know where our steps are taking us.
Even if the two (or more) roads seem to differ only slightly or insignificantly at
the moment, they may have significant and large effects, as the students in this
and the following chapter found out during their study of chaotic systems. A
metaphor for the instantaneous choices we make is this: If we are in a new country and without a map, we cannot predict what we will see, whom we will meet,
what we will learn, and how these experiences will forever change us. For another image, we might also think of entering an unknown, completely darkened
room, or even of the game where one has to find out what is in a bag solely by
exploring it through touch. In these cases, we do not know where to go first and
we therefore begin moving here and there. We explore, continuously moving on,
and map the territory at the same time that we cover it. In the end, the path we
have taken, the cumulative history of our trajectory, is unique; it is the one less
traveled by, the one that has made all the difference. Even if we returned to
some point in the room or with our hand in the bag, it would not be the same
point given that we have had experiences since we last had been at the physical
place and therefore know it as part of a larger whole, even though we can never

know what the whole is as a thing in itself. We no longer experience the revisited place in the same way, because *we* have changed since; we no longer face the same kind of instance that Frost describes in his poem. If we were to take the same physical route over and over again, would become increasingly articulated, and in this articulation, would become familiar to us. It soon would seem natural to take a left turn at some point along the road, and we could give reasons for taking the left turn. We quickly forget what it means to travel this road for the first time.

The students who come to our science classrooms are, in effect, asked to travel territories that they do not know. We ask them to look and understand, but they do not know what to look for and therefore how to integrate it into their understanding of how the world works. In laboratory situations, students' explorations involving materials that they had not used before and their creation and exploration of unknown phenomena has much in common with traveling in unfamiliar countries without a map, exploring an unknown darkened room, or investigating a bag of items by touch alone. For a while, students have to keep exploring in the same direction and then, as the poet says, they may take another approach that seems just as fair. And yet, teachers are upset when their students do not take the one road that they had mapped out for the learners, the one learning trajectory that appeared so natural during the teacher's planning stage.

In this chapter, I am fundamentally concerned with showing the contingent way in which explanatory language arises from students' science activities as these unfold in real time. At the beginning of their investigations of new phenomena, students know neither the phenomena nor the language that they will ultimately find useful for describing them. Both perceived phenomena (that is, the phenomena as they appear to the students) and language emerge in the course of students' engagement with the materials provided by the teacher. But, as I pointed out in the previous chapter, these materials do not tell students *what* language to use or evolve. This does not mean that a decision about which language to use is entirely arbitrary or that the language used during the investigation is an expression of ideas already within the student. Rather, new phenomena, new language, and new skills, gestures, and so on are interactively stabilized as students engage with the material world. This constitutive intertwining of embodied practices and the responses from the material world has come to be known as the "mangle of practice" (Pickering 1995).

In this chapter, I will use one case study to articulate how explanations emerge in contingent ways from students' engagement in activity, which is always mediated by their use of language for the purpose of moving the activity ahead. This case study is particularly interesting because it shows how a "wrong" theory, that is, a theory undesired by the teacher, may arise from serious student engagement determined to comply with goals set by the teacher. That is, students may construct unwanted theoretical language despite the best intentions of students and teacher, and despite the presence of well-designed and

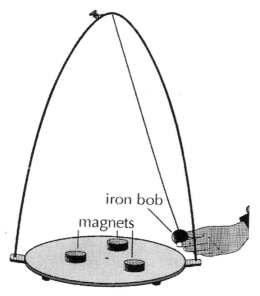

Figure 3.1. Despite repeatedly releasing the pendulum bob at "the same place," students do not succeed in predicting over which magnet it will come to rest. As part of this unit, they come to learn that this pendulum is a chaotic system, where small perturbations anywhere along the trajectory make exact predictions impossible.

experimentally tested curricular resources. My case study shows that the entire development of this unintended explanation, here referred to as "Foucault's pendulum," has great internal coherence, plausibility, and logic.

ETHNOGRAPHIC CONTEXT AND CURRICULUM

The events described below occurred during an experimental curriculum designed to teach some of the fundamental ideas of chaos theory to tenth-grade students in a German grammar school (Gymnasium) as an extension of their regular physics curriculum. Michael Komorek, a doctoral student at the time who had already completed a study of students' conceptions about chaotic systems, taught this unit. The goal of the unit was to assist students in developing an appreciation and understanding of the limited predictability of chaotic systems. In the first activity of the curriculum, students find out that the final resting position of a pendulum mounted above three magnets (figure 3.1) can only be known probabilistically: Theoretically, the pendulum bob comes to rest at a

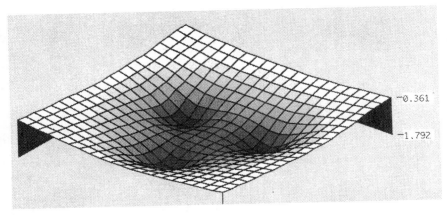

Figure 3.2. Gravitational and magnetic forces in the pendulum create a potential as shown. The bob comes to rest near one of the three magnets, because the potential energy is lowest there—like a ball rolling into the lowest point of an uneven field. The ridges between the hollows are critical, because immeasurable perturbations can take the bob into one rather than another hole.

particular magnet in one-third of the trials; by averaging across all trials conducted, the class arrives close to these probabilities. The students find out, through experience, that the magnetic pendulum is a system with limited predictability. This behavior can be explained as follows.

The gravitational and magnetic forces create a potential field shaped like a shallow bowl with three deeper depressions, one for each magnet (figure 3.2). Like a ball that a child releases on uneven terrain, which rolls along the steepest descent to the lowest possible point, the bob will eventually end up in one of the three depressions. However, the ridges that separate the three depressions are critical points in the system, because even one immeasurable perturbation of the bob somewhere along its trajectory can make the bob end up above one rather than another magnet and therefore endpoint. Think about it in terms of this one special situation. Imagine that the bob has slowed down so much that it just makes it come to a halt on top of one ridge. Everyday experience tells us that this is an unstable equilibrium, and much like a nail that we try to balance on its tip, immeasurable influences make the bob go down one or the other side. However, it really does not matter whether the perturbation comes exactly at the moment that the iron bob is on the ridge or elsewhere along the trajectory—which students come to understand in the second half of the unit through explorations with a computer model of the pendulum. In the popular science literature, this has come to be known as the "butterfly effect," whereby the wing beat of a butterfly in Asia is said to bring about changes in the weather in North America. It is important to keep in mind that in any real system, there is not just

Figure 3.3. During the early part of the lesson, the teacher provided each student group with two drawings representing a ridge and wall, respectively. For someone who knows, the unstable equilibrium of the balls in the drawings corresponds to the unstable equilibrium on the ridges of the potential field.

one perturbation; rather, there are many perturbations, continuously influencing the magnet and therefore its overall behavior.

Before the events described in the following sections, the students, who worked in groups of four or five, had explored the pendulum for two lessons. They had come to describe the pendulum as unpredictable. They also had identified the force field by bringing the bob to various places in the system and noting the direction in which it had moved and by sprinkling iron filings on a transparency sheet placed above the three magnets. One student had noted that this field resembled a "Mercedes star," where the arms constitute sensitive zones that correspond to ridges in the potential field (figure 3.2). In the lesson presented here, the teacher wanted students to arrive at an explanation for the unpredictable behavior of the magnetic pendulum given that they had already identified sensitive zones that take the shape of a "Mercedes star." The curriculum materials for this lesson included two drawings (figure 3.3) and one plaster bowl shaped like the potential field, but the teacher introduced these materials only after students had worked for some time on the task. In the course of the two-lesson (double) period, one group of students (Aleks, Janine, Katrina, Kiki, and Nikki) came to explain the chaotic pendulum in terms of Foucault's pendulum. My analysis brings out the contingent nature of the birth of this theoretical language. That is, following a path that had great internal coherence, plausibility, and logic, the five students failed to arrive at the teacher-desired explanation. This undesired outcome emerged despite the best intentions of students and teacher and despite the presence of well-designed and experimentally tested curricular resources. Before getting into the story, here a brief explanation of the Foucault pendulum.

A Foucault pendulum consists of a bob suspended on a long string, itself anchored on the top with a universal joint that allows it to swing freely in all directions. Once set in motion, the pendulum will, like any gyroscope, always move in the same universal plane. Because the Earth rotates, it will therefore move with respect to the plane in which the pendulum swings. As a result, the plane traced out by the pendulum string moves with respect to a dial constructed below the pendulum. That is, the pendulum seems to continuously deviate from the direction in which it had been originally set.

FLEXIBLE PERCEPTIONS

Most instructional design assumes that students view artifacts and texts in the way intended by designers and teachers. However, students who do not perceive artifacts and texts in the intended way cannot describe the scene in terms of the desired language or develop such a language. Thus, we cannot expect physics students who saw movement in a teacher demonstration to come up with the same explanation as those students who did not see this movement (Roth, McRobbie, Lucas, and Boutonné 1997b). This therefore has serious consequences for specifying and constraining the trajectories along which students develop theoretical languages. Teachers and analysts should not assume that the artifacts provided during instructional sequences are perceived and interpreted in the same way by all those present in a classroom; it is more appropriate to assume that these artifacts are viewed differently, which puts the onus on us researchers to explain the conditions that favor shared ways of perceiving and explaining. Most notably, we should assume that these perceptions might differ radically from those of teachers and textbooks. Even the best-designed instructional artifacts can therefore not assure that students come to view and therefore describe the phenomena in the scientifically sanctioned way.

The present episode began just after the teacher brought the two drawings (figure 3.3) to the five students' table and suggested that they should see whether these drawings had anything to do with the chaos pendulum. From this moment on, all students but Nikki were actively involved in exploring the pendulum and in talking themselves through the task.

01 Katrina: What is it that these are supposed to depict?
02 Aleks: Butterflies?
03 Janine: We are *not* seeing a psychiatrist here!
04 Katrina: Well, I see a butterfly in this picture.
05 Kiki: If this is related to the magnet, and if this so=
06 Aleks: =This is first attracted by a partition; it is already attracted from the beginning, there.
07 Kiki: Then it can't go across, directly.

Here, Aleks and Katrina's contributions made salient the butterfly in each drawing. Janine's quip related the drawings to those that one may be asked to interpret as part of a psychiatric evaluation. Because there were no established linguistic practices around these drawings or the chaotic phenomena, the students' primary task was to work out a way of looking at and describing them—though they were unaware of their task in this way. They literally talked themselves through the issue at hand, but because they did not know the terrain, they were "laying the garden path in talking." That is, because these students were new to the phenomena, they could not know whether the butterfly was relevant to chaotic phenomena, and, if so, in which way it was relevant. It was only when students perceived events that bore some relevance to the situation (physics course, pendulum) that their descriptive language could develop in the desired way. Here, Kiki talked in a way that allowed the group to move in this direction by addressing possible relations between the initially introduced pendulum and the diagrammatic resources that they just received.

Students in this class did not spontaneously describe the scientifically relevant structure (morphology) of the situations in ways that would have allowed them to make the analogical relation to the equivalent structure of the magnetic pendulum, the target situation. Focusing on and talking about the butterfly made these students' conversation take a direction different than talking about ridge and wall did to the direction of other students. From an outside and after-the-fact perspective, the butterfly drawing had led them down the garden path, that is, in a wrong direction. Talking about the butterfly, in fact, moved the conversation away from producing observation sentences about ridge and wall, which are part of the morphology that the intended analogy to the pendulum requires. However, once the equivalence became apparent, there would have been two cases that could be described with the same observation sentences, which is a first and necessary step toward observation categoricals (generalizations across observations) and toward the emergence of a scientific language (Quine 1995).

When the students ultimately came to see and describe the chaotic pendulum and drawings in morphologically equivalent ways, a prerequisite for seeing the analogy, it was always an achievement. That is, in each case the analogy was not perceptually or otherwise apparent but was the outcome of the dialectic processes described here. Students viewed and described the drawings in flexible ways, often dramatically diverging from the intended structural features. The students began to describe what they saw in the drawings—butterfly or waves—or talked about the ball that could not cross the wall. Janine described the possible trajectories of the ball in the drawing ("Funny. It comes down here, and then it rolls down here or there.") and Aleks suggested something about magnets ("It could be the other magnet, it cannot . . ."). Later they laughed about their own descriptions of the butterfly as a wind indicator or as a critical influence on the ball's motion, and they interpreted the wall as a "wave." Disconcerted that the students did not talk about what he considered relevant, the teacher asked them to think about the referent of the drawings, that is, the entity or situation that the drawings are *about* ("What this is about. This is what you have to think about.").

But Katrina and Aleks responded by talking about centrifugal and magnetic forces.

From the teacher's perspective, the situation was self-evident. He had prepared what he considered to be an analogy so that the structural equivalence of the situation depicted in the drawings and the magnetic pendulum should be registered and recognized easily. However, the present situation suggested that this was not the case for these students. Their descriptions were so diverse that a structural (morphological) equivalence cannot be considered the norm. For the teacher, the butterfly was significant only insofar as it symbolized small influences. It also related a popular image associated with chaos theory: a butterfly in one part of the world that affects the weather in other, faraway countries. Some groups did not even articulate the butterfly in particular, or used language that associated it with very different things, such as an entity that was beautifying the drawing, a wind indicator, and so forth. That is, whereas the teacher expected the structure of the drawings to be self-evident analogies, the data suggest that this was not the case for these students. They began talking, and in talking explored both the phenomenon and language. Because the students were new to the materials and phenomena, their talk not surprisingly concerned perceptually more salient features. The language used was rooted in students' phenomenological experiences of waves and butterflies. Because of the historical and contingent nature of conversations, these languages can subsequently become constraints on the type of explanations students develop; they constitute a precedent, a trajectory taken, and little would make talk and language suddenly become something very different.

In this situation, the students did not dwell for too long on talking about the butterfly but moved from topic to topic. Coincidentally, the words and language they used changed substantially. Over time, however, a more structured language emerged, much as structure emerges from chaos. That is, new degrees of order arose from more chaotic situations where senses and referents were unstable and changed continuously. This instability and change arose from the considerable flexibility that existed for describing and interpreting the objects and events at hand.

This interpretive flexibility, as shown in chapter 2, is a positive phenomenon, because it allows multiple ways of articulating situations and framing representations and possibly destabilizes early commitments to fixed senses and referents. That is, this flexibility is one important source for new ways of seeing and talking to develop. But interpretive flexibility undermines curricular approaches that require students to have specific perceptions and develop structural descriptions such as in learning with analogies. "Structure mapping assumes that domain knowledge is in the form of symbolic structural descriptions that include objects, relations between objects, and higher order relations among whole propositions" (Gentner et al. 1997, 6). However, if students do not perceive objects and describe the source and target situations in the way required by structure mapping, the success of the instructional unit along the path of the intended curriculum is constrained. Telling students what they are to see and describe does not eliminate the problem, because words are also interpretively flexible, still requiring students to work out relevant structure and descriptive language.

To understand the processes of learning a science language from experimenting, we must therefore understand what learners attend to and how the scenes they attend to are changed through experience. We also need to understand the language that they bring and which constitutes the starting point not only for talking themselves through the task but also for establishing the task in talking.

STABILIZATION OF DESCRIPTIONS

In the previous episode, different conversational contributions brought out different morphology (structures) in the focal artifacts and representations. This begs the question, How do students ever come to perceive and describe curricular artifacts and texts in convergent ways? In the present episode, I describe and discuss the process of interactive stabilization. This process allows students to arrive, through their interactions, at common observation sentences and observation categoricals. Common observation sentences emerge from, are developed through, and are grounded in social interaction. From here, they may be appropriated into private languages and become resources that individuals use even without the presence of their group members. Other descriptions stabilize at first but are subsequently destabilized and abandoned; still other interpretations never find resonance within the group.

Because the drawings themselves did not lead students to talk about those issues he had hoped for, the teacher asked students more directly to talk about the drawings by focusing on the ridge (figure 3.3).

08 Teacher: Yeah, but when you arrive exactly on the ridge?
09 Aleks: In principle, it will be exactly the same.
10 Teacher: What will be the decisive factor?
11 Aleks: It tips here, yeah.
12 Katrina: The loss of balance, kind of.

Here, Aleks made a first connection between the drawings and the magnetic pendulum (line 09). Encouraged by the teacher to talk about the drawings, she proposed that something was "the same"; she elaborated this response in her next utterance which made it clear that she saw the sameness in the tipping (line 11), which Katrina expressed as a loss of balance (line 12). This was a continuation of Janine's earlier utterance that described the two possible trajectories of the ball, "here" and "there." Together with Janine, Aleks continued exploring language and phenomenon, elaborating observational language concerning balance and remaining on a trajectory along the narrow ridge (a line).

13 Aleks: What will be the decisive factor? This is on the line. But it can't remain on the line now, it can't remain on a precipice, it can't lie on a precipice.
14 Janine: But it depends on the plain, is this a plain or what?
15 Aleks: No (??)
16 Janine: Yes, but what kind of plain is it? Because, look here, it does not remain in balance, it has to go to one, of course, what do you think?

Responding to her own question, Aleks worked out some detail about the ball in the ridge drawing that remains on a narrow ridge, and then suggested that this was impossible (line 13). Here, students had not yet arrived at a common way of seeing the situation, that is, which of several features in the drawing they should focus on still seemed too ambiguous (e.g., the "plain"). Nevertheless, Janine added that the ball could not remain in balance and had to go to either side. A few utterances later, Kiki proposed a distinction with considerable influence on the subsequent conversation: The motions could be considered from a theoretical or practical perspective.

17 Kiki: One would have to reckon if one should theoretically or practically.
18 Aleks: Yeah, you could treat this theoretically.
19 Kiki: Yeah, this is what I intend, the pendulum moves on the line, in equilibrium.
20 Katrina: That's fine. You can do this theoretically, because practically it is impossible. What does this tell us?
21 Kiki: When the point mass moves, directly on top of here. ((She points to the ridge.))
22 Aleks: And is there in balance, coming up there. ((She points to the ridge.))

Kiki proposed a new way of talking about the phenomenon of a ball moving on the ridge that consisted in distinguishing between theory and practice (line 17). Aleks and Katrina considered the distinction worthwhile to be discussed— making the orientation that their language should take itself as the topic. The implicit agreement in their respective contributions (lines 18, 20) stabilized the topic. Not only were both contributions to the same topic, but they also made it possible to make further contributions on the same topic. This constitutes an interactive stabilization of the topic as an achievement; it was not achieved, for example, for the butterfly (lines 02, 05) or the psychiatrist quip (line 03). Contributions that made salient different topics or perceptions were thus competitors that had the potential effect of destabilizing descriptions, even radically changing them as if a system was changing from one into another state in a sudden transition. Even metalanguage, that is, descriptions of previous turns such as "this has nothing to do with," harbors the potential to destabilize topic and descriptions without directly providing alternatives.

So far then, the students had raised two major issues. First, they talked about an equilibrium condition that has to obtain so that an object can move along an infinitely narrow ridge. Equilibrium and "being in balance" are important phenomenological primitives that people draw on in their talk about stability and instability (diSessa 1993). Second, students explored in their talk distinctions between what is theoretically thinkable and practically possible. Implicit in the conversation was the acknowledgment that both the ball in the drawings and the magnetic pendulum moved. Other students adopted these descriptions immediately after these were proposed, which led (because of implicit agreement) to a stabilization of this way of describing.

Katrina continued by introducing theory talk of resultant forces that act in the system ("Couldn't you do something with resultant forces?"). Though reasonable, talk about this idea was not developed much further even by Katrina. Kiki's critique added to the demise of Katrina's way of talking and had tremendous potential to destabilize the present topic and lead to confusion (line 23). Aleks, Janine, and Katrina attempted to reject the critique (lines 24–27).

23	Kiki:	But this has nothing to do with the magnetic pendulum, but with the inertia of the mass.
24	Katrina:	No, now watch.
25	Janine:	It has to do with how much force the things has.
26	Aleks:	How, exactly, how it flies.
27	Janine:	The centrifugal force, how fast it, how fast it is, then it comes up here, but the less, the less force it has, it can't, it can't make the hill.

The combined effort of Aleks, Janine, and Katrina averted the destabilizing critique for the moment. They brought into the talk the force of the moving "thing," "how it flies," "centrifugal force," and "how fast it is." This varied talk did not capture the phenomenon in a consistent way, but explored the talk as much as it explored the phenomenon that they were looking at. Through such explorations and stabilizing moves on the part of individuals to stick with some idea, specific ways of talking emerged, stabilized, and were concurrently explored. Other ways of talking never resonated within the group and were abandoned. In the present situation, the language can be characterized in terms of three phenomenological primitives: inertia as a resistance to motion, [centrifugal] force as a mover, and motion that dies away.

Any conversation, and with it the entire activity, emerges from the instances of interactive stabilization against destabilizing influences. These notions of interactive stabilization and destabilizing influences allow a symmetrical description of emergent language. In this, destabilizing influences are not to be seen as something negative. Rather, stabilization and destabilization are the outcomes of dialectic processes in which each conversational turn may add new ideas that elaborate and modify current ways of talking or shift to new and different ones. Each turn therefore has multiple potentials: destabilizing current descriptions, getting a group off a dead end (i.e., a garden path that they had been led down), stabilizing current descriptions, and so forth.

Destabilizing influences allow agreement on common ways of talking to emerge as achievement, a product of interaction, rather than the result of a consensual world. Researchers cannot, in principle, know in advance all relevant experiences that students bring to or remember during a learning situation nor predict the dynamics of a particular conversation. This leads to the emergent character of students' activities and associated conversations. Because of the emergent properties of any conversation, it cannot be established a priori where a particular topic will lead or how a destabilization will affect the development of an explanation. It is only after the fact that particular strands of ideas can be shown to have been present in a conversation. But such explanations are scientifically unsound because of their teleological nature. Furthermore, because the students had not yet developed a stable scientific language, even they could not know whether some observation sentence they arrived at was significant in, or consistent with, a scientific description of the situation.

From the perspective of an unfolding activity, we cannot know whether something being said by one or several individuals will leave traces in individuals. That is, we cannot know beforehand whether the semantics of some conversation will actually be reproducible by individual students in a different context (e.g., interview). In this episode, which is centrally concerned with the behavior at the critical points of the different systems under consideration, I observed instances where developments at different levels interacted. For example, in lines 17–20, Kiki, Katrina, and Aleks proposed that the problem needed to be considered both in practical and theoretical terms. When all influences can be controlled (i.e., in the "theoretical" case), the pendulum bob and ball should be able to remain in the labile position of the critical point. The students in this group brought their distinction between theoretical and practical considerations into the subsequent (public) whole-class conversation. Theory–practice distinctions are central to everyday ways of talking (what is possible "in theory" versus what happens "in the real world"), and therefore embody commonsense distinctions between ideal and real systems. The students' achievement here consists in making this form of talk relevant to the current situation.

In this situation, students also brought in and evolved talk about nonlinear systems in terms of theoretical (ideal) and practical perspectives; it turned out that this way of talking became especially fruitful in a subsequent lesson when students used a computer simulation of the chaotic pendulum, affording control over the perturbations. Being fruitful is one condition that contributes to the stabilization of a way of talking and may lead to the abandonment of the competing language. When there were no random perturbations and for the same starting position, the nonlinear system was completely predictable. In the classroom, this became a case exemplifying the theoretical situation; all other cases modeled the practical cases students encountered during their investigations. Here, one group's language for distinguishing systems shaped ways of talking in the classroom and therefore constituted an important social representation that was stabilized in the larger community. In chapter 4, I will analyze in greater detail the relation between the languages used by individuals, groups, and the class as a whole.

The interactive stabilization of new ways of talking is an interesting phenomenon that also elucidates the issue of intersubjectivity. Even if one student took a first step of talking in new ways, it is inherently understandable by others. In fact, language as a phenomenon requires that something said, even in new ways and with new language, is already a feature of collective life. There would not be any reason to say anything if speakers did not presume that what they said was understandable. That is, at the very moment an individual attempts to share a personal idea, he or she assumes that others already understand the idea, that is, find the associated ways of talking intelligible. Communication presupposes the shared nature of what it is about; communication is a pointing out, a telling, and an articulation of that which stands out or has the potential to stand out for the participants. Students' conversations therefore constitute processes that align them to linguistic and perceptual features that they already distinguish or have the possibility of distinguishing.

THINKING IN PUBLIC: WITH EYES AND HANDS

The value of hands-on activities to learning observational and theoretical language is one of the major unexamined presuppositions in science education. Although there has been significant amount of research regarding sensorimotor development, there exist few studies that show how kinesthetic experience interfaces with the theoretical language characteristic to science. The previous section showed that interacting with one another and with their teacher allowed students to evolve and ground new ways of talking in social interaction. Here, I examine how material resources contribute to the stabilization of descriptions. Laboratory activities, especially those that focus on conceptual language rather than mere measurement issues, situate and provide constraints to students' language, much as laboratory activity had provided constraints to Faraday's emerging language about electricity (Gooding 1990). The present episode illustrates

the interactive stabilization of student language in interactions with the curricular materials. It constitutes the continuation of the previous excerpts.

Following Janine's utterance articulating (centrifugal) force and the ball
making it up the hill, Katrina then brought the theoretical model or idea into the
conversation. Here, the topic of theory stood as a figure against the unarticulated
background of practical situations that had figured earlier in the conversation.

28   Katrina: No, watch, with the magnetic pendulum, because this here ((Points to
                drawings)) is a theoretical idea, this is the theoretical model that we
                want to have ((Points to drawings and moves finger down ridge)) and
                that gave us thingy, thingy. Theoretically it would be possible that it
                rolls down the crest, and ⌈exactly on the edge.⌉
29   Janine: ⌊This is impossible⌋in the middle, there is
                nothing.
30   Kiki: It is like this, that when I come through here ((Moves the pendulum
                across set-up center, midway between two magnets))
                ⌈it can't stay on the line– ⌉
31   Janine: ⌊T h e n   i t   i s   n o t –⌋
32   Katrina: It is not the crest then, it can't stay there, can't stay there.
33   Kiki: Remains on the line.
34   Katrina: It can't, it can't stay there, it can't stay there, guaranteed, and some
                time–
35   Kiki: But that doesn't help you here.
36   Katrina: Exactly, it doesn't remain, and an air draft.
37   Janine: Don't shout that much so that we can see where it will go.

The students repeatedly articulated and thereby pointed out the impossibility of the pendulum moving along a line between two magnets (lines 28–30, 32,
34, 36). On the line, the bob is "in balance" and the two opposing tendencies
(forces to the left and right) cancel each other, a description that is consistent
with the experience of dynamic balance. But perhaps more importantly, at issue
was the difference between the ideal and real situations. As Katrina proposed, it
would be possible for the ball in the theoretical model to move on a narrow
ridge (line 28). Two issues are salient in this excerpt. First, by pointing to the
drawings and by moving the pendulum, respectively, Katrina and Kiki explicitly
made material resources in the setting part of their communicative action, and in
this, elaborated and enhanced its verbal features. Second, both used language
that distinguished between theoretically possible but practically unachievable
motions of balls on infinitely narrow ridges.

While talking about the theoretical model that they wanted (line 28), Katrina moved her finger along the ridge in the drawing (as in figure 3.4). This
movement of her finger suggested movement of the ball, thereby constituting an
animation. She talked not about a moving ball in some abstract sense, but,
through her finger, *became* the moving ball on the drawing before the eyes of

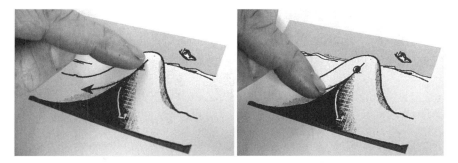

Figure 3.4. Katrina moved her finger along the ridge as indicated, initially touching the ball, then following the arrow. Her finger, taking the place of the ball, thereby enacted an animation against the image as the ground.

her peers. In the same way, Kiki did not just talk about the pendulum moving on a line of no net magnetic forces between two adjacent magnets (which they measured the previous lesson and discussed earlier in the same lesson). Rather, she took the pendulum bob and moved it midway between two magnets, along the invisible line between the two magnets (line 29). As she did this, she talked as if she *was* the pendulum, "When I come through there." She had taken position, oriented to the system, becoming the pendulum bob that could not remain on the infinitely narrow ridge. "When I come through here" made no distinction between her movement and that of the object. It is a language of relations.

In a language of relations, which also characterizes our early experiences in unknown settings, objects do not yet exist as things that language is *about*. Rather, language articulates relations without distinguishing people from objects and setting (Buber 1970). In Zulu, the equivalent for "far away" is "where one cries, 'mother I am lost.'" That is, the person is implicated in relations that the English expression articulates independently of persons and settings. Such ways of talking abstracted from lived experience emerge with, and even require, the detachment of the self. But here, their language and physical action show how students take up position without distinguishing their selves from the objects and the setting.

Talking from within a relation may come with a cognitive advantage. In the previous chapter, where students' talked about computer-based representation, fingers and hands were used in two ways: to make salient specific aspects of the display and to articulate salient aspects in front of the monitor display. The present situation exhibits these two aspects as Katrina pointed to the drawing and gestured the trajectory on the ridge (line 28); but there was also a new form of engagement with the world. Rather than re-presenting the situation, Kiki (line 30) let the pendulum be its own representation and moved it along the desired trajectory. Thus, rather than pointing or representing the trajectory, Kiki re-enacted the trajectory by actively moving the bob. This difference is important, as the number and range of constraints on the movement thus represented is different than if the representation was in another form (e.g., drawing or computer animation). The cognitive advantage comes from the fact that the equivalence between the two cases, the moving bob and the ball in the drawing, are perceptually available in the setting and do not have to be imagined or otherwise made present again. The participants do not have to imagine or represent in propositional form what the talk is about. Furthermore, the presenting student does not have to construct a complex set of propositions that would describe the two situations and argue their equivalence. Thus, having the two models available in material form allows communication to be distributed across the environment, in perceptual, gestural, and verbal form. In this situation, the *re*cognition is an emergent phenomenon that was facilitated by locating the material configurations into the world.

In this episode, the material resources provided particular constraints to students' observation language and actions. Katrina and Kiki not only articulated and talked about pendulum and drawing but also enacted the movement of the pendulum bob and ball along the respective loci of critical points. These physical enactments have the potential to make salient perceptual similarities crucial to observation sentences and observation categoricals about chaotic systems. Physical enactments have this potential because they provide bridges between different presentations.

The earlier emergent distinction between theory and practice also was an important issue in this episode. Janine (line 29), Katrina (lines 28, 32, 34, 36), and Kiki (line 30) emphasized that in the real world, an object could not remain on a narrow ridge as shown in figure 3.4. Janine's and Katrina's comments related the drawings; Kiki's comments involved the pendulum. An activity during the following two lessons (double period), which involved computer simulations and whole-class discussions, allowed them to further work on and elaborate these notions that are at the heart of an understanding of chaotic systems, that is, systems of limited predictability. From a physicist's perspective, chaotic systems are also deterministic but differ from classical systems in that minor perturbations can dramatically change their dynamics and ultimate fate at bifurcation points. Katrina and Janine's comments made mention of small variations that could disturb the magnetic pendulum in front of them (air draft, shout).

As a result of the episode, there existed a structural equivalence between the two systems (at least implicitly); the chaotic pendulum that Kiki traversed with her hand motion and the diagram of the ridge that Katrina moved along with her finger. In both situations, the actors placed themselves on the ridge and articulated the behavior of the system from that perspective. This episode also shows the relationship between the developments at the level of the local activity and those at the public, classroom level. The conversation about whether the pendulum can remain exactly midway between two magnets recapitulated results of an earlier activity and the whole-class conversation. There, the class had come to an agreement that on the midway lines between neighboring magnets, the pendulum bob is subject to minor, unpredictable air movements that make it go left or right. In recapitulating, students employed a resource, which was offered first in the public discourse of the whole-class conversation, to the local level of their small-group conversation. In the next chapter, concerned with the development of discourse at the whole-class level and with the interaction between public and private discourses, I will articulate the relationships between these two levels in greater detail.

MATERIALLY CHANGING THE SETTING

People actively change their environment and thereby change problem spaces and cognition (Snow 1992). Such active changes are a form of "jigging" the environment. Jigging brings additional degrees of freedom to tasks and may constrain activities in two ways. First, if the material resources allow jigging, deviations from teacher-planned activity trajectories and therefore to the observation sentences and theoretical languages that students evolve are possible. Second, because jigging constitutes a variation of given circumstances, it increases the potential for the emergence of analogical relations. That is, jigging creates the possibility for variations that entail sudden changes in the trajectory of the conversation, and therefore in the trajectory that cumulatively leads to learning. In this part of the lesson, students further capitalized on the opportunities residing in material resources by actively changing the pendulum and therefore making the analogy explicit by means of perceptual similarity.

So far in the unfolding events concerning the construction of an explanation for the chaotic pendulum, the five young women had found it difficult to relate the drawings to the pendulum. In this episode, the students actively changed the magnetic pendulum's setup. This change ultimately facilitated the establishment of a language that made salient the equivalent structures shared by the drawings and the magnetic pendulum.

38   Katrina: So, you don't notice it, and it will hardly decide for one of the magnets, because the variations are minimal. There we have to have three magnets; then everything changes, because we have to have magnetic fields, then it works.

39   Janine: Just think, it is, see, we have ⌈one here and here.⌉

40   Katrina: ⌊N o ,   n o ,   n o⌋ you can, this one here ((She removes one magnet)), watch. You let the pendulum swing, now ((She swings the pendulum to and fro between two magnets)), now it runs up and down. ((Holds the ridge drawing. She runs

the pen up and down ridge. She follows the movement of bob
demonstratively with her head.))

41   Kiki: These are the normal ways they can go; these are the lines that have
              to exist here. But it is impossible.

In this episode, students first removed one magnet, giving them a two-
magnet configuration (figure 3.5), and then returned it to reproduce the original
setup (figure 3.1). While the gravitational-magnetic potential field was invisible,
the geometry of the setup suggested (at least) a left/right difference from the
perspective of the pendulum bob. There is a ridge in the potential field perpendicular to the connecting line between the two magnets and halfway between
them, assuming they are of equal strength. Janine and Katrina accompanied their
talk by the corresponding geometric placement of the magnets and referred to
this geometry. Katrina also paralleled the motion of the pendulum by simultaneously following the ridge in the diagram with her finger. Her head, rocking in a
similar back-and-forth movement, further underscored this aspect of motion and
suggested an up-and-down movement (the pendulum bob moves on a circular
path, closer to the bottom plate in the middle of the trajectory, farther away at
the ends). The other participants (as the analysts) could discover an iconic rela-

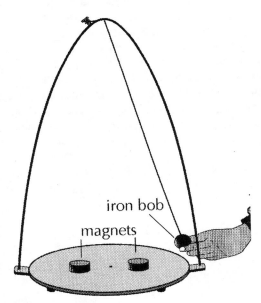

Figure 3.5. In this episode, the students removed on of the magnets. From a physicists'
perspective, this gives rise to a potential field with a ridge halfway between the two magnets and perpendicular to the line connecting them. This situation is therefore, once one
knows about it, equivalent to the wall and ridge situations.

tion between the back and forth of the finger (as in figure 3.4) and the simultaneous back and forth of the chin. Kiki's remark, "These are the normal ways they can go, these are the lines that have to exist here," could be heard as tying the topic back to the practically impossible (unstable) equilibrium of an object on a ridge.

Here, students accompanied their talk concerning the geometry of the situation with modifications of the number of magnets on the plate. That is, they were not reasoning in some abstract way, but drew on the material resources present in front of them to support their analysis of the system. In the immediately previous episode, they had talked about the situation in which an object moved along a ridge. But the three-magnet situation provided more than one ridge and therefore in its entirety did not have the structure that they had come to articulate in the drawing. Katrina proposed that a three-magnet situation would change the situation. Janine, who started her own explanation, added a third magnet, but was interrupted by Katrina who took the magnet away to elaborate her description of the situation with two magnets (line 40). Thus, Katrina modified the geometry of the system to be explained so that it had the same symmetry as the theoretical model she saw depicted in the drawing. That is, she structured the material world in front of them to produce the same binary geometry (left–right) that was depicted in the drawing. In addition, however, she set up a structural equivalence. On its trajectory, the pendulum bob approaches, and recedes from, the tabletop. This feature was suggested only partially in the drawing, but was elaborated in Katrina's comment of "running up and down," which was animated by the tip of her pen moving up and down the ridge similar to the finger in the earlier situation (figure 3.4). In the first part of her rejoinder, Kiki agreed that along the ridges (lines), there are the "normal" trajectories (ways) along which the two objects (pendulum, ball in drawing) had to move. Her description of "normal" trajectories, which contrasted the subsequent "but this is impossible," implied the trajectories were the ideal or theoretical ones that she and her peers had described earlier.

This case can be understood partially in terms of structure mapping—its component processes are restructuring, re-representation, projection, and highlighting—if one accepts the assumption now widespread in cognitive science that the world is its own representation (e.g., O'Regan and Noë 2001). At first, Katrina restructured the initial situation (configuration of pendulum) and thereby changed the target situation (magnetic pendulum) itself. She subsequently enacted a structural equivalence between the two situations, magnetic pendulum and drawing. Her moving finger highlighted the (relevant) aspect, the trajectories on the narrow ridge and in the drawing (line 41). She then made a candidate inferential statement, possibly on the basis of prior experience, that the pendulum cannot move on the narrow ridge ("line") previously identified. Thus, although she did not articulate the desired analogy between the provided artifacts, Katrina enacted analogical reasoning. The analogy was correct in the sense that she identified an analogous morphology, but it ultimately let them work on a new problem rather than that initially posed by the teacher.

At this point, then, the new configuration of the magnetic pendulum supported an analogical description to emerge as the achievement of students' interactions with each other and the materials at hand. By changing the setup, the students had achieved the closing of a gap, leading from unlike symmetries in the problem space (star, ridge) to morphologically analogous situations. That is, the material resources provided a positive constraint on the evolving observational and theoretical descriptions. As became clear in the next episode, this configuration subsequently led the students to elaborate a theoretical description that was not among the desired (by the teacher) outcomes of the lesson.

"FOUCAULT'S PENDULUM": EMERGENCE OF AN EXPLANATION

Because artifacts and talk are inherently dialectical and therefore flexible in nature and because students can change the configuration of the artifacts, the resulting conversations should not be expected to follow unique trajectories or have common results. Even in the case of collectively elaborated observation sentences and observation categoricals, these may be inconsistent with contemporary scientific standards. Students' theoretical articulations of phenomena emerged from the interplay of many elements: past experiences and their context, curricular context of the present activity, setting (physics class), or objects and events at hand. Given these contingencies, one should expect a broad array of actual outcomes within a class, even though *all* students were exposed to the same instructions, doing the same activities, and using the same materials. Local contingencies determined the degree to which the emerging observational and theoretical descriptions were interactively stabilized. From this perspective, one expects different groups of students to arrive at different results; common results therefore demand explanations rather than being the norm and causal consequence of a deterministic curriculum. Among the contingencies were forces that contravened the formation of and destabilized existing interpretations.

In a brief part of the conversation omitted here, I attempted to direct students to focus on the nonlinearities in the drawing and magnetic pendulum. Janine tried to set up the system with the pendulum at rest. After a quick exchange about being able to accomplish the task, the following conversation ensued.

46   Teacher: Isn't there a similarity with your drawing?
47   Kiki: Yes, but there is, uh hm::::.
48   Teacher: In this? ((Points to ridge))

49	Kiki:	That it has to decide if it wants to roll left, right, or along the middle. Okay, when it is, when it is here, then she'll be on a line, isn't it?
50	Teacher:	Yeah, and the drawing?
51	Janine:	That is certainly incorrect.
52	Kiki:	It has to decide, right, left, or straight ahead.
53	Katrina:	That's true. It doesn't work.
54	Janine:	((Watches the pendulum)) It never comes to a rest, because the Earth turns, and then the pendulum also always turns, that is impossible.
55	Katrina:	We investigated Foucault's pendulum!
56	Kiki:	((Shakes her head in disagreement))

Here then, students arrived at an observation categorical. Janine articulated a theoretical description that provided an explanation for the events—"It never comes to a rest, because the Earth turns, and then the pendulum also always turns"—and Katrina named it "Foucault's pendulum." During the following five minutes, they elaborated and more fully articulated why a Foucault pendulum provided the appropriate analogy in the present situation. The talk stabilized and the students decided, in their actions that did not further develop the topic, that they had come to the desired outcome of the task.

Up to this point, their conversation had been concerned with the possibility of a real object moving along a narrow ridge. In the case of the pendulum, the question then was whether the bob remains swinging in the same plane that bisects the line connecting the two magnets. Kiki and Katrina already had established that moving along a ridge was impossible in practice. But in the exchange between Katrina and Janine (lines 51, 53–55), a theoretical articulation arose that accounted for the movement off the ideal (theoretical) trajectory. Rather than the earlier discussed influences—air currents—they now explained the pendulum's movement off the ridge (in the potential) in terms of the rotation of the Earth underneath the fixed plane in which a long pendulum moves with respect to the planetary system.

This explanation emerged from the interaction of a number of different elements that led to a unique history of the conversation across different instabilities. The activity of finding an explanation for the motion of the pendulum and the unpredictability of its end state was part of the unit on chaos theory. After students had tried to construct an explanation for a while (which itself came after two other activities on finding a pattern and measuring the force field), the teacher had provided the group with two drawings and suggested that these might be helpful in the construction of their explanation. In the course of their deliberations, students focused on the drawing of a ball moving down a narrow ridge. They recognized it as a theoretical model, a situation that was impossible in practice. What they had not yet established was why the pendulum would move out of the plane of its initial swing, or how it was related to the drawings. The influences of air currents or of shouting had been brought up but were not seriously discussed as sufficiently large to bring about the chaotic behavior of the pendulum. To the contrary, Katrina suggested that the variations were too small to affect the pendulum.

Before these events as background, Katrina and Janine conjured the image of a pendulum that appears to rotate over a dial on the ground. Janine, who contemplated the pendulum while others talked (lines 40–50), suddenly suggested that the pendulum could not swing in the same plane because the Earth turned (line 54). Katrina named this explanation Foucault's pendulum. The subsequent conversation showed that four of the five women had been to the physics museum in Berlin. In this museum, they had seen an example of a Foucault pendulum made from a bob on a long wire that changed its plane of swing during the course of their stay in the museum. The image of the Foucault pendulum was part of their prior experience that became relevant when one student happened to remember it.

This description had immediate appeal. It provided an explanation of why the pendulum could not remain on the bisector between the two magnets: the rotation of the Earth would bring it off. The images and explanations associated with a previous experience in the physics museum of Berlin provided resources for dealing with the present situation. Situating the conversation in the overall context of students' experience provides further hints why a Foucault pendulum felt appropriate as an explanation. They found themselves in a physics course. The teacher had asked them to construct an explanation for a particular phenomenon. This provides a frame for the kind of observational and theoretical language that is appropriate in such situations, thereby constraining the range of explanations that are plausible. In fact, it is possible that this frame contributed to the plausibility of the theoretical description that they have evolved. The explanation that the group had come up with seemed plausible because, among other reasons, it was appropriate for another phenomenon known to be scientific. Here again, the similarity between the two settings ("physics") provided a constraint that afforded the emergence of a specific explanation. Furthermore, the development at the level of individuals interacted with the development of the ongoing activity by providing support for the interactive stabilization of the Foucault explanation. Although Foucault's pendulum does not qualify as a metaphor, it took the role of a metaphor by assisting students to orient to the world in ways that allowed for coordinated, socially distributed inquiry to progress despite the fact that the theories to be discovered could not yet be known or defined.

The explanation was not just due to the materials in front of the students, their previous experiences, the language they commanded, the teacher's questions, the drawings, and the history of the activity (especially the conversation). Rather, there was a dynamic that dialectically constituted this activity in relation with the setting. In their interactions, talk concerning the geometry of a line with its division into left, right, and remaining on the line became a central feature. It led to an emergent goal of these students' activity—such emergent goals that are used as resources in action are often articulated only retroactively. Rather than arriving at an explanation for the chaotic behavior, they had evolved a theoretical description why the pendulum could not swing continuously in the same (bisector) plane along the invisible ridge between two magnets (established during the previous lesson and discussed earlier in the same lesson). Central to this effort was the manipulation of the system, reducing it to one that only had two magnets to be considered. Katrina moved the bob along the centerline and thereby took a position. She became part of the setup in front of the students, becoming part of the bob that moved back and forth. This was further underscored by the person-centered descriptions they used for describing the movement of the pendulum; it suggested thinking through taking the perspective of the moving object ("it must decide").

DEMISE OF FOUCAULT'S PENDULUM

This case study shows how a theoretical description emerged as a contingent achievement. To understand why the Foucault pendulum was considered a reasonable explanation, one has to account for these students' prior experience in a physics museum, the artifacts before them (pendulum, drawings), and the emergent and self-integrating nature of the activity, its goal, and the languages that emerges. Though the data did not reveal any irrational activities and language along the way, students offered what was to the teacher an unreasonable (and undesired) result. In the process, students manipulated the pendulum setup, which allowed them to establish a structural equivalence with one of the drawings, but also led to the emergence of a new goal. Rather than explaining the original pendulum, the students explained why the pendulum could not move along a line where the net force of neighboring magnets is zero. Students had changed the physical aspects of the focal situation to be explained, changing goals and solutions. This new setting was generative in that it made visible the isomorphism between two different entities (i.e., pendulum and drawing). Although there were different ways of talking evolved in the discussion, only some of them were actually tested; others, though desirable from a teacher's perspective, were rejected or never stabilized as conversational topics. The Foucault pendulum and topical cohesion were maintained although potentially destabilizing propositions were made and questions were raised.

Despite the stabilization the Foucault pendulum received during the five-minute period following its first mention, the students eventually abandoned the explanation they had arrived at. Why did they abandon the explanation in the absence of counterevidence? For one thing, Kiki was critical of the new explanation. At first, she shook her head to indicate disagreement; then she suggested that the effect of the Earth's rotation was not large enough to be noticed in their experiment. However, the three other students contributed in a positive, supporting way, thereby stabilizing the explanation interactively. The more they talked, the more certain the three seemed to become that their explanation was what the teacher had wanted them to arrive at; their interactions stabilized the explanation.

A major destabilizing element existed in the teacher's reception of their achievement. In his reactions, the teacher made known to the students that Foucault's pendulum was not the explanation that he expected in this classroom (irrespective of the relation between what happened in this classroom and contemporary professional standards). The teacher's positioning with respect to the students' result was part of the extant frame of schooling that always allows students to make assessments about their work. In the case of the Foucault pendulum, the teacher appeared cool and little interested and asked critical questions. Sometime after the students had called him, the teacher approached the group. Excited, Katrina shouted that they had found the answer:

57   Katrina: The principle of Foucault's pendulum.
58   Teacher: Good that you know it!

The teacher's response was almost snide. Furthermore, after the student had presented an elaborate description, he merely responded, "Is that so?" This contrasted with the immediate interest he showed to student achievements that were in line with his goals:

59   Teacher: Can you provide a one-word description for [the pattern]?
60   Rani: Mercedes star.
61   Teacher: Mercedes star! I'll write it right down. Good!

The form of responding constitutes a frame with stabilizing or destabilizing features. In the case of the Foucault pendulum, it may have led to the demise of the explanation even in the absence of evidence that would have shown the limitations of the Foucault pendulum as an explanatory resource. It is important to keep in mind that the explanation constructed by the students was not destabilized and deconstructed on the grounds of empirical evidence or through significant counterarguments. Thus, although the students had arrived at what appeared to them a reasonable explanation for the pendulum's departure from its trajectory on the ridge of the potential field, and although they were confident about their work, the context was set for other criticism to emerge. That is, although there was very little interaction (and may be because of it), the teacher's questioning raised shadows of doubt. The explanation simply lost support and was no longer maintained by group members.

Throughout the analysis of the unfolding conversation, I make salient how developments at one level provided resources (positive or negative) to discourse developments at another. For example, the theoretical–practical distinction formulated by this group was carried forward to, and became a central resource in, the (public) classroom discourse about nonlinear systems. The prior (private) experiences of individual students in a physics museum influenced the stabilization of the Foucault explanation in the developing activity. Finally, the curricular artifacts provided specific constraints for the kind of topics covered in the unfolding conversation, to the development of individual conceptions, and to the classroom discourse in its entirety. These constraints, however, did not always work as intended, because additional elements were introduced such as the "force" and "Foucault" explanations. The students in this group covered most of the conceptual framework that the teacher had intended for them to cover in their activity, and yet, they had not arrived at the teacher-desired end results.

EMERGENCE AND CONTINGENCY

In this chapter, I provided a case study designed to help in understanding the processes by which particular student explanations and language arise from activity. The case study shows that the students' activities were highly contingent, their course unpredictably emerging from local contingencies. There are dialectic processes in the course of which interpretively flexible objects, events, and (observational) descriptions were interactively stabilized. That is, although there may have been differently perceived and described phenomena, interactions eventually led to a stabilization of one way (or a small number of ways) of looking at, describing, and explaining the relevant events. Active manipulation of materials provided material constraints on the kind of language that might be useful.

From a first-time-through perspective, the nature of students' observations and explanations was difficult (even impossible) to predict. The unfolding activities and embedded conversations were historically contingent, and often took unpredictable courses. Only after the fact was I able to say that this or that student experience came to bear on the evolution of language about chaotic systems. Given the inquiry orientation, it was not surprising that students began by using observation descriptions inherently pertaining to surface rather than deep features. Associated with simple observation sentences, students drew on personal experiences, such as force as mover or dynamic equilibrium, for talking things through and developing the issues at hand. However, such characterizations of student talk are insufficient for understanding the emergence of explanations. Which aspects of a setting were perceptually salient was virtually impos-

sible to predict, leading to varying trajectories of the conversations that we recorded. Furthermore, students' everyday language already made available certain phenomenological primitives, so that their observation sentences were inherently individual and social simultaneously.

Each utterance not only contributed to the unfolding activity but also
changed what was available as a resource to subsequent actions. But each utterance was also a response to the present situation so that future utterances responded to future situations rather than to the present ones. This gives any conversational setting an emergent character, because no participant can predict
what the next person will say, how this will develop the topic, and ways of talking. But by the time a person comes to talk, the previous person's utterance has
changed the context to which participants orient physically, emotionally, or intellectually. This case study also shows that students actively changed the material setting, which allowed them to take new orientations or, in fact, similar orientations across two different situations, the pendulum and the drawing. Both
Katrina and Kiki took up positions, moving their finger or hand along salient
features and articulating the impossibility to remain on the narrow ridges where
they had placed themselves.

In the end, the students had arrived at a way of describing their chaotic pendulum in a language suitable for a Foucault pendulum. Their talk of the side-
ward movement of their pendulum, which could not remain on the ridge, and the
rotating plane in which a Foucault pendulum swings were sufficiently close at
the moment to make it sensible to move the linguistic resources across into the
new situation. The talk about moving along the ridge had contingently emerged
from their inquiry after Katrina had removed one of the three magnets and
moved the pendulum bob along the invisible ridge between the two remaining
ones. In this moment, the students had taken another road, "as just as fair, and
having perhaps the better claim," in the words of Frost. But taking it, the road of
their inquiry diverged from another possible one in which the three magnets had
remained in their place. But the students, to quote the poet, "took the one less
traveled by, and that has made all the difference."

Why do students take one road over another? This question has no answer,
because, as I show in my personal examples in the introduction, what becomes
salient to us while navigating unfamiliar terrain emerges from our activity. Even
if there are multiple ways in which we continue, not knowing where either one
will lead, choosing one is as good as choosing the other. Most frequently, we do
not even choose but, to paraphrase Frost one more time, keep on the first for
another day.

If we take the perspective I develop here, science education finds itself in a
quandary. It assumes that lessons, curricular artifacts, and teacher practices will
lead all students to talk science in standard and legitimated and legitimized
ways. But this way of viewing learning is inconsistent with the way in which
intellectual development proceeds, when viewed as the evolution of language

constrained by structures in the sociomaterial world. What we need is a non-teleological view of intellectual history, whatever the level of the system that we describe. Language and culture are contingencies, "as much a result of thousands of small mutations finding niches (and millions of others finding no niches) as are the orchids and the anthropoids" (Rorty 1989, 16). In the same way, the languages students develop even in the most carefully designed and taught curricula are the contingent outcomes of situated trajectories that begin with but are not determined by the linguistic and experiential resources that students bring to class. Thus, although many students in this class had been to science museums or heard or read about a Foucault pendulum, this group of five girls was the only one that had ended up using its imagery and language as an explanation for the chaotic pendulum. This language seemed suited at the moment to fill a void, the absence of a theoretical language, and it appeared to handle the segment of the world containing the chaotic pendulum quite handily.

Not having arrived at the teacher's desired ways of talking and the negative reception requires our attention, for students find themselves in a contradictory situation where they are asked to develop some theoretical talk but then are cut short if they do not come to the forms of talking that the teacher has expected. This is even more of an issue in a class where teachers allow students to engage with epistemological issues and come to hear about constructivism. In a context where schooling is all about getting good grades, it comes as no surprise that students can both reject open-inquiry laboratory situations and have adopted a (social) constructivist epistemology.

4

Public Language, Private Talk

In saying something, an individual concretely realizes a way of talking that exists at the collective level. Yet the collective possibilities inherent in language are not exhausted by the sum total of concretely realized ways of articulating them. Furthermore, each utterance or book also expands the collective possibilities of talking. Readers will have encountered this phenomenon in their lifetimes, such as when new words and new ways of talking, produced somewhere, sometime, by someone, all of a sudden sweep a culture. Thus, things and people were not always "cool." Now, however, the word "cool" is used even in German and French, where "that's cool" translates into "das ist cool" and "c'est cool," respectively. There is therefore a dialectical relationship between concrete realization of language and generalized, collective linguistic possibilities.

In everyday life, newcomers to a culture appropriate its language, which, as far as the individual is concerned, is relatively stable. One therefore often speaks of the enculturation of newcomers into existing practices through the dialectic of legitimate peripheral participation (see, e.g., Lave and Wenger 1991). Although the collectivity (e.g., community) changes with each new participating individual, the development of the collective practice occurs at a time scales much longer than the development of individuals because of the sheer size of the linguistic community under consideration. Investigations of language change in discourse-oriented school science classrooms, on the other hand, have to be centrally concerned with continuously and rapidly changing collective practices. This does not change the dialectical relation binding collectivity and individual; rather, individuals find themselves in a continuously changing context to the evolution of which they themselves contribute in more or less substantial ways.

In this chapter, I will describe three levels of development important in understanding learning from physics laboratory activities by drawing on materials from the same tenth-grade physics classroom that readers encountered in the previous chapter. These three levels include the development of conversations in real time, development of individual students' ways of talking, and development of ways of talking at the level of the classroom. At the classroom level, specific descriptive language arose in the context of (and sometimes disappeared with) specific tasks, where it was used by an increasing number of students. These ways of talking emerged from ongoing local activities where they were stabilized by means of interactions within groups and experience with the materials and tools at hand. From these interactions, and in the context of the community, individuals evolved their ways of articulating and describing relevant phenomena. It is important to note the heterogeneity of these developments. Groups evolved different descriptions, individuals developed different ways of explaining phenomena and at different rates, and the language varied at the public (classroom) level. Thus, although students' language was generally consistent with the conceptual framework used to organize the curriculum (figure 4.1), there were considerable variations in how the relationships among the concepts were concretely realized in language in specific situations and by individual students.

SENSE, REFERENCE, MEANING

In this chapter, I am centrally concerned with the relationship between public, collective language and private, individual ways of talking. Existing research frequently uses the concept of *zone of proximal development* to explain how a child or student comes to use the language of his or her culture. In received theoretical approaches, words, ideas, and meanings are produced somehow, in a public arena, on an interpsychological plane, from where the individual appropriates it, so that the entity (word, idea, or meaning) comes to appear at the intrapsychological plane. This creates not only a sequence of but also a dichotomy between the collective and individual language practices.

There is also an unexamined problem with the notion of meaning and its relation to sense and reference. Science educators sometimes use the concept of *meaning* as synonymous with *reference*. Thus, the meaning of a word is said to be the thing it stands for—the material object *magnet* is said to be the meaning of the word "magnet." Such a use of signs is common in the sciences, where the equivalence between language and the world is a fundamental presupposition (Latour 1993). Other science educators use the concept of *meaning* in terms of *sense*. Thus, the meaning of a term is given by its synonyms or equivalent ex-

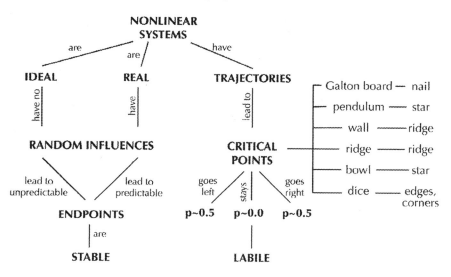

Figure 4.1. This semantic network expresses the key elements of the curriculum. The nodes, links, and examples to the right are explicitly incorporated in the various tasks that students complete in the course of the unit.

pressions, such as the drawing or gesture of a magnet being synonymous. Finally, it is common science education practice to write about the meaning of words, as if there was something attached to words. Students are said to "make meaning," without explication of what it is that they are making. Furthermore, such a way of talking and talking about meaning is inherently problematic, as pragmatic and phenomenological philosophers have pointed out for a long time. Here, I clarify the relation between the three concepts in terms of activity theory, which is fundamentally concerned with the relationship between the individual and the collective (Leont'ev 1978). Activity theory is a relevant frame because, conceptually, utterances are actions that have the same function of bringing about changes in the sociomaterial world as any material action.

In activity theory, three levels of events are used to analyze events: activity, action, and operation. Communities of practice motivate activities such as farming, building detectors, or researching fundamental particles; thus, the object or motive of activity is always collectively established. In the practical realization of activities, subjects (individuals, groups) set specific goals that orient their actions. Actions do not exist independently but always occur in the context of some activity. Thus, the significance of "doing a polymerase chain reaction" is very different when the action is completed by a high school student as part of a unit on genetic identification, a graduate student in biochemistry as part of her thesis work, a senior laboratory instructor preparing a demonstration for a lecture, a professor of microbiology in the process of completing data collection for an article in process, or a research scientist analyzing hair supplied by police working on a murder case. Activities and actions are therefore dialectically related: actions concretely realize activities but activities provide the context that orients the specific sequencing of actions. The relation between the activity and action is therefore one of *sense*.

Actions are realized by the sequencing of operations. Operations emerge as responses of the human body to conditions below the level of consciousness; having emerged in the course of living in a culture, operations constitute unconscious collective consciousness. Again, the relation between action and operation is dialectical. A sequence of operations concretely realizes an action, but the sequencing requires the action (goal) as its orientation. The turning of the right hand at the wrist is part of many actions, such as doing a titration. However, *when* to turn the hand, and preceding and succeeding which other operations, depends on the action to be realized. An action (oriented toward a goal) serves as referent for the operations that concretely realize it.

Sense and *reference* are dialectically related: this relationship is termed *meaning*. Meaning therefore is never an attribute of a word, nor an entity that is a stable outcome of an action. Rather, meaning is the relation of the two relations *sense* and *reference* that exist only in action, that is, in the course of some unfolding process. The "reference relation" grounds meaning in the individual body, the "sense relation" grounds meaning in collective activities. To concretize this discussion, let us return to a brief excerpt from the previous chapter, the moment when the analogy of the Foucault pendulum first emerged.

54   Janine: ((Watches the pendulum.)) It never comes to a rest, because the earth
             turns, and then the pendulum also always turns, that is impossible.
55   Katrina: We investigated Foucault's pendulum!
56   Kiki: ((Shakes her head in disagreement.))

Katrina's utterance "We investigated Foucault's pendulum!" constitutes a speech act. Its significance cannot be established without the surrounding actions—here, Janine's articulation of the behavior of pendulums and Kiki's head shaking, which articulates her disagreement. This action sequence is part of the realization of the task, formulating an explanation for the chaotic behavior of the magnetic pendulum. That is, sense is the relation of this utterance to the preceding and succeeding utterances, which concretely realize the task of evolving an explanation for this chaotic system. However, the utterance is realized by a sequence of words together with body position, gestures, intonation, and speed that accompany any unarticulated visual images of the speaker. None of these aspects are normally conscious when students speak in a science classroom, and they therefore constitute operations. (They may be consciously attended to in other situations: by actors during rehearsals, secret agents preparing for a mission in a foreign country, or a person with a speech defect during a therapy session.) These words, in this sequence, accompanied by a prosody that could be experienced as expressing excitement, emerged as unconscious responses sequenced by their reference relation to the speech act as it unfolded. Each operation, the word, speed of speech, inflection, gesture, body orientation, and unarticulated images are materially grounded in the body. Meaning existed in the simultaneous grounding of the speech act in the physical body and the collective culture. In this chapter, I am concerned with the evolution of ways of speaking, simultaneously grounded in collective activity and bodily operations. That is, this chapter focuses on the enactment of sense and reference relations, which, in turn, enact a relation that is called *meaning*.

COLLECTIVE WAYS OF TALKING

An explicit aspect of the unit on chaotic phenomena in the German tenth-grade physics class was the back-and-forth between small-group investigations and whole-class discussions. At the classroom level, a refinement of the language related to deterministic systems and systems, with limited predictability could be observed over the time of the unit. This refinement pertained to the number of relevant concept words employed and to an increased differentiation of the language with respect to the course content. The emergence of new language elements was tied to particular activities. Figure 4.2 displays the usage of six predicates for aspects concerning the events when a moving object passes a sensitive area. The first three (canceling forces, neutral, indifferent) relate to forces acting on the objects, the second triplet (labile, stable, out of balance) to the state of the object at the critical points in chaotic systems. The figure shows how the frequency of particular expressions changed with time. For example, the predicates "indifferent," "labile," "stable," and "out of balance" were not used during the first two periods on October 24; similarly, on October 31, the day students explored a computer simulation, the six predicates useful in the context of real chaotic systems, were no longer used. Hence, although all student activities related to chaotic systems in which nonlinearities (instabilities) cause apparently stochastic behavior, observational descriptions developed and were used in contextually specific ways. Useful descriptors carried over into new situations (e.g., "labile" and "out of balance"), while others were never used again (e.g., "indifferent"). Some of these new language elements were stabilized and therefore became part of the collective ways of articulating and talking about chaotic systems, whereas others were discarded and never reused in future activities (or interviews). Thus, the development of talk in activity and at the class level interacted with each other: There is a dialectical relation between the two levels in

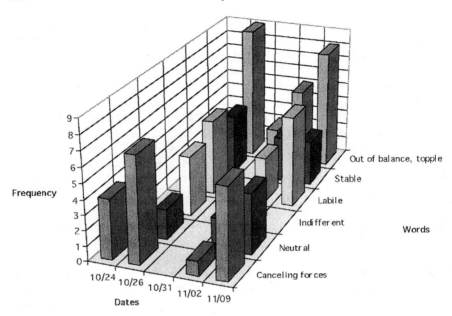

Figure 4.2. The number of students using certain words in the context of the instabilities of chaotic systems changed throughout the course (October 24 to November 9). The frequencies are subject to the dialectical relations linking words, sentences, and tasks.

that students often encountered new ways of talking in collective settings but concretely realized these ways in small-group settings.

An interesting case is the notion of "indifferent" tested by two groups as a possible candidate for describing force equilibria. This notion was intensely discussed in these two groups as a descriptor for the situation where the net forces on a steel ball or pendulum are zero; at this point, the objects are in a labile equilibrium. This description was not used (at least not recorded) during the activity of measuring the forces on the pendulum (October 24) and was never used again after October 26 in either the lesson or the interviews (figure 4.2). During the discussion where students tested it, the term "indifferent" appeared plausible. But in the end, it turned out not to be a fruitful descriptor. That is, "indifferent" emerged from a particular activity, but evidently was not a resource in the context of constructing an explanation for the magnetic pendulum. The second tier of terms, "labile," "stable," and "out of balance" came into use on October 26 while the students worked on generating an explanation for the chaotic pendulum. The third of these three descriptors appeared to have been more accessible and useful. How students test and ground new descriptive language for the phenomena they are to explain is the topic of the next section.

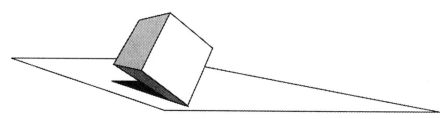

Figure 4.3. Because immeasurably small influences can make the die end up in one of six different end states, it was treated as an example of a chaotic system of immediate appeal and intelligibility to the students.

In the course of the unit on chaos theory, students had many opportunities to ground their discourse in experience and to work out how to talk about some of the phenomena in a more specialized way. Students' frames when they first explored the chaotic system frequently were in terms of stochastic systems such as dice and lotto, or in terms of occult practices (predicting the future from the movement of a pendulum). They also framed the possibility of specific sequences of outcomes (like the same final state five times in a row) in terms of their prior experience with stochastic systems such as the dice (figure 4.3) or the lottery machine—students compared its mixing arms to sensitive ridges for the balls. In the course of their involvement with the activities, students' discourse changed in specific ways and according to the affordances of the activities (artifacts present). These activities, especially when there were concrete materials to be worked with, allowed students to evolve a language, inherently social, correlated with their concrete physical experiences with material objects.

One of the teacher-supported expressions for talking about chaotic system was the notion of "Mercedes star," a one-word (in German) iconic description for the locus of force equilibria, which students had identified in the task asking them to explore the magnetic field of the three magnets using the pendulum bob. The teacher had noted the results of student investigations on the chalkboard and then asked them to use a one-word description to summarize it.

01   Teacher: So can we simply describe this using but one word?
02   Rani: Mercedes star.
03   Teacher: Yea?
04   Rani: Mercedes star.
05   Teacher: Mercedes star, I am writing it here, *Mercedes star*. ((Writes the word on the overhead.)) Good!

The teacher first repeated the word Rani had uttered and then wrote it onto the transparency, uttering the term one more time, with emphasis. His comportment expressed satisfaction with the student answer, which was further reified

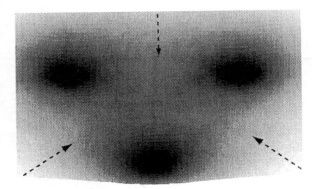

Figure 4.4. The iron filings provided an image in which the sensitive zero-force zones between the magnets showed up as white lines (see arrows) in a way that the students in this study, as well as in a previous study, likened to the shape of the star featured on Mercedes-Benz cars as logo of the company.

by the qualitative description, "Good!" (line 05). That is, without further discussion, the teacher had accepted "Mercedes star" as the legitimate one-word descriptor. Rani then continued talking about the magnetic field, but unbeknownst to the two interlocutors, the student articulated a one-magnet situation whereas the teacher talked about the three- and two-magnet situations. He evidently wanted to return to his issue, the Mercedes star, and therefore suggested that they could also consider her scenario. In this continuation, he further reified "Mercedes star" as the desired word.

06   Teacher: But we can take a closer look at that, too. In any case, the result of
                   your research is now stated here, formulated in a sentence or two, and
                   before we continue, someone in your group had proposed to spray
                   iron filings over the three magnets, and we would get the same im-
                   age. I therefore brought iron filings and a glass plate. Is there some-
                   one going to help me? We can do it on the overhead projector.
07   ((A student sprinkles iron filings onto the glass plate sitting on top of
                   the magnets.))
08   Teacher: Now, do you see the Mercedes star here?

Initially, the teacher made reference to someone who had proposed to use iron filings rather than the pendulum bob for exploring the magnetic field. But evidently, he had already planned this demonstration, having brought iron filings and a glass plate to class. He asked a student to sprinkle iron filings onto the glass plate lying on top of the three magnets sitting on the overhead projector. The result was an image strongly resembling the three-armed star of the Mercedes-Benz logo, similar to my simulation of it (figure 4.4). "Do you see the

Mercedes star? The iron filings, what is happening to the iron filings?" The teacher summarized the whole-class session, including a reference to the Mercedes star, "And our third intermediate result, we just formulated it. It is there on the lines, on the Mercedes star that the magnetic fields of the individual magnets are equally strong, isn't it?" He then asked the students to construct a relationship between the Mercedes star, on the one hand, and the limited predictability of the final resting position and the apparent large effects of small random influences on the pendulum bob trajectory, on the other hand. He thereby set up an opportunity for students to use their personal experiences with equilibrium, for his description implies that the forces are not equally strong to the left or right of the lines.

The notion of the Mercedes star and the image that goes with it then become potential resources for the conversations in the small groups. Thus, Janine proposed a theoretical articulation that was to explain the motion of the pendulum right at the critical zone. As described in the previous chapter, she made the distinction between the ideal (theoretical) and real case.

> The pendulum is equally attracted from both sides. ((Gestures attraction)) When you have a real, yes when you have a real, I mean, this is not ideal. ((Points to the pendulum.)) But if you had a real Mercedes star, then, then the pendulum is attracted on both sides. And because they are both equally strong, it stays in the middle, and it is not a broad line.

Janine provided a description centering on the equilibrium between the forces tugging on the pendulum on both sides. It is only in the ideal case that the equal forces cancel and produce something like an equilibrium state. She then used the Mercedes star to reference the locus of these equilibrium positions, but noted that it did not represent a "broad line."

Other groups equally drew on Mercedes star as a way of talking about the system (i.e., as a theoretical description). For example, Tatiana summarized the results of her group in terms of the theory–practice distinction, the Mercedes star, and the small influences that make the final resting point of the pendulum unpredictable:

> When there was no influence on the pendulum, that is, if there were a perfect trajectory, then the trajectory of the pendulum would theoretically always remain the same. That is, it would, if it gets into motion, it would always come to rest on the same magnet. Because of the changing influences, the outcome becomes random. And because the point on the Mercedes star is so small that you can't calculate it, so that you cannot exactly calculate the starting point, so that the pendulum always starts differently, it will always end differently, that is, at random.

In the group including Rani and Chris, the Mercedes star did not seem to be a useful way talking about chaotic systems. Thus, after they had worked on developing a theoretical description, Rani questioned what all of this had to do with the Mercedes star.

09 Rani: But what has this got to do with this stupid Mercedes star?
10 Chris: Nothing. We have just seen that in these cases, that on these lines the forces cancel each other.
11 Rani: But they get equal impetus. Yes, it goes, let's say, like here, from here, every time.
12 Chris: But this is self-evident. Here, it doesn't have much to do with it, I guess.
13 Rani: But he particularly said we should, that it was important, we do– we have to do it with the Mercedes star.

Neither Chris nor Rani (nor any other one of their three groupmates) found any use for the Mercedes star as a way of talking about the phenomenon at hand. In suggesting that the phenomenon might have something to do with the Mercedes star, the teacher had provided a frame within which it would be suitable to arrive at a description in which the word was used. But as the transcript shows, that Rani (line 09) and Chris (line 12) came to conclude that the notion was not a useful way of talking. Nevertheless, subsequent whole-class (public) discussions provided additional opportunities for students to use the notion or hear it being used by others.

The teacher continued insisting on using "Mercedes star" as part of the way of talking about chaotic systems. If it was not used, he mentioned the notion and asked how it was related to whatever students had just said. If a student speaker used the notion, the teacher greeted it with a nod.

In the subsequent whole-class discussion, the teacher asked one student from each group to read out the statements that they had arrived at. These statements were the endpoint of a search for taking a position in the world with respect to the chaotic pendulum; but, because the students were only at the beginning of their investigations, these statements constituted a form of muddle, although the members of the community could not realize it as such at that particular moment. For example, Svenja read from the sheet in front of her.

We divided our discussion in to theory and praxis. Relative to praxis we found out that there are different influences, and these influences cannot be determined in an exact manner or not be determined at all. These influences act on the object at hand, that is, the sphere, and these influences cannot be eliminated in praxis. Therefore, you cannot predict the results. And theoretically it is like this: if the influences could be determined exactly and infinitely far, or eliminated completely, then you could predict it quite exactly.

It is clear that the students were groping to come to grips with the problem at hand. Their talk was as much a search for coherence of language as it was language about the chaotic pendulum. They were still articulating the setting as much as they searched for explanations. "Mercedes star" was one element especially flagged and therefore standing out, but its usefulness for talking *about* chaotic systems had not (yet) become apparent to most students. It is not surprising that the term was not equally salient in the descriptions by the other students. Therefore, while attempting to construct two concluding sentences to be written on the chalkboard, the teacher encouraged students to include the Mercedes star.

14 Teacher: And so now, you need to bring in what happens on the Mercedes star. Why is it important? We need to get this sentence completed. It may sound strange, but I know we are getting there. Hauke?

15 Heiko: When you are on the Mercedes star and then a bit away, and the magnetic forces and the external influences, which can no longer be calculated.

16 Teacher: Yes, but what is going on exactly on the Mercedes star? Equally strong, can we get the sentence completed?

17 Hauke: The forces cancel each other. And then there are only the external influences.

18 Teacher: But these are equally strong. Can we get that sentence? Let's look again at the Mercedes star. We said that there is a balance of forces. So, and some of you brought in the notion that is important to the balance of forces. Heiko, you said it before. What kind of equilibrium do we have on the Mercedes star?

19 Heiko: A labile or indifferent one.

20 Teacher: A labile one did you say? OK. Or indifferent? But *la*bile is all right.

Although the notion of Mercedes star was originally entered into the classroom discourse by a student, it was not automatically used by others as a way of talking about chaotic systems. Rather, the teacher repeatedly reintroduced the notion back into the conversation when students did not make use of it. As a result, the notion was reified and legitimized as a resource in the language about chaotic system. The stabilization occurred here through a process of recurrent use in conversations both at the whole-class and small-group levels. In other words, recurrent use brought ways of talking into circulation as resources in the construction of observational and theoretical description. However, being available as a resource did not necessarily entail students' use of them. Resources are just resources, available for use, constituting possibilities without implying their own necessity to the situation at hand. In some instances, despite extensive discussion and attempts to make them part of a discourse, an individual ends up not finding a representation useful. In other instances, students adopted a new way of talking about and telling apart as a discursive resource but employed them in ways inconsistent with those of this community or the scientific community.

A holistic reading of the transcripts provides the sense that this unit allowed students to develop and refine ways of talking about chance and necessity and chaos and order. Table 4.1 shows two clusters of ways of talking associated with this refinement, which in fact can be read as a differentiation of ways of talking about equilibrium in the context of chaotic systems. For example, students increasingly distinguished deterministic physical systems as those that exist primarily in theory—an understanding later grounded in their experience with the computer simulation, an ideal world—and chaotic systems as those that exist in practice—an understanding grounded in their experience of real chaotic systems. The use of this distinction of things possible in theory and in practice arose in several groups—one of which we documented in the previous section—while considering whether an object could move along a infinitely narrow ridge. During the interviews following the unit, all students made use of the theory–practice distinction as part of their distinction between deterministic and chaotic systems (see figure 4.2). That is, a development at the level of the (public) classroom had supported a development at the level of the (private) individuals. At the same time, the public language was concretely realized as individuals talked about chaotic systems.

Whole-class discussions allow newly developed ways of talking about phenomena to become known to other students. Ratification of ways of talking at the public level legitimizes them, so that they become resources for private conversations. If ways of talking are not ratified in the public forum, such as the talk about the Foucault pendulum in the previous chapter, then the incentives to use this resource in private conversations are also lowered. That is, all linguistic resources are only potential rather than definite resources. Once accepted and circulated at the classroom level, they can become useful resources for the conversations at the private level. However, whether new ways of talking will be widely circulated in the classroom community is not entirely predictable and appears to depend on a range of constraints. Some of the new language elements, as with the notions of theoretical and actual systems, or the description of labile and stable equilibria, appeared to be plausible and fruitful to others and were therefore accepted—though individual students may not adopt particular discourse elements. The notions of "labile" and "stable" proved to be fruitful from both the students' and teacher's point of view. Drawing on these notions in the course of the activities meant that students usually described the (from the teacher's perspective) crucial aspects of chaotic systems. In this sense, observational descriptions containing "labile" and "stable" easily allowed students to construct analogies between familiar and new cases. Pragmatic studies of discourse at the classroom level with respect to specific disciplines are still rare. In chapter 6, I will show that the adoption of new discourse elements does not depend on who introduced them (teacher or student), but rather on the family resemblance of the new discourse elements with resident discourses.

Table 4.1. Descriptors contrasting deterministic and chaotic systems

Deterministic systems	Chaotic systems
Order, law(-like): Physics consists mostly of *laws* that can be applied to every case . . . but now we deal with disturbances, which we always treated as nonexistent. The *disturbances* are crucial for the results.	**Chaos:** And chaotic is where the influences, minimal influences, have large effects so that it is no longer predictable, and the bob is moving *chaotically*.
Necessity: By and large, the things in the world work the same by *necessity*. Everything is given, when I do *this* then *that* will happen. I flick the switch and the light comes on.	**Chance:** There is *no chance* if you can *compute* everything, but we have influences here that you cannot compute. If you could compute these influences, you could predict what would happen.
Predictable: If you could *compute*, and with the die it is the same thing, if you could exactly compute the die, then you could *predict* it.	**Unpredictable:** You *cannot predict* [the balls on Galton board]. First, you do not know whether it is *exactly even*; and second, the balls are *never in order*, you can never get them in exact order.
Ordered, regular: If there were no magnets, the trajectories would be very *regular*.	**Random, irregular:** There was no series, *no regularity* in the movement.
Theory: *Theoretically*, the trajectories are the same, as we saw on the computer. *Theoretically*, without the influences, you should always get the same result.	**Practice, praxis:** In *practice*, it is not chance, but in theory you can calculate [systems] but not in *practice*, because of the minute, *noncalculable* influences.
Ideal case, ideal experiment, model: On the computer, we saw this *ideal* world, and there it works in the way you want, it just works in the *ideal*.	**Real world, student experiment:** In the *real world*, we cannot predict [the endpoint], because there are influences that we *cannot compute*. And on the computer, I would say, without disturbance, the trajectories are *exactly even* and it always stops on the *same* magnet.
Exact, exactly equal: If the *exact same* conditions prevail, we would get the same, as was shown in our first experiment [on the computer].	**Inexact, unequal:** In the lotto machine, the balls, when they bump into each other, they are *no longer exact*, and you *can't* assume that they are *equal*.
Measurable: Like with the weather, *immeasurable* influences, like when a butterfly beats its wings, lead to all sorts of things, like hurricanes.	**Immeasurable:** If you knew all influences, you would be able to calculate where the pendulum bob stops. But it lies outside of what we can *measure*, the influences, so we cannot compute it.

NEW LANGUAGE AND EMBODIED EXPERIENCE IN AND OF THE WORLD

Actions (material or verbal) are bound up in a double dialectic, making them concurrently an aspect of collective life, actions inherently are social actions, and of the individual life, actions inherently embodied. In this section, I show how ways of talking come to be connected with the bodily experience of and in the world. Talking about stability is not just using some arbitrary word, "stable" in the present situation, but is using the word across particular settings where what we know as the phenomenon of stability is an invariant. This usability of ways of talking across situations and settings is a central aspect of the power of language. In the present context, developing useful and appropriate descriptions of nonlinearities was essential for the development of a discourse about chaotic systems. Once students articulated the nonlinearities as some kind of critical zone where the trajectories diverge, the step was small to arrive at a complete theoretical description of chaotic systems. That is, perceiving critical zones in chaotic systems and using "out of balance," "labile," "on the edge," or "precarious equilibrium" as ways of articulating the situation provides opportunities for making an association in the two partial descriptions of the analogical situations provided in the curriculum, that is, pendulum and drawings: small influences that have significant effects at the nonlinearities.

The teacher had asked the students to describe different kinds of equilibria in some way, and Chris had introduced the terms "stable" and "labile." The teacher confirmed these as suitable and left the table. Rani then asked Chris to explain.

01 Rani: Explain, for stupid people.

02 Chris: * Stable!

03   * Labile!

04   So you drill he hole through * here

05 Rani: Yeah
06 Chris: And * there is a screw through it

07 Rani: Yeah.

08   Chris: And then you can * turn this on it.

09   Rani: And when it hangs, downward, when it hangs
               exactly down, it is stable down it is stable
              ⌈down it is sta⌉ble.
10   Chris: ⌊* It is stable⌋
11   And * *this* way it is labile. Then it can fall over the
              side. ((Wiggles pen back and forth.))

12   Rani: So is * this labile? Labile forces or what?

In conjunction with the teacher's question about types of equilibria, the students brought into their discourse two new descriptors, "stable" and "labile" (In German, the words are "stabil" and "labil"). Whereas Chris used the terms comfortably, Rani was uncertain about their use in this situation. What made them a good way of talking here? That is, for Chris there existed a grounding such that the word "stable" was anchored in the resource situation, the pencil. Following Rani's request for an explanation (line 01), Chris attempted to communicate this anchoring by emphasizing the different first syllables (sta- [line 02] and la- [line 03]) while concurrently showing different configurations of the pencil (hanging [line 02] and standing [line 03]) so that the contrast in the two words and two positions was made salient simultaneously in each situation. Chris literally correlated each of the two words with their corresponding situations: a sound goes with a perceptual experience. These sounds (words) would allow them to tell these two (and perhaps other) situations apart and thereby better handle two different types of equilibrium situations.

The transcript shows that with his subsequent actions, Chris reiterated and elaborated on his earlier explanation (lines 04–17). He first described a different material arrangement that the listeners had to imagine: drill a hole in one end of the pencil (which was made salient as he grabbed the upper end concurrently with uttering "here") and insert a screw (line 06) so that the pencil would be free to move around the screw (line 08) in the direction indicated by him. At this point, Rani joined into the explanation providing her description of a stable configuration; this description was ratified by Chris' overlapping utterance of "stable" while holding the pencil in the stable position (lines 10–11). He continued to reiterate the utterance of "labile" while simultaneously holding the pencil in the unstable position (line 11), elaborating the earlier description by mentioning that in this position, the pencil will topple (line 11). The rising tone in Rani's voice signaled that Rani attempted to use the term "labile" to the starting situation, the drawing of the ball on the ridge to which her index finger and reoriented body pointed (line 12).

This episode provided opportunities for all group members to ground both terms in an *experiential* way but in, at least as seen by Chris, an analogical situation. That is, Chris explained these notions by gesturing two concrete situations for which they were appropriate as descriptions. The number of material elements in the situation was small, consisting of a pencil that was held in two ways. Chris thereby decreased the interpretive flexibility of the focal situation and increased the likelihood that Rani could pick out which aspects of the situation were appropriately labeled "stable" and "labile." Rani, who had asked for the explanation, appeared to be satisfied at first; her utterance can be heard as a confirmation that in this situation, she felt comfortable using the two terms. However, at the end of the episode there is some evidence that Rani was not yet certain about the way the two terms related to the other two situations, pendulum and drawing. She had not yet perceived the invariant physical structure that would make the use of the same ways of talking sensible. Whereas the ball in the drawing was indeed in a labile position, Rani's descriptive language was not appropriate from the perspective of standard physics. In line 12, she tentatively suggested labile forces. However, stable and labile are not appropriate for describing the forces; rather, ball and bob are in a state of labile equilibrium under the influence of the gravitational and gravitational plus magnetic forces, respectively.

Despite the small number of elements in the situation (i.e., a pencil hanging or standing up), it is not evident that all students perceived just those material aspects that constitute the object as stable or labile. This became evident in Rani's question of how the terms related to the drawing. She pointed to the ball on the ridge and asked in which way the ball and the pencil could be seen as similar (line 12). That is, while the hand movements and the material constellations of the pencil contributed to Rani's grounding attempts, they could not guarantee them. In part, the problem was rendered even more problematic because Chris asked his audience to picture a different situation where the pencil was attached to a screw around which it could pivot. This explanation was in part not about stability, but about constructing a system that had labile and stable states. Although his hands animated the focal situation at hand (lines 04–08), the system was not so permanent that it could be pointed to. Some of the communicative problems may have arisen from this complexity. If the system Chris described had existed in material form, he could have then demonstrated how the pencil always falls out of the labile position and into the stable one. Chris partially animated the pencil to do this as he wiggled the pencil back and forth (line 11) but this demonstration was insufficient for Rani to bring the two language elements to her embodied experience of how the world works. Chris had used the words "stable" and "labile" in this specific context; despite being copresent, Rani did not perceive the pertinent material configuration and therefore make the link between configuration and language. Chris used the two words to articulate something, that is, to tell it apart from other things, but his words failed to attune Rani to the corresponding elements. At this point, Chris and Rani failed to focus on the same things in a world of significations. Their ways of telling the situation apart was not the same, so they could not ground references in the same way. This resulted in a conversational breakdown, technically speaking. Rani therefore took Chris to the task of providing additional descriptions that might allow her to bring focal situation and talk to a convergence.

At the end of the episode, however, in conjunction with the teacher's question about types of equilibria, the students brought into their discourse two new descriptors, "stable" and "labile." Students grounded the meaning of both terms experientially as they described something about the pencil Chris held in front of them. That is, Chris explained these notions by showing two concrete situations for which they were appropriate as descriptions. Rani, who had asked for the explanation, appeared to be contented at first; her final utterance can be heard as a confirmation that for this situation, she felt comfortable employing "stable" and "labile." However, the issues were not settled and were discussed again by the students in this group when they looked at new situations.

MULTIPLE AND BODILY GROUNDING

Science educators and teachers often assume that the mere fact of manipulating materials allows students to understand conceptual issues. That is, there is an assumption that manipulation somehow allows abstract ideas to emerge, perhaps by means of a process that has been called "abstraction." However, even in situations when students create material analogies on their own, they may not take this way of talking to new situations. This language therefore is not (perhaps not yet) fruitful. Additional work is then required, for example, by attempting to structure additional situations in ways that the same invariant property becomes salient across situations; the same words can then becomes useful for articulating these invariant properties.

Neither the teacher's drawings nor Chris's explanation of stable and labile equilibria led the group to evolve a satisfying explanation of the pendulum's chaotic motion. The teacher then provided the group with a chaos bowl (figure 4.5), a plaster bowl with ridges that display a physical equivalent to the invisible ridges that explain the potential field in the chaotic pendulum (see figure 3.2). The bowl can therefore be structured as a material analogy of the chaotic pendulum. The behavior of a steel ball in the bowl and that of the pendulum bob are similar; a further aspect of similarity between the two systems arises from the salience of the ("Mercedes") star-like arrangement of the ridges. As they pored

Figure 4.5. The combination of gravitational field and chaos bowl provides a potential field to the little ball that is similar to the field of the chaotic pendulum. It can therefore be used to make inferences about the magnetic pendulum by means of an analogical extension.

over the new artifact, Chris invoked again the linguistic elements "stable" and "labile." Rani signaled her uncertainty for the referents of these words in the context of the bowl.

13	Rani:	But how would *, how is this with the ball?
		When is the ball labile?
14	Chris:	When it is up there, its–
15	Rani:	=Stable?
16	Chris:	You *see*! And it is labile when * it is here.

| 17 | Rani: | Then it rolls either * this way. |

| 18 | | * this way |

19		* or this way.
20	Lars:	*There,* it is right on the working point, because here the, yeah, the different effects are felt.
21	Rani:	Yes, this is clear now.

Similar to the pencil situation, Chris's use of the words "labile" and "stable" co-occurred with holding the ball in particular positions in the chaos bowl. As he began his explanation (line 14), Rani immediately tested her use of "stable" (line 15), which Chris confirmed as appropriate (line 16). By holding the ball in the labile position, he fused reference and ostensive designation. He immediately proceeded to offer the contrasting situation by holding the ball on the ridge in the chaos bowl and indicating in gesture and utterance the three possible directions for the subsequent trajectory (lines 16–19). Lars elaborated his talk by articulating an explanation sentence, produced by the connective "because": the place where Chris last held the ball was a "working point" in which different small effects (observed and discussed during an earlier lesson) make the ball go unpredictably in any of the three directions (line 20).

In this situation, Chris first established a reference (of "labile") by ostensive designation. He held the ball in the position where it would be labile if released. This "would be" was not realized; however, Chris then elaborated, again through ostensive designation, where the ball might roll if released: to the right (line 17), left (line 18), or straight on the ridge (line 19). The adjective "labile" for the ball's state (line 16) is appropriate not because of intrinsic reasons but because of the consequences arising from the position. The precarious nature of the ball's position (or that in line 19) was further elaborated in Lars's comment about the working point (lines 20). ("Working point" is an expression used much less in English than its German equivalent "Drehpunkt," especially in the sense of fulcrum.)

In this episode, the importance of the unspoken background is evident. Chris indicated three possible trajectories for the ball in the chaos bowl from its present position (lines 16–19). At the level of the utterance ("this way"), the three ways to the left, right, and straight ahead are the same. To understand the three ways, we need to know the gestures that Chris used to distinguish the three "this way" utterances. However, what Chris said went beyond a simple combination of utterance and gesture. The "ways" were not only different but also gained further significance from the unspoken but taken-for-granted shape of the bowl. The videotape does not clarify whether the significance ascribed to the situation by each student would have been the same had they actually talked about it. Here, two of the "ways" were trajectories down the sides of the ridge, whereas the third "way" suggested a trajectory along the narrow ridge. Lars expressed the differences between the "ways" in his notion of the "working point" and thereby associated these working points with labile states. That is, these students created different focal situations in which the relations "is-stable" or "is-labile" held, relations that were central in the curricular framework (figure 4.1). Coming to use and describe these relations appropriately (i.e., "understanding" these concepts) then amounted to a situation-type abstraction. Despite the apparent dissimilarity between the different objects in the two episodes (pencil, pendulum bob, steel ball), something can be made salient and constructed as similar. Listeners following Chris's explications had to disclose this similarity for themselves. Pointing and gesturing assist in the process, but only partially establish the reference for "labile" because it is not available to be referenced by ostensive designation.

Rani indicated again that this made sense to her, which suggested—in the context of her question about the use of "labile" and "stable" concerning the steel ball in the bowl—that she accepted this description as intelligible and plausible (line 21). However, she was not happy with this, but also wanted to know how the two notions would apply in the case of the pendulum (line 23).

22	Lars:	Down here ((Points to the bottom of the bowl)), there is–
23	Rani:	And wherein does the pendulum lie, when it is, when it is on the thing?
24	Chris:	When it is labile or stable?
25	Rani:	There it has to be stable, the position of the pendulum I mean. Now here–
26	Lars:	When it is on the Mercedes star or what?
27	Chris:	Yes, on the Mercedes star it is also lable.
28	Lars:	Yes, it is, because there is no gravitation.
29	Chris:	And stable it is exactly in the middle, like when it is in the center.
30	Rani:	Stable it is also, above all, later on the magnet, or not?

Rani's question was a request for both Chris and Lars to follow up because it was not apparent to her what the expressions were to articulate in the situation. Both agreed that on the Mercedes star, the pendulum would be in a labile position. Perhaps, the teacher's earlier ratification of the two terms "labile" and "stable" suggested to Rani their usefulness or correctness so that she therefore pursued understanding how they were useful in the complex of situations before them. The conversations about labile and stable positions in different situations continued. Rani repeatedly asked how the three others would use the two adjectives in the context of the drawings, the bowl, and the pendulum (lines 23, 25, 30).

Here, "labile" was grounded in a double sense, that is, in terms of sense and reference relations. First, it became a way of talking with others about an important structural aspect of chaotic systems; that is, "labile" was grounded in social interactions. Second, it was also materially grounded in that it referred to aspects in the physical world and students' own bodily experiences of finding themselves in "labile" positions. The recurrent descriptions of object motions from the perspective of an agent who makes decisions in which direction to, further underscore this interpretation. The notions of stable and labile are interesting from the perspective of earlier work. First, the intuitive notions of stability and instability appear to be important to developing an understanding of chaotic systems in general (Nemirovsky 1993). Second, equilibrium and dynamic balance constitute a powerful human experience in the world, which is then metaphorically extended (Johnson 1987). It is important to note that in this study, equilibrium and dynamic balance did not act like driving forces of students' activities. Rather, when the notions of labile and stable were used, they emerged from the social and material interactions as tentative articulations, which were the achievements of the group. That is, the present case study shows how stability and abstract imbalance resulted from students' situated inquiries and emerged as evidence of their work, rather than being primarily generators of the activity and discourse. It is through their recurrent experiences in an increasingly familiar world that their talk found a place and stable structure. It is at this point that they also had the experience of sense, reference, and meaning.

Initially, Rani did not find it meaningful to use "labile" and "stable" as a way of talking about the chaotic systems at hand. That is, she heard the words and knew that her teacher wanted her to use them, but this way of talking lacked a corresponding perceptual articulation. Both sense and reference relations therefore did not exist for her; she could mouth the words but initially did not find invariants in the physical or social situation for the recurrent use. Repeated articulations in the group against changing material configurations appeared to have allowed her to both perceptually isolate an invariant structure (perceiving something as something is an operation) in which a way of talking (social resource) turned out to be useful.

As in other situations, communication in these episodes clearly had a material basis. Communication was not *just* socially constructed and a matter of talk but was fundamentally intertwined in the coordination of talk, hand movements, and shifting gaze against the lived-in world. The coordination work was done over, about, and against the material background of the pendulum, drawing, and bowl. In other words, the explanation arose by networking shifting gazes, body movements, and hand gestures and thereby achieving a convergence with the co-occurring utterances. Their confluence allowed a convergence that reduced the flexibility associated with artifacts and utterances. However, the significance of the utterances and pointing gestures did not come from their properties as signs in themselves, but from the unspoken relationship established by the students' movements against the stable background of their respective interactions. Moving their bodies in space and before an always-present background allowed students to articulate objects and events practically and perceptually, then with words, and subsequently to arrive at observation categoricals, that is, to talk about them. Laboratory situations therefore make particular allowances for gestures that cooperate with speech in creating new themes or continuing old ones. Using their bodies, students construct relations and connections that are not necessarily explicit in talk, but are afforded by the physicality of laboratory situations. The artifacts were not just topics of talk but also part of the background against which students' verbal and physical actions were to be heard, and aspects of which the actions made salient. However, although gestures and ostensive designation were present, they could not completely remove ambiguity.

CLASSROOM LANGUAGE CONSTRAINS DEVELOP-
MENT OF ACTIVITY IN UNFORESEEN WAYS

So far, I have largely described the positive ways in which developments at the whole-class level constrained the development of individual activities. However, such developments may also support developments at the other levels inconsistent with the curricular framework, that is, may lead to inappropriate ways of talking. Individual students may associate ways of talking accepted into collective ways with different perceptual features than those that are salient to their peers and teacher without these differences being apparent to the interlocutors. In an everyday way of talking, such situations are characterized as "talking past one another," for although interlocutors participate in conversation, the referent situations, that is, what they are talking about, may differ. The interlocutors nevertheless assume that they are articulating and talking about the same thing, an inherent contradiction that often is not apparent. In science classrooms, teachers often think that students understand because their contributions to the classroom-level interactions seem to indicate so; even when teachers listen to small-group conversations for brief moments, they may think that students understand and that they are "on the same wavelength." Yet when teachers look at what students write on an examination, they may then be surprised about the inappropriate ways of articulating particular scientific phenomena. This was also the case in this classroom, which I exemplify with one of the teacher-favored expressions, the Mercedes star.

One notion that turned out to be problematic was that of "Mercedes star." As noted earlier, Rani originally introduced the notion as the asked for one-word description of the geometric shape produced by iron filings sprinkled on a glass plate posed over the three magnets in the magnetic (chaotic) pendulum under investigation. The teacher, who had found the term useful in an earlier study on learning about chaos theory, received the term positively and supported and encouraged its further use in whole-class conversations and small-group interactions. As the earlier part of this chapter documents, the teacher expended a lot of effort to have students use the term. This contributed to its circulation during whole-class, public sessions, and it subsequently found widespread use in small-group, private conversations.

The transcripts show that the term was used in different ways—without signs in the transcript that anyone was aware of this contradiction. The teacher used it as a way of talking whenever he wanted to articulate (i.e., make salient) a sensitive zone that introduced nonlinearity to a system, which causes it to show chaotic behavior, irrespective of the geometric shape of the locus of all instabilities. Some students, however, used it to describe geometric properties of the system or trajectories. For example, during the activity that asked students to

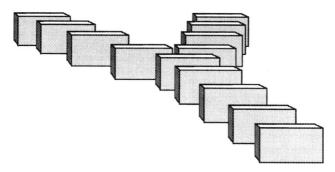

Figure 4.6. Janine brought dominoes to class to show her example of a chaotic system. The key feature articulated in her talk was the Y-shape where two branches of dominoes continue the original line. The strong similarity between this arrangement and the "Mercedes star" in figure 4.4 is apparent.

design their own system with limited predictability, the group of five young women picked up a proposal by Janine: a chain of dominoes arriving at a point where it branches into two. The main part of her argument was that the system had the shape of a "Y" or "Mercedes star" (figure 4.6). Although classmates (supported by the teacher) suggested that "a small air movement won't change the direction in which the last domino falls," the women were not convinced that that they did not have a system with limited predictability. For example, Alex argued, "But very straight, they won't touch each other exactly in the same way, and with time they will be more crooked."

During the posttest, when asked to identify what she meant by "Mercedes star" in one of the drawings (the wall in figure 3.3), Janine noted the Y-shaped trajectory. Similarly, during the post-unit interviews, she articulated a geometric configuration on the Galton board that looked like the Mercedes star (figure 4.7). The Galton board consists of a board with nails in a triangular configuration. Steel balls released onto the board will bounce off the nails and end up in one of many trays at the bottom. Janine spontaneously pointed to the Y-shaped trajectories rather than to the critical points where the ball is in an unstable equilibrium. That is, in the chaotic pendulum (and the bowl), the locus of all points where the bob (ball) is unstable takes the shape of a Mercedes star; on the Galton board, however, the equivalent locus are rows of points with a geometric distribution identical to the location of nails. Interestingly enough, the two drawings of figure 3.3 featured trajectories that are Y-shaped in the same way Janine indicated on the Galton board; the lessons had not made salient that in the two drawings, each point along the ridge and wall constitutes a critical point.

This case shows that although ways of talking are used collectively, some students may associate them with different perceptual features salient to others

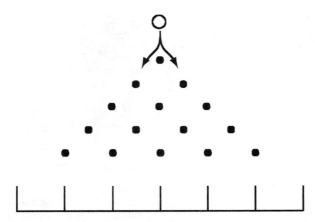

Figure 4.7. A Galton board consists of a triangular array of nails through which balls are dropped. Every time a ball hits a nail it has a probability of 50 percent of falling to the left of the nail and a probability of 50 percent of falling to the right. The possible trajectories of the ball are in the shape of an upside-down letter "Y."

(students, teacher). That is, although ways of talking are the same, meaning is not understood in the same way. In general, there were three ways that the term "Mercedes star" was used in conversations: denoting (a) instabilities, a topological feature; (b) two-dimensional shapes (geometric feature); and (c) the locus of all instabilities in a system (topological and geometric). Only in the first form can the word be generalized to all chaotic systems. Because it easily engenders uses that could be summarized and denoted as a so-called misconception, the use of "Mercedes star" should be considered unfortunate; or rather, the curriculum might foresee a discussion of the geometric shape of the locus of critical points in different systems, which would turns out to be star-, wall-, and point-like in the systems that the students articulated and talked about. Here, members in the class had taken the Mercedes star as part of their common ground. Because there was no striking evidence to the contrary, no repair was instituted and its use was continued as described previously.

CLASSROOM (PUBLIC) AND INDIVIDUAL (PRIVATE) LANGUAGE

In this section, I am concerned with the nature and function of the ways of talking as individual students employed them while talking to the researchers in post-unit interviews. That is, I am concerned with the interaction of development of individuals, on the one hand, and the earlier-described developments at the whole-class and activity levels against the background of the curricular framework. Although students participate in small-group and whole-class conversations and subscribe to ways of talking consistent with the curricular framework, there may be considerable (and idiosyncratic) variations in the individuals talk in different situations, such as with a researcher during an interview. That is, individual differences are expected when students use a discourse for their own intentions. Individual development occurs in the context of the development of collective activity—during which ways of talking emerge and are grounded—and development of ways of talking in public that both enable and constrain the development of collective activity.

Before presenting what some students said during post-unit interviews and the ways of talking they employed, a brief comment on the inherent contradiction of using interviews as a way of assessing what individuals know. During the lessons, students participated in one kind of activity—learning physics as part of getting a high school certificate. During an interview, they participated in a different activity, producing data for a research study. Different activities, however, constitute entirely different context, mediating what is said and done in different ways, focusing on different outcomes, and so forth, and therefore lead to very different cultural practices from which researchers infer what students are said to know (Roth and Lee 2004). Consistent with the stance I am taking in the book as a whole, I do not consider interviews as a way into the mind of an individual. Rather, each interview constitutes a social situation that produces a recorded and transcribed text, but this text is the product of collective rather than individual activity. Whatever is said and how it is said is an interactional rather than psychological feature of the interviewee—even under the most controlled and rigorous conditions intended to keep the context the same for all research participants (Suchman and Jordan 1990).

Having presented the development of an aspect of classroom discourse and how discourse emerges from and is grounded in the interactions arising from ongoing activity, I illustrate how three students figuring in my account—Chris, Lars, and Rani—talked about chaotic systems during post-unit interviews. Broadly conceived, all three had developed ways of talking consistent with the curricular framework (figure 4.1), but they varied considerably in the details of their language even if many, as shown in figure 4.2 (November 9), used the same words (which, of course, is partially an effect of the interactions with the researchers). The three cases presented below show how individuals eventually used certain linguistic elements—developed during local activities and stabilized during public whole-class conversations—across settings, that is, with different interlocutors. Rani's case also shows us that despite extended interactions with others that included the terms "labile" and "stable," these ways of talking about chaotic systems had not become part of her discourse.

Chris

Over the course of this unit, Chris (with physics achievement in the middle tier) developed a rich and varied language to talk about chaotic systems. For example, he used the term "Mercedes star" to denote those points in which the objects experienced an equilibrium position, where forces canceled. In the following quote, he described the critical points of the chaotic pendulum in terms of the zones where neighboring magnets cancel, leading to the unstable equilibrium of the pendulum bob.

> At the Mercedes star, there are in theory, the magnetic fields of two magnets are in effect on this line, and these forces cancel, like in magnitude, like this means, the forces are still acting, from both sides, like when the ball is in this position ((Holds pendulum bob halfway between two magnets)), then it is labile, it is not attracted to one or the other magnet, but to the center.

One can see the relationship between what he said in the interview and how he had explained the words "stable" and "labile" to Rani during the unit, despite the differences between the two situations. Chris also used the descriptions of "deadlock," "apex," "turning point," "neutral zone," "edge," and "summit." He appropriately used these same descriptions for different chaotic systems, including the chaotic pendulum, chaos bowl, Galton board, wall and ridge images, lotto drawing, and kneading dough. It is unknown where this last example had come from, but kneading of dough is a standard example in the physics of nonlinear systems and therefore constitutes an appropriate extension of the situations that had been talked about in this classroom. Any pair of arbitrarily close points in phase space will be, after a small number of stretching and folding operations, far apart. Stretching the dough corresponds to the motion of the magnetic pendulum, folding to the motion across the ridge. He also identified the "deadlock points" as one characteristic of all chaotic systems. Similar to his peers, he continued talking using a person-centered language to describe the ball movement on the Galton board: "Why do the balls arrive differently on the bottom? Because they seek different ways, through the forest of nails there."

Lars

Under his regular teacher, Lars ranked in the middle third of the class in terms of his physics achievement. In this unit he developed a very rich and varied language for talking about chaotic systems. In the end, he had developed the richest language of all interviewed students (i.e., half of the class) for talking about chaotic systems. He was the only person who talked of chaotic systems as characterized by nonlinear relationships that could not be approximated by systems of linear equations. This language was grounded in his prior experiences and in those made during the unit. An excerpt from his explanation of the critical points in one chaotic system illustrates this:

> The forces of two opposing magnets cancel on the Mercedes star with respect to magnitude. When the forces are canceled with respect to magnitude, then it is like in a tug-of-war, when two equally strong teams pull, there will be no movement. At this moment, the forces also cancel with respect to magnitude. That is, the pendulum is pulled equally to the left and right, but is also attracted to the center of the Earth. . . . With the dice, we again have this labile point, that exists in all chaotic systems, this labile point, the edges of the dice, and when you throw it, at some point it stands on an edge. . . . And there is this point where it does not know, should I fall forward or should I fall backward, because it is labile, and the forces are canceled, and then it depends on the perturbation, the influences from the outside.

Lars drew on the activity where he qualitatively determined the size and direction of forces on the pendulum bob at various locations to explain why the "Mercedes star" causes the curious motion of the bob. He drew on an everyday example, a tug-of-war, to elaborate his description. This experientially grounded language allowed him to articulate and talk about chaotic systems in many different ways, provide self-generated analogies, and use the same discourse in different situations (drawings, pendulum, chaos bowl, dice, lotto, roulette, Galton board, weather). He characterized the points on the Mercedes star in several ways. These included "points where objects are susceptible to influences," "points of zero force," "where forces from left and right are equal," "where the steel balls are labile," "labile points," "where forces are canceled," "where the lotto balls are on an edge, are about to topple," and so forth. Referring to the chaos bowl, he articulated the critical situation in terms of the butterfly's wing beat:

> When the steel ball is right here on top [as in figure 4.5], there may be a small disturbance, like the butterfly, which is exactly at the moment, the disturbance has to be exactly at the moment when the ball doesn't know to go left or right, so that it rolls down on the front or the back.

Two features should be noted. First, Lars pointed out that the disturbance had to influence the ball at exactly the moment when it lies on the critical point. This is not the case, a physicist would say, for any disturbance along the ball's trajectory prior to reaching the critical point will have the same effect. Here, the image of labile equilibrium may have mediated his way of talking about the timing of influences on the ultimate fate of the ball. Second, Lars articulated the critical situation in terms of a decision process, where by the ball "doesn't know to go left or right," so that its fate will be determined by the minutest of disturbance, such as a wing beat by a butterfly. Here, Lars used a person-centered description of the system rather than a way of talking that has evacuated all agency.

Rani

Like her peers, Rani had developed a rich vocabulary for articulating and talking about chaotic systems. It was interesting to note, however, that she did not use the descriptors "labile" or "instability" for articulating and talking about the die standing on the edge. In fact, she did not use the terms "labile" and "stable" at all, although they had been, as illustrated, the focus of intensive discussion in her group not only among her peers but in the interactions with her. A considerable number of her peers had taken up this way of talking, but Rani, who exhibited difficulties establishing how they related to the phenomena at hand, did not continue using them after the lesson.

> There are no forces here, on the Mercedes star, where it is susceptible to forces. Exactly on the middle, I mean it is improbable that the ball remains exactly in the middle. This is like the dice that does not stay on the edge, although it would be possible in theory. I would say, this is in principle the same for the pendulum, which never comes to rest. It is improbable that it comes to rest somewhere in the middle where it is so sensible.

On the one hand, this quote illustrates Rani's competent idiom for articulating and talking about chaotic system. She described different systems, here chaotic pendulum and dice, in the same or similar terms, thereby showing how she structured them in equivalent ways. Instead of using "labile" to characterize the state of the various objects, she described the systems in terms of "where it is sensible to external influences," "where the forces cancel," "where there are no more magnetic forces," where forces "act in opposite direction," "balance of forces," "susceptible for external influences," or "where it rolls this way or that way." On the other hand, the quote also shows that in her description, the external force had to occur at the moment that the moving object was at the critical point, consistent with the pencil situation that Chris had explained and demonstrated to her. Lars had evolved the same way of talking, which suggests a possible relationship between the ways of talking during the interview and the previous conversation during the lesson.

She also extended the newfound ways of talking to articulate aspects of life. Asked whether it bothered her that there are phenomena that can be predicated only to a limited extent, Rani answered:

If it was different, it would have repercussions for the entire life, as I already said– I don't want to say that my life was diminished if lotteries didn't exist, but there are so many things that we don't usually think about, and which are chaotic, like the dice. I mean, all games would be down the tube if you were able to predict them. So I think that it is a good thing that you cannot predict some things. But in perfect worlds, everything is possible. But I am not bothered at all that you cannot predict the outcome of a game of dice.

In this chapter, three levels of development important to understanding ways of talking emerge from physics laboratory activities: the evolution of talk in real time, development of ways of talking individual students draw on in an interview situation, and changes of way of talking at the classroom level. At the collective level, specific descriptive language emerged from and sometimes disappeared with specific activities; an increasing number of groups and individual students used these ways of talking in the more private small-group and interview settings. The descriptive language emerged from ongoing activities where they are stabilized by means of social interactions and engagement with the material world. It is important to note the heterogeneity of these developments. Different groups evolved different descriptive ways of talking, individuals developed different ways of explaining phenomena and at different rates than groups, and the ways of talking changed at the collective level.

d

5

Mediating World, Articulation, and Science Talk

In the previous chapters, I have shown how ways of talking evolve from initial articulations of structures to science talk. At the outset, learning to talk science is therefore an aporia, a problem that seems perplexing because it is rooted in the dialectical relation of two things (i.e., a chicken-and-egg situation). *Meaning* is the dialectical relation of *sense* and *reference*, which presuppose one another. For sense to exist there has to be reference, and for reference to exist there has to be sense. This aporia, however, is an artifact of classical logic embodied by much of Western thought. Aporias become understandable within dialectical logic, which includes the identity of nonidentical things as a central aspect. Which came first, chicken or egg, if each presupposes the other? In classical logic, this aporia cannot be resolved. In a dialectical approach, however, chicken and egg are nonidentical aspects of the same thing. We can think of it historically, a typical method of dialectically oriented social sciences. At some point, there existed an organism that did not reproduce by means of eggs. Eventually, however, the single-state organism (reproduction by cell division) evolved into a two-state system (sexual reproduction, two-parent system). Such an evolution can be described mathematically using the same language as the one that describes the chaotic pendulum (Roth and Duit 2003). That is, the same mathematical language of catastrophe and chaos theory describes the existence of multiple stable points and the evolution of the total number in response to environmental pressure (context, experience).

Teaching is an activity that provides resources that enable and constrain the evolution of ways of talking. How this might occur, given the fundamental aporia that hearing a word does not tell students to what it refers in the perceptually world accessible to them, is at the heart of this chapter. In essence, it involves a process that physicists call "bootstrapping," a developmental process that gets itself going. I therefore view teacher and students as a system that contains the resources to develop: students come to use language and articulate the world, although the two will eventually appear to presuppose one another. We can think of the two as mutually constraining elements of the same world that coevolve until they can be articulated as separate.

An equivalent aporia exists for the development of sense and reference. For example, to see some structure in the world, a corresponding perceptual schema has to exist, but the perceptual schema only exists as a result of seeing the structure in the world. A widely varying body of literature—ranging from the brain sciences to philosophy—shows that the two corresponding structures coevolve as a result of activity, itself subject to biological structures. That is, activity—or rather agency—and structure are related dialectically, giving rise to a bootstrapping process after some critical branching point in the evolution of the system. What are such critical branching points during the teaching of physics?

WAYS OF TALKING AND TEACHING

So far in this book, we have seen, with some exceptions, students interact with the social and material world almost completely on their own. We have seen that in these situations, often facing new materials and new phenomena, they structure (articulate) both world and language in the process of finding new positions and orientations. The new perceptual and linguistic structures arose from their activities. The language initially was not so much about a world, its objects, and events, but a form of action that helped them in articulating the scene, in separating it into figure and ground. In this, the world did not tell students a new language; nor did language tell them what the world would be like. They had to find both. New language and new ways of seeing arose as stable and recurrent features from their articulations in activity, where, faced with particular situations, students lost the habit of using some words and gradually acquired the habit of using new words. They did not have choice over the words and ways of talking as these emerged, for initially their material and verbal actions were more like groping in the dark than like repeated, routine actions in a familiar world.

Whereas the world does not tell students which linguistic resources to draw on and how to talk about it, other human beings can. In the previous three chapters, I showed how new ways of talking emerged from and were stabilized largely in student–student interactions, although I also pointed out the pressure existing in the teacher's continued insistence on the use of certain words such as in the case of the term "Mercedes star." In this situation, the new linguistic elements and new ways of telling in situation materialized for the first time, the students' prior experiences and language at hand constituted the surface of emergence for the new way of talking. Within the groups, different ways of seeing and talking became apparent as students sought orientations in talk, action, and gesture. These variations made for a fertile ground for the evolution of new ways of seeing and articulating, just as genetic variation creates a fertile ground for the rapid, mutual evolutionary adaptation of animals and niches. In this, the gradual, trial-and-error creation of new vocabularies and ways of talking were not discoveries of how students' prior language resources fit together. Students could not reach new forms of talking by inferential processes in which they coordinated familiar linguistic elements and the new phenomena that they perceived. They could not achieve new ways of talking based on premises formulated in their old ways of talking, their familiar or root discourses. Even those people whom we celebrate as the greatest minds—Galileo, Hegel, or Einstein, for example—did not create new language based on premises formulated in old vocabularies.

> Such creations are not the result of fitting together pieces of a puzzle. They are not discoveries of a reality behind the appearances, of an undistorted view of the whole picture with which to replace myopic views of its parts. The proper analogy is with the invention of new tools to take the place of old tools. To come up with such a vocabulary is more like discarding the lever and the chock because one has envisaged the pulley, or like discarding gesso and tempera because one has now figured out how to size canvas properly. (Rorty 1989, 12)

Inventions, however, are not derived on the basis of inferences but rather on the basis of insights, which impose themselves more or less suddenly after having primed oneself through extended activity with the elements at hand. Students are not entirely in the situation of having to evolve new forms that do not exist in humanity but rather, find new ways of talking that are heretofore unfamiliar to them but already exist as possibilities at the societal level.

In most everyday situations, we learn new ways of articulating as we enter some existing community with its own local dialect pertinent to the activity at hand. Thus, when I moved into a small isolated village on the coast of Labrador to teach mathematics and science, I came face to face with the culture of fishermen who also built their own boats. Everything that I know about boat building, the specialized language for boat parts, how to seek and choose the appropriate trees and roots, I learned by participating with others. That is, I was a newcomer to an existing culture into which I immersed myself but which changed little during my two-year presence. There were many people who knew about boat building, and of course everyone knew fishing through their lifelong experiences. Many people helped me, were models of cultural ways of talking, corrected me when I described something inappropriately, and provided feedback while I built my own boat. That is, I acquired the new language by means of access to and simulations of the perspectives of more-advanced users of the language in the midst of practice, a crucial component in the process of language acquisition (Gee 2004).

In schools, however, the relationship between existing culture and newcomers is different. There is only one teacher who can give feedback, make a small correction by repeating an utterance but with a slight change, or propose a new word when students attempt to articulate some feature. Telling students how to use new linguistic elements has as much chance of changing their ways of talking as selling a tool has chance of changing the material practices of the buyer. That is, teachers and textbooks are but resources providing students with opportunities to find existing ways of talking that they can try out, as they would go to the hardware store to purchase a tool that they have not used before. But trying out the language, students have to do on their own.

In this chapter, I provide examples for teacher–student interactions in the context of Interactive Physics, which allowed me (the teacher) to mediate students' access to the microworld and to fruitful ways of talking. However, even though teachers take important roles in the students' lives—as evaluators of their work and as gatekeepers into science—whether they do integrate new orientations and viewpoints proposed by the teacher and make it their own cannot be predetermined in advance. How we use the tools we acquire is determined neither by their structural properties nor by other people's usage. Rather, my use of a tool constitutes at the same time a reproduction of culture and, in the (slight) variation of enacting them, the production and change of culture. However, teachers can mediate how I articulate the tool and how I come to talk about using it. Here, I focus on the possible role a teacher can play in the emergence of new forms of seeing and talking as students explore new (micro-) worlds. In 1991, having just read *Talking Science* (Lemke 1990) and having used other activities that engaged students in focused conversations, I recognized the potential of Interactive Physics to focus student–student conversations. I had recorded the interactions because, as the teacher, I was interested in understanding how students evolved new ways of talking and in how interactions with me would mediate the development of their conversations and ways of talking. We return to the same classroom and to the same group of students that featured in chapter 2.

TEACHING FOR ADAPTIVE CHANGE IN SCIENCE TALK

Besides students' free explorations of the microworld (using Interactive Physics), the conversations with me became for many groups a significant aspect in evolving standard ways of talking about the microworld phenomena. The present case study of the interactions between Glen, Eliza, and Ryan, on the one hand, and myself, on the other, documents two important aspects of teacher–student interactions. First, I needed to assess the students' learning, that is, to identify their ways of seeing and talking about the microworld phenomena. Up to the point of the first episode, I had spent about equal amounts of time with all student groups so that I had not heard much of these three students' conversation. When I interacted with the students, I frequently approached them so closely that I had the possibility of accessing the mouse and touch the monitor (figure 5.1). This allowed me to orient in the way they were oriented and vice versa.

To assess student progress, I engaged them in conversations. Here, students oriented to the microworld, articulating objects and events in their material, verbal, and gestural actions, thereby articulating the world. In other words, by joining their groups and orienting to the microworld in ways that at least on the surface resembled their orientation, I could find out if and to what extent their actions and ways of talking resembled mine, a trained research physicist. This aspect of teacher–student interactions is illustrated in the episode below. The two aspects of teacher–student interactions were also prevalent in the transcripts from all other groups (and were so in the interactions not recorded), but depended in quantity on the groups involved. For example, with the group in this case study, there were three occasions in the course of one sixty-minute lesson

Figure 5.1. When I interacted with students, I placed myself right among students. In the middle picture, my head is visible on the bottom left. On the right, Ryan's pencil is just entering the frame in the process of gesturing the motion of the object. On the left, one can make out Glen's arm in the process of making a gesture toward the image on the monitor.

of helping students articulate the microworld such that they came to see it in the culturally sanctioned way. During the equivalent lesson with the other three groups, there were one, two, and two such occasions. All interactions with students included the dimension of identifying students' ways of seeing and talking.

If the probe was positive, that is, the students' science talk seemed appropriate, I would move on to another group. (Little did I know about how ways of talking can appear appropriate when we teachers only spent a few moments with each student group. This is the aporia of teaching that to do the good job we are supposed to do requires spending entire lessons with each small group.) However, if the students' discourse was inappropriate (from a standard physics perspective), as it was in these students' case, I would take some action that created new resources available to students for use, hopefully moving them off the current trajectory and into a new one more consistent with the standard ways of seeing and talking about the microworld. This aspect of teacher–student interactions is documented in the episode described in "Making Forces Visible." The final episode, contained in the section "Coming to Terms," provides data extending those in chapter 2 in support of the claim that the students had developed stable and recurrent ways of talking in the microworld situation without my presence and assistance.

The videotapes show that all four groups I videotaped arrived at standard ways of talking that are illustrated in the "Coming to Terms" section during the period of data collection. As far as I could ascertain from my interactions with the students that were not videotaped, they also achieved this competence (given the limitations of a teacher in making such assessments, especially in the course of the ongoing lesson where other concerns compete for his attention). That is, they literally and metaphorically came to terms with the microworld phenomena.

IDENTIFYING STUDENTS' WAYS OF SEEING AND TALKING

This episode shows how students' talk about the microworld was elicited. Through this talk, the students made available the data on which my subsequent teaching intervention was based. I had just approached the three students, who were oriented toward the monitor where something like a multiframe photograph of a ball moving along a parabolic trajectory was displayed. In each position of the circular object, there was also a single-line arrow attached, which changed in length and direction along the trajectory. These stood for the velocity of the object, but because students did not use or describe it as such, I denote the arrow as «velocity». Near the end of what was visible, a second arrow in outline form (which I denote here as «force») attached to the last ball in the sequence. Glen said, "It carried it up again" (line 01). Overhearing this utterance, I asked the three students what they had found out (line 02). Still in the presence of the same screen display, Glen and Eliza responded.

01 Glen: Let– * See it carried it up again.
02 Teacher: Well, what did you find out?
03 Glen: The longer the arrow– (1.2)
04 Eliza: The longer the big arrow is, the higher the veloc-
             ity, like this– see it's steeper. ((Glen resets the ex-
             periment.))

05 Teacher: * Which one do you think shows you velocity?
06 Eliza: The ⌈b i g a r r o w.⌉
07 Glen: ⌊The big arrow.⌋
08 Ryan: The big arrow.
09 Teacher: Shows us velocity? ((Glen moves «velocity» into
             new position.)) *
10 Ryan: Oh, no because it carries the redirection.
11 Teacher: So what does it take to carry something?
12 Glen: If you have the little arrow in one direction and the
             big arrow in another direction then the little arrow
             will be like the whole trajectory or whatever will
             go the way the big arrow is pointed in.

From the video, I later found out that when I approached Glen, Eliza, and Randy, they had just run another simulation. Glen remarked that the object ("it") moved up, carried by «force» ("it," line 01). To answer my question about their findings, Eliza first used the term "velocity," which, as a consequence of a longer "big arrow," would be higher (line 04). However, she appeared uncertain about it and began to articulate the steepness of the trajectory in an observation sentence (line 04). That is, her utterance consisted of one observation categori-cal, followed by an observational predication whereby something is steeper. But the two parts of the utterance stood side by side, in time, and were not explicitly connected by means of the kinds of connective that makes language characteris-tically scientific.

At this point, Glen reset the display so that it now simply showed the object and the two arrows (experimental preparation). My subsequent question, "Which one do you think shows you velocity?" expressed uncertainty as to which arrow Eliza was looking at when she said "velocity." All three responded by uttering, "the big arrow" (lines 06, 07, 08). I questioned, "Shows us velocity?" Here, the students already had indicated to which entity they referred when using the term "velocity." My questioning can therefore be also heard, as the next turn shows, as a critique, a doubt about the relationship between the word and thing so denoted. Ryan began his utterance with an, "Oh no," which indicates a revision, a recognition that something was not in the way that it had appeared in earlier talk. Ryan then apparently rearticulated (line 10) what Glen had said earlier in a slightly different way (line 01). In the next turn, I then asked what it took to carry something. There had been no time to reflect, but the question appeared to have been designed. From the perspective of those who know Newtonian physics, it is evident that the question aims at eliciting talk about force. In response, Glen articulated a situation that began with the "little arrow" oriented in one direction and the big arrow in another; the trajectory and the little arrow would reorient to "go the way the big arrow is pointed in" (line 12). There was nothing in the utterance to suggest that Glen was talking about several instances. Rather, the entire utterance consisted of observation sentences, articulating the orientations of the two arrows prior to the simulation and the change in the orientation of one of them in the other. There was no connective that would have made one of the two arrows (standing for) the cause of the changes in the other, nor was there a connective that would have linked several different simulations (e.g., in the form, "Whenever . . . it . . ."). There was also no connective between "trajectory" and "the little arrow," which, from a physicist's perspective exists, because the instantaneous velocity, denoted by the velocity vector ("arrow") is tangential to the moving object's trajectory at any current position.

Nevertheless, the excerpt shows that students had begun developing a way of talking in the context of particular screen displays that they felt comfortable with. They used "it carried it up again," "it's steeper," "it carries the redirection," and "the little arrow . . . will go the way the big arrow is pointed in." This excerpt also indicates that students used a common way of articulating the situation, a way that they developed during their interaction with each other and the system. On the other hand, the students appeared to be much less confident in their use of the term "velocity." When asked, "Which one do you think shows you velocity?" Eliza and Glen had responded, "the big arrow." Eliza had used the term in response to my initial question about what they had found out, while Glen and Ryan did not use the term at all. However, their talk about a "carrier of redirection" and, at least in Eliza's case, the feature responsible for the increase of «velocity» bore some family resemblance with the standard ways of talking— force is responsible for a change in velocity, both its direction and its magnitude (speed). At this point, the step from the "carrier of redirection" and "change in «velocity»" to force seemed small. My question, "So what does it take to carry something?" (line 11), has to be seen from this perspective; it had arisen from my orientation to the situation, including both objective student talk and screen display. The use of their way of talking, "What does it take to carry something?"

can be understood as an attempt to help students make the switch from talking "carrier" to talking "force," and thereby about the cause-and-effect relationship that exists between force and velocity. The question therefore had the potential of mediating students' ways of articulating the situation, particularly of evolving the ways of talking that are typical of physics and include observation categoricals.

The transcript of this part of the conversation contains several indicators of a high degree of common ways of talking among the three students. First, Eliza repeated and then completed a sentence Glen had started (lines 03, 04). Then, all three responded to my question, "Which one do you think shows you velocity?" (line 05) in essentially the same way, and all three of them answered almost in unison (lines 06, 07, 08). Finally, Glen (line 12) elaborated Ryan's statement (line 10), which if joined together would not only articulate observations but also explain what they had found out about the microworld and what language they were using in common. The transcript shows that I differed from students in at least two ways. My question suggests that I was unclear about what the students denoted by "big arrow" and "little arrow," and I did not share the students' notion of velocity that led them to use it as label for «force» (line 05). To find out how students were oriented when they used the word, I used the students' own talk as a starting point. When Ryan stated that the big arrow "carries the redirection" (line 10), I asked in the next turn, "What does it take to carry something?" (line 11). In this effort to establish a common way of talking, our conversation became a collective achievement. I did not attempt to tell students anything. I apparently attempted to find out how students' shared ways of talking related to the situation at hand, but the students also had to find out how my way of talking related to theirs.

A crucial point in teaching was the identification of what students were currently attuned to, that is, the identification of how they structured the relevant aspect of the setting (things on the monitor) so that I could design appropriate interventions. Here I use the notion of "designing intervention" to denote teachers' everyday ways of orienting to students and engaging in teaching without having time out for reflection and theoretical considerations about what to do next (Roth 2002). The design occurs on the spot, oriented to the world as it presented itself, students and their objects of inquiry taken together. This spontaneous designing has much more similarity with an athlete making a next move in some competition (where there is no time out for reflecting) than with the architect who, for the hundredth time, designs a townhouse for a rapidly growing suburban area. The necessary identification of students' current orientation, their ways of seeing and talking, had to occur through communication. The difficulty in this process lay in the fact that the students and I did not see nor talk over and about objects and events in the same way—sometimes unbeknownst to us, for we hear specific utterances, particular words, as they would appear in our own language rather than how they are part of others' patterned ways of communicating. But, if we teachers want to make appropriate assessments, we need to go beyond hearing the presence of particular words and assess orientations and ways of talking, both of which extend single utterances.

In this situation, my reactions to student talk shows that I realized discrepancies between our mutual orientations and ways of articulating them in words. Students' talk, however, was based on the default assumption that we perceived the same entities in the same way. There were also differences in the students' and my talk. They drew on linguistic resources (velocity, speed, force) in everyday folkways, while I used the same linguistic resources in ways characteristic of the physicist community at large. The way particular words are used, how they orient people, and how they are connected with other words differs between folk and scientific settings. My task was therefore to identify students' ways of articulating the microworld before I could design an intervention. That is, I had to begin with their talk ("What does it take to carry something?"), before shifting to more scientific modes of talking. In fact, the physical presence of the animated diagrams mediated our conversations.

Despite the fact that teachers do not have the luxury of time in a situation such as the episode describes, they need to find a way of engaging that promotes development toward more appropriate (from a curricular perspective) ways of talking. Because teachers while teaching do not also have time or resources to conduct research about what students might intend, the best way to think about what the teacher has to do is the development of a passing theory. The passing theory is about students' current ways of articulating the world, based on what the teacher knows in advance and the kind of data that he can gather by interacting with students as I had done. In effect, students have to engage in the same task, for my own ways of talking may appear strange to them. To converge in their ways of talking, what

> two people need, if they are to understand one another through speech, is the ability to converge on passing theories from utterance to utterance. Their starting points, however far back we want to take them, will usually be very different—as different as the ways in which they acquired their linguistic skills. So also, then, will the strategies and stratagems that bring about convergence differ. (Davidson 1986, 445)

Such a theory is passing, "because it must constantly be corrected to allow for mumbles, stumbles, malapropisms, metaphors, tics, seizures, psychotic symptoms, egregious stupidity, strokes of genius, and the like" (Rorty 1989, 14). At the moment, therefore, I was concerned with the passing theory I needed for designing an intervention on the spot. Thus, based on my passing theory, I could modify my actions, which produced resources that students use for modifying their own language. All a teacher in such a situation can do is to hope that this new way of talking not only fits the phenomenon but also converges with the standard ways of talking. Such a theory has to arise from the teacher's situated practice; he adjusts them to the contingencies of the ongoing conversation. The teacher thereby becomes a situated analyst of situated talk rather than a user of a general theory of cognitive frameworks.

MAKING FORCES VISIBLE

This episode illustrates how interactions with me, the teacher, provided students with resources that allowed them to articulate a crucial aspect of object motion that they did not perceive initially. However, without seeing this aspect, the language that describes the relationship between the two arrows «force» and «velocity» becomes inconsistent, impeding the evolution of language toward the standard Newtonian language, in which force and velocity are linked in specific ways. My interactions, therefore, allowed students to become attuned to an aspect that they had not been attuned to before, and subsequently to include the notion of "force" into their ways of talking about «force». Here, I set up a critical situation in which the two arrows «force» and «velocity» pointed in opposite directions and asked students to hypothesize the outcome of the experiment (line 13).

13   Teacher: What if you had that point up? (3.5) And this one would
                 be pointed like this? ((Moves first «velocity» then
                 «force» into configuration shown.))

Readers may notice the particular up-and-down orientation of «force» and «velocity». On the surface, the microworld does not have a preferred orientation. This simulation would run in the same way whatever the global orientation of these two arrows as long as they are aligned but in opposite direction in the way they were. However, the orientation that I had used for setting up the simulation provided a resource to draw on the human experience of living in a gravitational field that makes vertical orientation a powerful experience that is metaphorically extended, via language, to many other experiences (Lakoff 1987). However, students may not perceive such a configuration as that resource intended by the teacher. That is, although to me the direction of the arrow and the experience of living in a gravitational field are aspects of the same world, teachers cannot assume that students would relate «force» to their experiences. The teacher's task therefore consists of contributing to the interaction with students in such a way that they come to perceive the display in one rather than any other way.

This pedagogical move enacts the initial part of the predict–observe–explain method, in which a teacher asks students to hypothesize the unfolding of some event, based on their existing understanding, then observe the event, and finally explain what they have seen. All of the stages require students to articulate the subjective intelligibility of the events they expected and had seen, making available to the teacher their ways of telling things apart and talking about the objects and events thereby made salient. My intuition about the need to listen to students in this way turned out to be right. In a research project I conducted many years later in an Australian twelfth-grade physics classroom, my colleagues and I found out that there were many situations in which students saw different events occurring while watching demonstrations or creating some phenomena on their desks. The problem was not that they had expected and seen different things, but that there were no opportunities for talking about what they had seen and thereby revealing to those present (teacher and students) that different perceptions were the norm. Everyone in the classroom listened to the teacher and talked to peers as if they had articulated the focal situation in the same way.

But the process also includes the act of perception, itself a form of action that has been formed in past experiences. Because of the flexible nature of language, however, the teacher has to be alert to the fact that students use words differently, thereby articulating different worlds. Words such as "backward" and "forward" may not articulate the same situation for different individuals, thereby opening up the possibility for a different sense of what is happening. Further, because people do not normally reflect about their concurrent experiences in the world and form theories about them, they do not automatically have a means for checking whether they actually have passing theories about another's utterances. Rather, we take the world in the objective way it appears to us for granted and inherently shared with others in the situation. This may give us a false sense of being attuned to and understanding the segment in the same way as the others.

We now return to the episode. In response to my question, both Glen and Ryan suggested that the circle would go down (lines 14, 15), an observation that Eliza contradicted as the experiment ran its course (line 16). In effect, Eliza stated an observation sentence ("it went") that was framed as a contrast "first, though." That is, this statement did not contradict the previous statements in general, but only insofar as it pertained to the first part of the object's trajectory. There, "it went backwards." My next turn ("But first?") reiterated doubt about an observation in the first part of the event. This statement did not contradict what Eliza had just said, but rather pertained to statements that were incorrect or did not refer to the initial part of the event. Because Eliza had just made such a statement, my comment could be heard as questioning Glen and Ryan's prediction, a hearing reified by the ensuing revisions of observation sentences. Ryan was the first to respond (line 18). He suggested that the "initial velocity went the way the little arrow goes." Assuming that he was in fact attuned to «velocity», his way of talking still sounds odd from the perspective of a physicist, who uses vectors ("arrows") to stand in for the word "velocity" for referring to an object's speed and current direction of motion. "Initial velocity" and "little arrow" are therefore synonymous expressions.

14	Glen:	It would go straight down.
15	Ryan:	Yeah, it would go downward. ((Teacher runs the simulation, which results in the screen display depicted to the right.))
16	Eliza:	* I think it went backwards first though.
17	Teacher:	But first?
18	Ryan:	The initial velocity went the way the little arrow goes.
19	Eliza:	Didn't it go backwards first? and *then* go forwards?
20	Ryan:	I think so (1.3)

From a structural perspective, Ryan had uttered a tautology. Pragmatically, however, he may be heard to have made a statement about the initial movement of the object, which was in the direction of «velocity». In the subsequent conversational turn, Eliza stated two observation sentences about consecutive moments in the object's trajectory; the structure of the sentence signaled disagreement, "Didn't it go backwards first?" (line 19). In this, she both responded to my own question about what happened first and uttered an observation sentence that contrasted Ryan's statement. Why might she have uttered a contrast, if in fact Ryan was talking about «velocity», the arrow that was thin and narrow? But, as the screen image shows, while «velocity» was given as a single line with an arrowhead, and therefore "little" in some sense, it was also longer than «force». Eliza's utterance makes sense if you are attuned to «force» as the "little arrow," where the predicate "little" pertained to its length rather than width.

Despite the contrast that Eliza's statement constituted with respect to his own previous utterance, Ryan expressed tentative agreement with her observation sentences, "I think so" (line 20). In this, agreement was achieved, and the source of the previous disagreement was no further explored, which might have brought to the clearing the unexamined and unnoted differences in using the predicates "little" and "big."

At this point, then, I may have realized that the students had not perceived the object to go upward initially before moving downward. Furthermore, although the motion seemed to suggest a ball thrown into the air, I might have thought that the students did not relate what happened on the screen to their personal experiences of objects thrown into the air. However, what I might have thought was not relevant to the unfolding of the situation. Rather, what matters is how we, the students and I, provided one another with resources, opportunities, and constraints for developing the conversation. The question "Is there something in real life?" (lines 21, 23) requested such a link be made between the salient screen display and something else, denoted by "real life." In fact, the question is a request to seek an observation invariant, a perceptual analogy, between two different situations.

```
21   Teacher:   Like this? (1.4) Is there something?=
22   Ryan:      =Yeah, see.
23   Teacher:   Is there something in real life?
24   Glen:      Yeah, when you spin a hula hoop and the–
25   Eliza:     Towards ⌈you. ⌉
26   Glen:             ⌊Yeah,⌋ towards you.
27   Teacher:   But here?
28   Glen:      And it sort of goes ((Hand moves forward and away from
                him)) that way and it comes back to you. ((Hand returns))
                (1.2)
29   Ryan:      No.
30              (4.5)
31   Eliza:     It reminds me of a yo-yo=
32   Ryan:      =That's gravity, that's the gravity
33              (2.1)
34              'cause when you throw it ⌈u p – ⌉
35   Glen:                               ⌊What⌋ goes up, it must come down.
```

Glen and Eliza together elaborated the description of a hula hoop that is spun "towards you" (lines 24–26). After the fact, it is not clear whether they had finished their description, for I already took the next turn, which could be heard both as a question and a critique, "But here?" (line 27). How, the question seems to ask, does a spun hula hoop relate to the situation that currently is the focus of the conversation? In the next turn, Glen provided an answer. His hand motion suggested that the hula hoop moves away from the body first and then returns, a description that makes sense against an unstated background experience of a hula hoop (or any other circular object), spun toward the person before being thrown away, that rolls back to the throwing person because of the rotational energy embodied in the spinning motion and friction with respect to the environment. After a short pause, Ryan said "no," but it is not evident what he negated. There was a long pause. Rather than evaluating what students had said, which is a common teacher practice (Lemke 1990), I was not taking the turn. By not taking a turn at talk, I not only refrained from evaluation but also provided space for student talk and expressed that I wanted the three to continue articulating responses to my question.

Eliza then suggested a resemblance with a yo-yo (line 31), without, however, articulating the aspects in which the present situation resembled a yo-yo. The fact that Ryan latched in taking the next turn left no space for Eliza to elaborate. His voice expressing excitement and something like an "aha" experience, not unlike Katrina's expression when she first articulated Foucault's pendulum, Ryan called out "That's gravity, that's the gravity" (line 32). There was a pause, which no other participant in the conversation took as an opportunity to take a turn at talk. It could have been an opportunity for me to enter, because, from a naive teacher perspective, Ryan had used the "magic word," gravity, which could transition the conversation to take a trajectory toward standard ways of relating force and velocity. If the circular object were a ball, then gravity would make it come down when it has been thrown up. This pause was therefore also a call for further elaboration of the previous statement, which Ryan then provided, "'cause when you throw it up." Ryan sketched such a situation, "when you throw it up" (line 34). He did not articulate what the "it" was, nor was there a referent that this indefinite particle might have pointed to. The articulation was such that it could refer to a real-world event that I had asked for or to the object in front of us. Structurally, it was therefore a suitable candidate for describing two situations, that is, an observation categorical, and therefore a move from simple observation sentences to an observation categorical, a first faltering scientific law. Overlapping his turn with Ryan, Glen explicitly stated such a law, "What goes up, it must come down" (line 35).

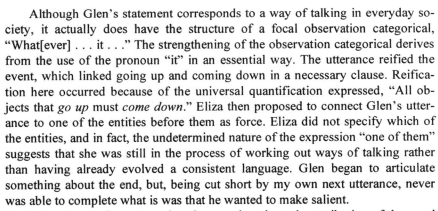

34   'cause when you throw it ⌈u p – ⌉
35   Glen: ⌊What⌋ goes up, it must come
          down.
36   Eliza: And then one of them is the force– (1.0) isn't it?
37   Glen: In the end you're, when the=

Although Glen's statement corresponds to a way of talking in everyday society, it actually does have the structure of a focal observation categorical, "What[ever] . . . it . . ." The strengthening of the observation categorical derives from the use of the pronoun "it" in an essential way. The utterance reified the event, which linked going up and coming down in a necessary clause. Reification here occurred because of the universal quantification expressed, "All objects that *go up* must *come down*." Eliza then proposed to connect Glen's utterance to one of the entities before them as force. Eliza did not specify which of the entities, and in fact, the undetermined nature of the expression "one of them" suggests that she was still in the process of working out ways of talking rather than having already evolved a consistent language. Glen began to articulate something about the end, but, being cut short by my own next utterance, never was able to complete what is was that he wanted to make salient.

My own question returned to the question about the attribution of the word "force" to one of the two arrows (line 38). The question referred directly back to Eliza's utterance, by requesting a clarification, "Which one . . . ?" which is in continuation of the student's "one of them . . ." that had left the exact referent open. The question also expressed confusion, for I had earlier asked them, "Which one . . . shows you velocity?" (line 05); the students' responses had been "the big arrow" (lines 06–08). Now I was asking them again, as if they had not already told me what one of them was. Surprisingly, perhaps, Glen and Ryan then responded with the same words that they had used responding to the earlier question, "The big arrow" (lines 39–40).

38	Teacher:	=*Which one would be the force then?
39	Glen:	The big arrow.
40	Ryan:	The big arrow.
41	Eliza:	Yeah, the little arrow–
42		(1.3)
43		wouldn't it?
44	Glen:	The big arrow.
45	Teacher:	I think=
46	Ryan:	=The force would be the little arrow.

The fact that Ryan said the same thing is an indication that they were attuned to the situation in the same way *and* produced the agreement in the social setting. Eliza, in the next turn, appeared to further add to the production of agreement, beginning her utterance with "Yeah" (line 41). But she continued, saying exactly the opposite, "the little arrow" (line 41). There was no inflection in her voice or any other indication that the listeners could have taken as a resource to hear her utterance as an opposition to the two previous statements. A conversationally long pause followed (line 42), and then Eliza took another turn asking, "Wouldn't it?" (line 43). This question articulated the difference as a difference, because it asked the peers whether it would not be the referential relation made in her statement that responded to my question rather than that made by Glen and Ryan. By initially articulating agreement before stating the association between the word "force" that I had used and the entity that she designated by "the little arrow," Eliza softened the fact that she contradicted the two male students.

Glen answered Eliza's question by repeating the statement he had made earlier, "The big arrow" (line 44). He used the predicate "big," which was in direct opposition to the predicate "little" that Eliza had used. Using different predicates to go with the same word "arrow," they appeared to articulate different perceptual entities. That is, the predicate suggested that they attempted to make different material arrows salient. I began an utterance but was cut off as Ryan made another association between the word "force," on the one hand, and the "little arrow" as an articulation of the perceptually available world, on the other (line 46). In this, he had shifted and now stated and produced an agreement with Eliza, without, however, elaborating why he had apparently changed the object to be associated with the word "force."

My next question showed that the situation was becoming confusing. While taking the mouse and clicking on «force», which highlighted the arrow, I asked, "Which one is this one?" (line 47). This change should have made salient which entity we were currently talking *about*. But Ryan simply stated agreement, "Yeah" (line 48). This was not what the question had asked for. In his previous turn, which immediately preceded my question, he had already associated a physical entity (little arrow) and a word (force). I now had highlighted «force», so his agreement signaled that the sought-for association between "force" and «force» had been made. Eliza elaborated the account by stating an association between "little arrow" and the arrow that I was currently highlighting, and Ryan followed with an utterance that stated agreement twice ("Yeah, that's the one"). It seemed then that the issue was resolved, for all three students used the terms "gravity" or "force" for talking about the motion—if any speaker had a sense that common ground did not exist, he or she normally would articulate this as part of the ongoing interaction. Here, this resolution was achieved in the assertion that a common term was used to denote force, where it mattered little whether the common way of talking was "the little arrow" or "the big arrow."

47   Teacher: * Which one is this one? ((Clicks, highlights, and points to
                «force» with cursor.))
48   Ryan: Yeah.
49   Eliza: Yeah, it's the little arrow.
50   Ryan: Yeah, that's the one.

Making one entity in the setting salient by changing its aspect, that is, the way it presented itself, while asking for the corresponding word, I implemented one part of an ostensive definition; students were to provide the second part. The highlighting occurred not only through the use of a pointing gesture, but also by means of the additional visual effect that clicking an object creates in Interactive Physics. The key factor in ostensive definition is *perceptual salience* (Quine 1995). Perceptual salience is implemented and enhanced by deictic (pointing) gestures in the direction of the intended part of the setting and by iconic gestures that draw on (previously inculcated and culturally characteristic) perceptual similarity between some part of the body and the intended portion of the scene. That is, my question was part of a pedagogical move that not only mediated between students and the world and between students and language, but also provided resources for aligning the two forms of articulation (perception and word).

In its entirety, this episode had mediated both the articulation of an aspect of the world and language. The students had made an association between the initial «velocity» and upward motion in the early part of the simulation, and they had made the association between «force» and "force." This conversation constituted an instructional situation in which the microworld and my questions provided constraints that became resources for changes from students' earlier folkways to more standard ways of talking. The constraints of the microworld are constituted by standard rules consistent with scientific ways of articulating the events (e.g., mathematical equations such as $\underline{v}[t] = \underline{v}[0] + [\underline{F}/m] \cdot t$, where the underlining marks the vector nature of the variables), but that are implicit and therefore not directly available to students. Their task was, in part, to evolve scientific ways of talking that implemented these rules. Thus, scientific descriptions of the microworld and real world are isomorphic, that is, a consistent mapping from one onto the other can be established. However, my research in classes around the world confirmed that such a mapping is not obvious for newcomers to physics.

Teacher-articulated constraints were evidenced by the particular experiment that I provided as focal point for the conversation and by the four questions I posed. The first question encouraged students to hypothesize and talk about the specific experiment in the microworld (line 13). Then I asked for a mapping of the microworld event onto the real world (line 23). Finally, I asked students twice to identify which object they described with "force" and "big arrow." Each of these questions constituted a new resource, which was both an opportunity and a constraint for new forms of (verbal) action. In the context of these resources, students' language changed so that they associated «force» with "force," the standard association to be inculcated by the curriculum. The episode made evident that this association was not in the microworld, there to be "grasped" by the students. Rather, the association emerged from the conversation, mediated by the microworld's range of possible events and teacher questions.

In the science classroom (just as in any other social situation), students and teachers may use the same ways of talking. But unless they are attending to and are perceptually attuned to the same entities in the same way, there is a vast amount of room for misunderstanding that may never be detected; or teachers and students may be attuned to the same global things, but attend to them in different ways—such as when interlocutors are talking about a graph, but they are attuned to its height and slope, respectively. Thus, a crucial aspect in teaching physics is that students and teacher focus on, and are attuned to, the same thing in the same way. In the present context, there were four processes of articulating objects and events. These consisted of (a) repeated motion in real time and slow motion or stepwise change, (b) the direct comparison between two parallel events that differed in one aspect (initial position, force and/or acceleration, initial velocity), (c) the study of critical cases (such as when the direction of motion changed), and (d) the mapping of microworld events onto the real world. The transfer of descriptive and explanatory language from one to the other situation mediated the articulation. This transfer itself occurred in language that was therefore not about the world but had as its major function the evolution and constitution of this language.

Each of the four processes provided opportunities for increasing the probability that students and I were attuned to the same aspect of the microworld. The first two processes were based on a juxtaposition of perceptual aspects, the first being juxtaposition in time (the same object at two instances), the second in space (two objects moving in parallel). In both cases, the teaching situation highlighted the crucial aspect to be talked about. Such juxtaposition assists in the attunement to the same feature, a figure against a diffuse ground, based on a variant–invariant dialectic. The juxtaposition itself was highlighted when combined with the third process, the consideration of special cases. For example, the change of «velocity» was particularly dramatic when its direction was reversed ("and it sort of goes that way and it comes back to you"), as in the simulation that I had constructed and run. In this setup, the arrowhead of «velocity» changes by 180 degrees at the pinnacle of the object movement. In the simulations that the students had set up, the direction of the arrow changed continuously, so that its change and the direction of «force» was not as salient.

The fourth situation was considerably different because it involved a process of mapping the microworld onto natural events. Sometimes, such as in the present episode, I asked students whether they could think of situations in their experience that resembled (perceptually) the events in the microworld. Here, students suggested the hula hoop, yo-yo, and an object in the air as situations where the direction of object motion is reversed in the course of an event. Often, however, students suggested such analogies on their own. For example, while observing a situation with decreasing speed, a student in another group commented, "'Cause the velocity, like your initial velocity and then it's just like you fire a bullet out of a gun and that's the initial velocity and then if there is a big wind, it pushes it back." His partner suggested, "That's just like our sails," relating a microworld situation to an experiment they had just completed in which a sail caused a cart to slow down. In chapter 3, the Foucault pendulum constituted a similar situation, as students related a situation to be explained to another situation that they had experienced previously. Thus, when students succeeded in structuring microworld and real-world events in a similar way so that their descriptive language carried across, they arrived at new ways to explain the microworld events. Here, mediated by my presence and my contributions, the analogies were such that they afforded the evolution of language to standard rather than nonstandard ways of talking. Eliza, Glen, and Ryan used «force» as "gravity" after Ryan and Glen realized that "what goes up must come down," and another student oriented to «force» by uttering "force" when he and his groupmates realized that what they saw was comparable to friction slowing down a bullet.

COMING TO TERMS

The first episode showed how I elicited student talk, which gave me indications of how the students were oriented to the microworld and their ways of articulating and talking about it. This prepared the ground for a teaching intervention. The second episode described this intervention, which mediated student articulation of the world (perceptually, verbally) and the way in which they came to talk *about* «force». The students used new ways of articulating and talking about the

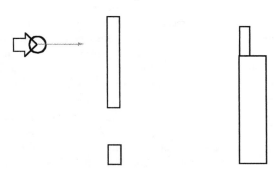

Figure 5.2. The object of this task was to set up force and velocity so that the ball would go through the hole in the wall and then knock the small rectangle off the pedestal.

world. Did they employ these new ways of talking consistently? Much of the three students' conversation between the foregoing and the next episode was spent on stabilizing (without my presence) their new conversational forms. This episode shows that the students had converged on common ways of talking within the group and that this talk was consistent with standard forms of talking.

The students worked on a particular task that asked them to knock a rectangular object off its stand by getting the circular object through a hole in a wall not in line between the circle and rectangle (figure 5.2). The configuration was such that the circular object had to move along a trajectory curving upward, rather than downward as a thrown object would in the world surrounding us. That is, the setup did not allow an easy association of the task with the everyday experience of throwing a ball—although, if perceived as a scene viewed from the top, one can make associations, for example, with curveballs in baseball or free kicks around a wall of opponents in soccer. Such associations, however, may interfere in the present situation, because the phenomena are based on the effects of spin on objects in flight. Nevertheless, Eliza proposed an analogy to the everyday world, or rather, a disanalogy—trying the simulation "on anti-gravity" (line 51). (Between lines the students look at the screen display.)

51   Eliza: I think we could try it on antigravity. (2.2) ((Laughs.))
52   Ryan: Hey, hey, hey (1.9) we're, like I went the wrong way.
53   Eliza: No, 'cause you've got gravity ⌈the w r o n g w a y–⌉
54   Glen: ⌊You gotta push the=⌋
55   Ryan: =I didn't finish, whatever.
56   Glen: You gotta push the=
57   Eliza: ='Cause you want gravity going * ⌈that way– ⌉((Us-
              ing pencil tip, points to
              «force», then moves tip upward.))
58   Ryan: ⌊You want⌋this

		line down. ((Places cursor on «velocity».))
59	Eliza:	Don't you want to click gravity?
60	Ryan:	Which way do you want to go this ⌐arrow?⌐
		((Places cursor on «force».))
61	Eliza:	⌐That's⌐ like antigravity, now
		you've gotta click the big arrow=
62	Glen:	=No, but see, ⌐push it, you wan' it go like this way–⌐ ((Gesture as in
		figure 5.3.))
63	Ryan:	⌐You want it so gravity kicks in to get it⌐ through that
		way. ((Gesture as in figure 5.3.)) (2.3)
64	Glen:	Pull the velocity! (0.9) Pull the long skinny one.

Ryan had run the simulation, resulting in the repeated bouncing of the circular object along the wall. Eliza jokingly suggested trying "antigravity." Ryan was still concerned with the failed attempt to move the circle through the opening and toward the target, articulating what he had perceived as going the wrong way. In the next statement, Eliza used the word "gravity" again to articulate an entity (presumably «force») and a part of an explanation (as indicated by the connective "[be]cause") for what Ryan had articulated as going the wrong way. Her statement not only was a response to Ryan, but also constituted an elaboration and rationale for her earlier remark. Twice Glen began to utter an instruction the meaning of which was unclear (lines 54, 56), but Ryan said that he had not finished moving "whatever" while working with the cursor on the direction of «velocity» (line 55). In her two turns, Eliza instructed Ryan to manipulate "gravity," the first time using her pencil tip to establish an ostensive definition that linked the word to a specific arrow indicated (lines 57, 59). At first, Ryan still manipulated «velocity» (line 58), but then asked Eliza for the direction she wished "this arrow" to take while using his cursor to highlight «force» in the

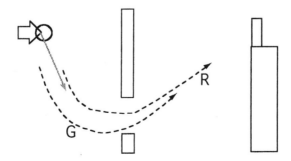

Figure 5.3. Glen (G) and Ryan (R) moved their index fingers along the monitor, gesturing trajectories that they wanted the ball to take. The situation therefore becomes an occasion for intersubjective, public thinking.

way I had done during the earlier episode (line 60). Eliza indicated that she intended «force» to act like "antigravity" and instructed him to "click" «force», which she pointed to again using the tip of her pencil (line 61). Ryan followed this instruction, but Glen was not satisfied. He suggested that they wanted the circular object to move along a specific trajectory, which he outlined moving his finger along the screen (line 62, figure 5.3). This, he suggested, could only be achieved by pulling "velocity," the "long skinny one" (line 64). But Ryan explained that his positioning of «force» would provide the necessary "gravity" to get the trajectory through the opening (line 63, figure 5.3).

This episode is evidence that the students' ways of talking were beginning to be compatible with the standard ways of talking Newtonian physics in this microworld setting, that is, they had come to use the standard terms to denote «velocity» (line 64) and «force» (lines 51, 53, 57, 61, 63) that are acceptable from a physicist's perspective. Eliza articulated and explained the situation on the display as a world governed by "antigravity," that is, a world in which objects moved toward the top of the screen under the influence of a force opposite to gravitation in the lived-in world. She consistently used the label "gravity" to describe «force», and in two instances used the prefix "anti-" to indicate that the direction of gravity in the microworld was opposite to that in her physical world. Similarly, Ryan and Glen used "gravity" and "velocity" to denote the respective vectors «force» and «velocity». The relative position and length of «force» and «velocity» before their next attempt to achieve the desired trajectory indicated that the students not only articulated the vectors appropriately, but also talked *about* the relative effects of the two on the motion of the circle in their microworld. Later in the transcript they described the shape of the trajectory as a "parabola" caused by a gradual change of «velocity» over time.

Although the students talked about the phenomena in their microworld in standard ways, there was one description that is uncommon in scientific language. Ryan (as did Glen in other parts of our data corpus) described the vertex of the object's motion as the point where "gravity kicks in." There are no indications in the data collected as to whether the students, despite contrary visual evidence, associated the notion of "kicking in" with a sudden change of «velocity»'s vertical direction. If such a notion did in fact persist, it could have indicated that students attended to the sudden reversal of direction rather than to the continuous change of «velocity».

The conversation in this episode shows that the students had developed a common language to articulate and talk about the microworld. They collaboratively decided about the relative position and magnitudes of «velocity» and «force» and had developed common ways of talking about these vectors as "skinny arrow" or "velocity" and "big arrow" or "[anti-] gravity." In addition, their language was compatible with that stated in the provincial curriculum of their course. Thus, the students had "come to terms" in two ways: they had overcome the differences between their individual descriptions of the microworld, and their common language had converged with standard ways of talking. At the end of their investigations in the microworlds, all students talked about the displayed phenomena in Newtonian terms. For example, faced with the task of designing an investigation that would help eighth-grade students to learn about motion, Ryan suggested:

> We'll design the experiment with the Newton's law . . . the opposing forces, one has two equal forces, there's no velocity, and this one is unequal opposite forces . . . they will accelerate in the direction of the greater force.

Following this excerpt, Glen provided a scientific observational and theoretical description of two situations. If there are two equal (in magnitude) but opposing forces, there is no change in velocity. However, if there are unequal and opposite forces, there will be an acceleration in the direction of the greater (in magnitude) force. At this point, students no longer needed the perceptual and gestural modes of expression to evolve their observational and theoretical descriptions. The verbal modality had entirely taken over the task of sign (sign complex, text) about some event in the (Newtonian micro-) world—the relationship between opposing forces acting on an object, on the one hand, and the velocity and acceleration of this object, on the other. Of course, we should not be surprised of this, for the pressure to succeed is equally a pressure to evolve ways of talking about salient events in particular ways, at least as long students find themselves in the particular setting.

In these terms, the setting—which included student interactions with peers, microworld, and teacher—provided opportunities and constraints that encouraged and supported changes in students' discourse to the desired standard forms. Students used the notions of force (gravity), velocity, and acceleration to describe and analyze the objects and events that they observed on the display. However, although students developed proficiency in talking about the microworld in standard ways, their talk continued to be highly indexical. I also observed that they, although referring to «velocity» as "velocity" (or even "speed"), continued to use indexical terms such as "it," "the skinny arrow," and "doohickey."

TEACHING AS MEDIATING ACTIVITY

Engaging students in science talk over the animated inscriptions of a Newtonian microworld allowed me to monitor students' actions and talk and to look for evidence of their adequacy in terms of the specified curriculum outcomes. If necessary, I could engage students in face-to-face interaction to make objects and events in this microworld salient and to model actions toward the microworld. Such interactions therefore mediated the collaborative construction of useful ways of seeing and talking; they also mediated my building of passing theories and on-the-spot interventions through practical analyses of the communication's success at each turn. As the conversations evolved, I provided minimal descriptions that could be elaborated when needed. The engagement of students in talk began in a period of exploration during which students could develop some shared way of talking about the microworld that arose from their own prior ways of talking. In the course of the interactions (with each other, the microworld, and myself), new forms of talking emerged that eventually converged on the standard ways outlined in the curriculum. I began by participating in students' ways of talking, and then introduced new language elements. Students could then incorporate such new elements in their own ways of talking, that is, use them for their own intentions, as Mikhail Bakhtin (1981) once had articulated it. These ways of talking constitute an articulation of intelligibility, themselves grounded in attunement and existential understanding.

Once we accept that students are intent on succeeding at a particular task, we can take it for granted that they are attuned to the environment in ways that are related to their previous experiences. Their attunement and their existential understanding about how the world works are inseparable. Their way of articulating the world is equally foundational, for it is associated with their attunement and understanding. The language they use as part of their initial exploration is an articulation of the intelligibility of the world. But if they structure the world in ways that are inconsistent with the science that they are supposed to learn, that is, if they perceive objects and events incompatible with standard physics, they will attempt to integrate perception and language—with disastrous results. Physics will not make sense and the students will likely discontinue their studies. If teachers want to have any hope that students will use standard physics words within standard ways of talking, they have to begin by mediating students' access to the world (figure 5.4). Teachers have to ascertain that students articulate (structure) the relevant aspect of the world in ways that their perceptions can serve as a suitable constraint to the evolution of their ways of talking. A specific way of talking, scientific language, is the target of the evolution that teachers are asked to mediate, and, at the same time, this evolution itself has to occur in language as the territory for the evolution to occur. Language is also the tool that mediates interactions to proceed, because it allows coparticipants to bring one another in tune with the entities that are currently salient to them.

Challenging Received Ways of Doing Science Education

All of these issues provide challenges to the received ways of doing science education, which has never dealt with the variegated ways students use language in real classrooms but has been instead overly concerned with their mental structures. These issues also provide challenges to the classroom teacher, who has to approach interactions with students by assuming that they are not similarly attuned to the objects and events and that their language articulates different worlds and a different intelligibility. Without knowing what students are attuned to and how they speak, a teacher stands little chance of mediating either students' access to the world or the standard language of science. I understand teachers' initial task therefore to be one of getting a sense for the world in which students find themselves. Subsequently, they can begin devising ways of mediating access to the world and standard language. However, teachers must be aware that even if students use standard vocabulary, the way they use it to make assertions, observation sentences, observation categoricals, and theoretical statements may differ substantially from the historically evolved scientific language. How teachers may do this in real time and when there is no time to reflect, even if they are very experienced, is not self-evident. It requires constant attention that resembles attunement to the situation rather than reflective distancing. Even more important to teacher educators is the question of how one can assist new teachers in becoming attuned to students and building the kind of passing theories necessary for designing instruction that mediates the evolution of student talk. Equally important is to allow new teachers to develop competencies in becoming attuned and building passing theories in *real time*, not on the drawing board and not in fake exercises in the university classroom.

Teaching is a form of mediation between student and world, on the one hand, and student and language, on the other (see figure 5.4). Language is also part of the world, and it is a tool used in the mediation of world and language. But there are other mediational resources available to the teacher. The communicative elements (words, sentences, gestures, body positions, and voice inflec-

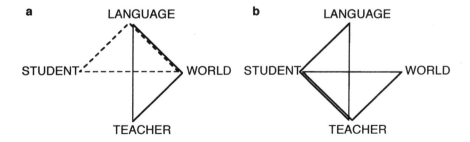

Figure 5.4. Learning to use new ways of talking is the outcome of two mediational processes. **a.** As a teacher, I already mediate my access to the world via language and, vice versa, I have experiences in the world that mediate my access to the language. Students have neither form of mediated access. **b.** In teaching, the teacher mediates both between student and text and between student and world, and thereby sets a context for the students' mediated access to world and text.

tions) provide structural resources that stand in certain relationships to those things that are the true subjects of a lesson. For example, if the point of the lesson is for students to perceive something, teachers can use their body orientations and gestures as resources that students can use in their efforts to make specific things salient in the focal situation (Roth and Lawless 2002b). Thus, teachers already mediate their access to an aspect of the world (e.g., moving balls, pulleys, and chaotic pendulums) via language; or, conversely, they have worldly experiences that they can bring to encounters with language (e.g., about vectors, chaotic systems, or simple machines). Students, on the other hand, may be unfamiliar with both linguistic resources for mediating their access to the world and worldly experiences to access the text (figure 5.4.a, broken line). Before I began my pruning adventure (described in the introduction), I had only my garden world. I did not know how to prune and, before purchasing the pruning book, had neither language nor any other entity to mediate my access to this world. In a sense, there was just the Michael–garden world opposition. After buying the book, I had language, drawings, and photographs as mediating resources, but these resources alone did not allow me to access the world of pruning. The book's language about pruning and the bushes and trees in my garden were somehow unconnected entities in my world.

While I was participating in the pruning workshop, language and trees came together in the actions of pruning expert. In his actions, he mediated my access to the text and to the world at the same time. He mediated other participants' and my access to the language by engaging with us in pruning talk, patiently rearticulating a phrase when the way of talking was inappropriate (from his, the expert's, perspective), and talking while making or not making particular cuts. In each cut that he made or did not make, he mediated our access to the world; he also mediated our access by pointing to other trees, for example, to show what an entire tree should look like after having been appropriately pruned, or to point out a tree where some years ago he had made some inappropriate cuts, the inappropriateness of which became clear to him only years after the fact. In the process, we walked from tree to tree and from row to row, each tree different than the previous one, even if it was the same kind of tree. Across these different situations, invariant perceptual structures slowly emerged for me, which I associated with invariant linguistic structures that he produced and I heard. My own access to the language and world of pruning (figure 5.4a) emerged following the mediational workshop in which the teacher provided me with resources to access the world and to the language. This episode therefore shows that even a motivated and educated person such as myself may encounter difficulties learning to do and talk pruning on his own. The language of the book, despite its apparent familiarity and despite the excellent drawings and photographs did not allow me to enter the pruning world. It does not surprise me therefore that students have difficulties appropriating new ways of talking by listening to teachers or looking at textbooks without the experience of articulating relevant entities and talking science.

Mediating Students' Languages and Experiences

In school science classrooms, students often gain worldly experiences by engaging in hands-on investigations that teachers set up and take students through; and students gain language experiences when teachers provide opportunities for talking through issues and talk about the events that they created and are supposed to explain (figure 5.4b). When the language is about the aspects of the world that students have had opportunities to engage with, the two mediational practices overlap so as to provide the activity structure for students to build their own mediated access to world and language. To strengthen the relationship between language and associated world, students not only listen to teachers but also engage first in talking and later in writing about experienced aspects of this world. I am suggesting talking first, because in situated verbal discourse, as this book shows, students still have all the means of ostensive reference by means of words, gesture, and presence of the talked-about entities themselves. Once they have developed more elaborate discourse, that is, discourse that relies less on visual and gestural means of representation, they have sufficient verbal resources to begin writing about the events. Being familiar in the double mediation of text and world, students have developed literary practices.

This example also shows us that language is not only the learning outcome but also the terrain where the learning occurs and a tool that makes learning possible. That is, language is a central aspect of the world to which students are oriented and attuned and in which they experience themselves. I made the split between language and world (figure 5.4) only with respect to the endpoint of the teaching and learning process: students use a specific language that is *about* a specific aspect of the world, useful in specific (scientific) situations. But this specific world is part of the world in general, and the language a microworld of language in general.

A central aspect of teaching for the changing of language *about* scientific entities was the aspect of language as a territory that permitted and assisted in orienting to and articulating the sociomaterial world in which students and teachers were embedded. Language itself was the territory that allowed language to be about something else than itself and the present situation. Although all interlocutors build passing theories about what others are attuned to, the teacher, concerned with the learning and development of his students, has to be concerned with building a passing theory about their world and language. This is a passing theory especially because the teacher never gets to spend a lot of time with the same student group but must move about the classroom. Having analyzed many videotaped teacher–student interactions, where I had a record of student conversation before and after the interaction, I know that teachers (including myself) often do not find out just what students are oriented to and where they are in the evolution of science talk. Their passing theories are not viable—I was embarrassed when I discovered this in my own teaching, realizing that had I spent more time with a group, I could have found out that my passing theory was inappropriate.

Building Passing Theories

One of the mediating circumstances for building a passing theory is the brevity of the possible teacher–student interaction when teachers have to attend to twenty-five or thirty students in one classroom. To find out what any group of four or five students is attuned to and what the extent of their current way of talking is, teachers have to listen for a while, tuning into the conversation. But with six or eight groups of students in the same classroom and sixty minutes, there are less than ten minutes available for engaging with students, even if a teacher did not have to have any other, organizational concerns.

Teacher educators may ask themselves whether it is possible to teach arriving at passing theories to future teachers and students alike. Here, the answer pragmatic philosophers provide is quite pessimistic (e.g., Davidson 1986). There are no rules for how to arrive at passing theories, just as there are no rules for arriving at new scientific theories, which emerge from activity and include a certain amount of wit, luck, and wisdom. Certainly, in the course of life each person develops private vocabulary and grammar, rules of thumb for figuring out how people use language in ways that differ from dictionary definitions. But,

> there is no more change of regularizing, or teaching this process than there is of regularizing or teaching the process of creating new theories to cope with new data in any field—for this is what the process involves. (Davidson 1986, 446)

Davidson concludes that there is no such thing as language, at least not in the way philosophers and linguists have been thinking about it. There is no difference between knowing a language and knowing one's way around the world there is no way in which we can learn a language or master it. There is no underlying structure that language users acquire and then apply to particular utterances in the process of communicating with others. Teaching therefore does not and cannot be a matter of linking words and things by means of ostensive definition. It is therefore an illusion to think that we could teach or even impart meaning without directly telling the student, who is brought to the point of giving himself the correct ostensive definition as by finding out how such words as "force" and "velocity" refer to the entities in the microworld.

We are so much accustomed to communication through language, in conversation, that it looks to us as if the whole point of communication lay in this: someone else grasps the sense of my words—which is something mental: he as it were takes it into his own mind. (Wittgenstein 1974, §363)

Pragmatic philosophers encourage us to be more relaxed about deconstructing the boundaries that separate language and world, without ever managing to bridge the abyss that separates them. In the final account, utterances are sound patterns, noise, and thus part of the material world; at this level, there is no difference between world and language. In this sense, therefore, language is an overprivileged part of the world. But, undoubtedly, language provides humans with enormous power, which it draws from its reflexive nature. Language is not only part of the material world but also a part of the material world that is about the world. We figure out how to perceive and make these sound patterns and noises in the same way that we learn to stand upright and walk—before having any notion of gravity or language to describe it. We grow in our competencies to have appropriate passing theories as we grow in our ability to use a tool like pruning shears or a software program such as MathCAD or Interactive Physics.

6

Adopting New Ways of Talking: A Question of Origin and Control?

Students come to school not as (linguistic) blank slates but deeply familiar with particular ways of experiencing the world, including familiar ways of talking in and about a variety of situations. These ways of experiencing and talking generally differ among students based on social class, gender, and race. In schools students come face to face with new types of situations and with languages that are, in mathematics and science, generally consistent with white, middle-class, Eurocentric ways of experiencing and talking (Gee 1996). Students' levels of success in schools are, to a great degree, mediated by their willingness and ability to cope with the various academic languages that they encounter including, when they are not from the middle class, the ones spoken in science. However, willingness and ability to cope are not sufficient; students need to be prepared to accept certain losses and see in the newly gained languages a certain gain. These losses are smaller whenever the difference between an academic's and a student's root language is small or, in other words, when the family resemblance between the two languages and the situations in which they are used is high. There are therefore frequent recommendations to design curricula in such a way that students can begin the learning process by drawing on their familiar experiences and language so that they can more easily cross the borders into academic experiences and languages (e.g., Giroux 1992).

The design activities that constitute the background for the present chapter were planned to provide just such a transition. A question one may be inclined to ask is whether the students in a science classroom would more readily appropriate new ways of talking when these emerge from one of their own than when a teacher introduces a new way of talking. In chapter 4, we can find a hint of a partial answer: the way of talking about situations in terms of "labile," "stable," and "indifferent" that evolved in one group was not readily adopted by all students. Some students grounded the language in the experience of objects in stable and unstable positions, whereas others, despite a lot of effort on the part of their peers to help them, did not adopt this way of talking. In the same chapter, we also found a teacher who successfully "pushed" the use of a particular term, "Mercedes star," in that students used it in varied situations to talk about chaotic systems.

The adoption of a new language and the associated design practices may be very slow compared to the evolution of other practices. Thus, in a fourth- and fifth-grade classroom, where the students learned about stability and material strength by engaging in architectural design, it took more than six weeks until a majority of students explained the stability of artifacts as arising from the use of triangular braces or used triangular braces to stabilize their own designs (Roth 1998). It is true that students were uttering the word "triangle" rather quickly. When cued ("What does it take to make things stable?" or "What is the magic word?"), students mouthed the word within the first two lessons of the introduction of the term to a whole-class discussion. However, being able to verbalize "triangle" on cue did not immediately lead to the use of triangles as a resource in practical design or in students' design language. The difference between saying "triangle" and explaining the use of braces for stabilizing structures clearly expressed the difference between a word as a piece of information (resource) and as part of a linguistic practice. The adoption of language was closely related to the enormous effort spent by the two teachers in teaching the concept. Conversely, when the effort was less considerable, the classroom community as a whole did not adopt new words into their ways of talking design, as I had observed with "catastrophic failure," which described the engineering technique of bringing structures to their breaking point to study weaknesses in their structural designs. Despite continued teacher insistence, the notion never become part of the public or private ways of talking design. One might think that the teachers' failure to inculcate the use of the word had to do with the distance of this language from students' familiar ways of talking and with the lack of experiences in which they could have grounded it.

At the time, I hypothesized that the differences between the wide adoption of sociomaterial resources and practices, on the one hand, and the linguistic practices, on the other, may reflect differences in the level of control students might feel they have in situations where they originated, as opposed to being pushed into using, new ways of talking. Outside of schools, people change their ways of talking continuously and purposefully as they participate in everyday activity, structure their interactions with the sociomaterial world, and change their interactions according to local contingencies. That is, people are in control of their activities and therefore over their learning in practice. I observed such purposeful learning as students participated in design activity where they had a high degree of control over the situation. Katrina, Janine, and Aleks found it useful to talk about the chaotic pendulum in terms of "Foucault's pendulum." Similarly, Chris and Lars found the notions of stable, labile, and indifferent useful for talking about a variety of systems whose behaviors could not be predicted with certainty. Students who had found a new way of talking useful, such as Chris, mediated others' access to this new language and corresponding situations, and therefore became peer tutors; the development of language—that is, learning—lay in their own hands. In contrast, the acquisition of curriculum-determined linguistic practices in the fourth and fifth grade was akin to traditional school learning; similarly, the resistance that the teacher experienced in getting students to use "Mercedes star" as part of their explanations of chaotic phenomena resembled traditional teaching. Because of their status with respect to legitimate knowledge, students in these situations were no longer in control of their learning or of the context in which they evolved. As a consequence, learning (and with it, teaching) was no longer effortless.

This research appeared to suggest that ways of talking introduced by the teacher were less taken up by the collective than ways of talking and doing things introduced by a student. I conjectured that practices introduced by students allow peers a greater degree of ownership than practices introduced by the teacher. In this chapter, I pursue this issue by providing examples from a study explicitly designed to test my earlier conjectures. After introducing the context of a science unit on simple machines, I will use two case studies to follow the transformation of language available in the classroom community. Although students invented a series of observation categoricals (laws or rules) to describe patterns of the behavior of simple machines, the associated linguistic practices were not widely adopted, despite my attempts to foster the process. The names of the different ways of talking that I had introduced ("Laura's law," "Riley's rule," "Aslam's rule," "Shamir's catapult lever") were readily available (as was the label "triangles" in the fourth- and fifth-grade classroom). I had explicitly denoted students' inventions of ways of talking to associate them with particular individuals and to characterize the ideas' origins within the student community rather than with me. These denotations were intended to facilitate the transformation of linguistic practices thought to reside in ownership or come from inventing. These denotations, and the postings describing them, were readily available as resources to community members, unlike the accompanying discursive practices. On the other hand, the notion of mechanical advantage, though I had introduced it during a whole-class conversation, was readily accepted and became a major way of talking in this classroom.

ETHNOGRAPHIC BACKGROUND

The episodes and materials in this chapter were collected in the same classroom where I had the debate with Shamir, the student who argued with or rather against me about how to set up a pulley system so that he rather than I would have an advantage in a tug-of-war (chapter 1). During a four-month study of learning in a student-centered science class, I was teaching a unit on simple machines as part of an arrangement with the teachers of an elementary school to assist them in transforming their science teaching to include hands-on activities. In exchange, I received the permission to have my research team document the science teaching and learning. This unit on simple machines was taught in a split sixth- and seventh-grade class. A considerable number of students experienced problems in academic aspects of schooling. Four of the students were classified as learning disabled (in one case paired with attention deficit hyperactive disorder), and one boy had muscular dystrophy and associated physical and cognitive difficulties.

The simple machines unit lasted from the beginning of October to the end of January. Each week, there were two seventy-minute and one fifty-five-minute lesson leading to a total of thirty-nine classroom hours. The unit included whole-class conversations on the topics of simple pulleys, block and tackle, class I (balanced) levers, class II and III levers inclined planes, work, and energy. Students conducted small-group activities with class I or class II and III levers, or summarized their ideas about specific simple machines on specially designed forms. Over the course of the unit, students designed four hand-powered machines. The first three machines were to lift loads, move loads horizontally, and displace loads by means of a self-propelling mechanism. In the fourth machine, students were asked to combine a minimum of four processes, two of which had to be based on simple machines discussed in the unit. Students presented their machines in whole-class sessions and directed subsequent question-and-answer sessions.

The unit began with a whole-class discussion of machines and their purposes, followed by a specific example of a pulley mounted in different configurations. After that, we followed the same pattern of activities. First, students took about three lessons to design machines and construct working models. I split the subsequent three to four lessons into two parts. During one part, I led whole-class conversations about a physics topic or small groups of students completed investigations or recorded their ideas on previously discussed topics. During the second part of the lesson, students presented their machines in whole-class sessions and then directed sense-making conversations. There were one or two lessons on each of the following: class I levers; class II and III levers;

pulleys; mechanical advantage; springs and elastics; inclined planes; and kinetic energy, potential energy, and work.

Different kinds of activities supported students' participation in talking science and engineering design, each with different amounts of structure provided. These four activity structures differ in terms of the social configuration (whole class, small group) and the origin of the central, activity-organizing artifact (teacher designed, student designed).

First, students spent about 30 percent of the unit designing and constructing, in small self-selected groups, models of machines that met a number of teacher-specified or classroom-negotiated conditions such as "Design a load-moving machine" or "Construct a model of the machine able to carry a 100-gram load over a two-meter distance." The students were invited to the design activity by means of a request for proposal (figure 6.1). I had chosen the design context, because designing artifacts constitutes an important learning environment that allows learning-in-practice as students pursue their own goals. Design tasks are not so much suited for transmitting specific facts as for participating in activities central to design practice (such as designing and testing artifacts, generating hypotheses, making presentations, describing systems, etc.). Because of the broadly unstructured nature of design tasks, students had opportunities to engage in specifying goals, framing troubles and breakdowns in the pursuit of these goals, and resolving problems. Furthermore, open-design classroom communities allow new discourses to evolve and circulate among student members.

To introduce each problem, the students received a one-page letter, which differed in content for each design problem but not in structure (figure 6.1). The letter, purportedly from a local company, invited students to submit proposals for machines that could be operated by hand if the gas-powered machinery failed to operate during its Arctic explorations. The letter described the purpose of the machine and requested designers to (a) submit construction plans, working models, and written descriptions and (b) demonstrate their model to the class, including a test that the machine decreased the effort when compared to moving the load directly. Students began to work on their design drawings using a design pad which, to scaffold planning, also included a field for listing tools and required materials; at the end of the first lesson, some students presented their ideas, which provided an opportunity to discuss principles underlying the designs. Subsequently, students moved through cycles of prototyping, building, and revising drawings. During these activities, I moved around the classroom asking students in individual groups details about their design, how they used the concepts presented in whole-class sessions that I chaired, and about problems they had encountered. I assisted students in using tools appropriately, including handsaws, power saws, electrical drills, and X-Acto knives; and, when I felt students needed to engage in explanatory talk, I recommended that they go to the poster board and study the copies of transparencies used in earlier lessons.

Northern Explorations Limited
1999 Downtown, Vancouver, British Columbia

October 7, 1994

Re: Machine for moving heavy loads

Dear Engineer:

Thank you very much for your interest in designing some new machinery for our company. As you know, we are exploring new opportunities for expanding our operations into the far north. There, we sometimes experience a failure of our gasoline-powered machines so that we have to resort to machines entirely powered by hand.

In this request for proposals, we encourage you to submit your design for a hand-powered machine that can move heavy loads from our storage areas to our exploration towers. As part of your submission we require the following:

1. A working model to illustrate your design. To illustrate its capabilities, your model should be able to move a 100-gram weight over a distance of 200 centimeters.
2. A proof that your machine actually makes it easier to move heavy loads. We are interested in making it as easy as possible for our people to continue their work; your engine design should thus decrease the force it takes to lift a load. That is, you want a <u>mechanical advantage</u>.
3. A construction plan allowing our personnel in the north to build a machine according to your design.
4. A written description that explains your machine when it is on display and a presentation of the design principles that affected your design.

We look forward to receiving your designs.

Sincerely,

Figure 6.1. Students were invited to respond to a request for proposal by designing a machine according to the specifications provided. After handing out the third of these, one student said, "You are making it all up. This company doesn't exist."

Second, students presented the machines they designed in whole-class sessions, with opportunities for other students to ask questions or make comments (about 30 percent of the unit). The presenting students directed these conversations (figure 6.2). I intervened only when conversations seemed to come to a halt, old animosities resurfaced, or other communicative problems surfaced. The inclusion of this activity structure was based on my previous research findings that students who are required to elaborate, explain, or defend their own ideas

Figure 6.2. Students presented their designs to a critical audience. In this situation, they also presented their fourth design in the library, where several classes of students were invited to comment on and critically respond to the designs.

tend to evaluate, integrate, and elaborate knowledge in new ways. I assumed that students were more likely to engage in these processes when questions and critiques came from peers than from teachers because students were more likely to develop common ways of talking, including the way in which standard science words are deployed. This way of structuring the activity also allowed students to take greater control over their participation in the conversations.

Third, to provide students with resources in their design activities, about 25 percent of the unit was taken up by whole-class conversations around simple machines and associated overhead transparencies that I had designed (including pulleys, block and tackle, class I [balanced] levers, class II and III levers, inclined plane, work, energy, and mechanical advantage). Some of these discussions followed students' own exploratory activities with a device (class I levers, class II and III levers), while others, because of time constraints, were treated in whole-class sessions only (pulley; block and tackle; inclined plane, including work and energy). In the course of these activities, I introduced new concept words from standard physics and graphical representations at opportune mo-

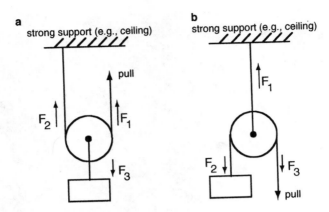

Figure 6.3. Throughout the unit, I used transparencies to display typical representations of the simple machines that were actually present at the same time. These transparencies were used to support whole-class discussions, for example, where they served as recording devices for student conjectures.

ments to facilitate communication about the simple machines at hand. For example, I moderated a class discussion (also analyzed below) about two different pulley configurations (figure 6.3). In one, the effort remained the same (figure 6.3b); in the other, the effort was cut in half (figure 6.3a). The purpose of the lesson was for students to develop accepted, standard ways of describing and explaining pulley systems: this includes the forces acting in the system and how they are denoted by means of arrows, labels for the different parts of the system, and ways of measuring these forces. For each pulley, I asked students to predict the forces, one force at a time, operating at various points in the system. After a number of students (about eight to ten) had made their predictions, and after tallying the commitments of other students, I involved students seated closely to the pulley in measuring the forces ("measuring" is a material practice). The magnitude of each force, along with student predictions, was recorded on an overhead transparency displaying key features of the system. I subsequently asked students to explain the outcome. The annotated transparencies of these lessons were copied and posted on a bulletin board set aside for science activities.

Fourth, I designed small-group investigations and discussions organized around simple machines, written instructions, and summary sheets to highlight important physics concepts (about 15 percent of the unit). These activities were to provide students with opportunities to manipulate and explore simple machines, develop familiarity, and come up with tentative explanations of the machines' functioning. For example, using class I levers, which we constructed from materials bought in a hardware store, a worksheet including a variety of

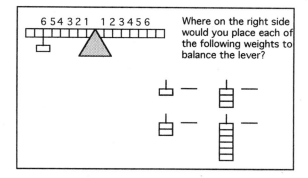

Figure 6.4. I designed activities that allowed students to work with simple machines in a more controlled manner. To answer the questions on this and similar worksheets, students used the respective simple machines. Subsequent to completing these activities, their answers would be discussed in whole-class sessions. Laura's and Riley's laws developed out of these activities and were publicly articulated during the whole-class sessions.

problems (e.g., figure 6.4), and a summary handout to scaffold students in producing observation categoricals from stems such as "The pattern we observed is . . ." and "Our reason is . . . ," I provided students with opportunities for first hands-on and conversational experiences. Because each self-selected group was asked to produce one agreed-upon answer, students had to work out differences in the ways they wanted to articulate observation sentences and observation categoricals. That is, students had opportunities to participate in more private conversations before going public and presenting ideas to the whole class. In these small-group conversations, they could develop and experiment with new ways of talking about and explaining the mechanical systems under study. After students completed their activities, the same artifacts (sketches and physical models) served as focal points in teacher-directed whole-class conversations.

LANGUAGE INVENTED BY STUDENTS: LAURA'S LAW

There were repeated situations in which students formulated a mathematical "law" or "rule" that could be used to answer questions related to the functioning of simple machines. For example, Laura proposed a product moment rule (LOAD times LENGTH on the left arm IS EQUAL to LOAD times EFFORT on the right arm); Riley had arrived at a ratio rule (LOAD on left arm DIVIDED by LOAD on right arm IS EQUAL to DISTANCE on right arm DIVIDED by DISTANCE on left arm) to equilibrate an equal arm balance; Aslam suggested a ratio rule for determining the relationship between effort and length of an incline; and Shamir suggested that a third-class lever (an example would be the baseball bat, where one hand serves to supply the effort and the other as the fulcrum) functioned like a "catapult." Hypothesizing that ways of talking originated by and associated with students would be more likely to be adopted by other students, I explicitly labeled these rules with the originating students' names. They were published on the bulletin board as summaries of the whole-class discussion—essentially the teacher-produced transparencies that had served as foci of whole-class conversations complete with student contributions, tagged with contributors' names. Being publicly available, these transparencies were therefore resources for anyone wishing to use them, even if they had forgotten the details of how they were expressed. These laws were highlighted and celebrated as the accomplishments of the class as a whole, and I did not attempt to teach more than what students in the guided whole-class discussion formulated. I wanted more than just a diverse set of answers; I was interested in the evolution of a language about simple machines by the students in this classroom more generally.

Initial Practice

We began our investigation of levers with a student-centered activity. In groups of two or three, students were asked to do twelve problems in which pairs of weights had to be balanced—the distance of one of the weights to the fulcrum was given (e.g., figure 6.4). After completing the problems, students were asked to write down any patterns they had observed. I then brought the students together for a whole-class conversation to have students generate a summary—assisted by me. Here, Laura explained her answer to a problem in which a three-unit weight at a three-unit distance had to be balanced by a four-unit weight on the other side of the beam. She said, "I think two point two five because, because three times three is nine, and two point two five times four equals nine." She had, spontaneously, figured out the product-moment rule. Riley, who had earlier used a ratio rule when the weights were in a two-to-one relationship, could no longer describe how his rule should be applied in this situation. Later, in answer to my request for an explanation of what Laura meant, Leanne said:

> I think she said, if there is three weights [sic] on, the numbers on three, and three, and multiply three by three and that's nine, and then for the other side, you try to find the number that you multiply by whatever number it's on, and then that's how you find out.

Because students could talk through the problems using Riley's (ratio) rule only when the relationship was two to one or three to one, I provided repeated opportunities for Laura to explain to others who said they did not understand.

Thus, while Riley's law was recognized as viable within this class, it was not applicable to all situations. My instructional move to emphasize "Laura's (product moment) Law" rather than "Riley's (ratio) Rule" was then based on my own previous (doctoral) research, which had indicated that many (older) students find it easier to develop a language related to the product moment rule rather than the ratio rule (Roth 1991).

During the same lesson, Laura had two more opportunities to explain how she did balance beam problems. At first, she described,

> I find the number that they are both equal like if there's four on three then that's where you can move, four times three is twelve, so you have to find something that two multiplies by to get to twelve.

Here, Laura articulated the procedure in terms of arriving at a number so "that they are both equal," without saying what she denoted by "both." But in the context where her audience is attuned to the same situation, a balance beam with a three-unit weight on a four-unit distance, the articulation of four times three not only describes what you have to do but also the counts of two salient features. The other given is a two-unit weight, for which she said, "You have to find something that two multiplies by to get twelve." In her next attempt, she also used the word "divide" and thereby provided the description of a modified procedure by means of which to arrive at the six-unit distance.

> Well, there is another way, is like, well, say three times four is twelve then, well, you need another twelve, and if you divide two by, divide twelve by two which is six, that's another way to get the number.

However, other students found Laura's new way of talking not very accessible. For example, in one episode during the following lesson while I was reviewing with the class, Leanne explicitly questioned Laura's account (line 06). The sequence began after I had shown an equal arm balance with four screws hanging from a wire at two unit-distances from the left arm and asked where I had to hang two screws on the right arm (figure 6.5). Being called upon, Laura's response was a laconic "Four." As always in such situation—because I wanted students to develop their explanatory talk—I asked Laura to provide her reasons.

```
01   Teacher:  What is your reason?
02   Laura:    Well, uh um, four times two is eight, and–
03   Teacher:  =Four times two is eight.
04   Laura:    And two times four is eight.
05   Teacher:  Two times four is eight. Leanne?
06   Leanne:   What is eight have to do with it, because there is no eight thing on
               here? Because there is six weights, not eight!
```

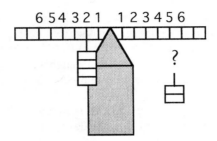

Figure 6.5. To review the results of a previous whole-class discussion, I set up an equal arm balance that students used as part of a task asking where on the right arm I would have to place the two-screw weight to make the lever balance.

Though we could hear Laura, she did not speak very loudly. Concerned that not every student had heard what she had said, I repeated her statements (lines 03, 05) before calling on the next student. Leanne exasperatedly asked what the "eight," a word in both of Laura's answers, had to do with "it," presumably the problem. She elaborated by means of an observation sentence, "There is no eight thing on here." She specified that there are six weights. Evidently, Laura's way of talking about the problem did not make sense to Leanne, particularly the number eight. The fact that there was a four weight on the two-unit distance and, correspondingly a two weight to be placed on the four-unit distance, was not in any way transparent to her. Rather, there were six weights before them, grouped into two and four, respectively. Upon my request, Laura articulated her method again, associated with a further example that I mounted. There was therefore repeated telling of the rule in concrete situations.

07	Teacher:	But, Laura, what are you doing? You're looking at two things at the same time. Can you explain that again for the class?
08	Laura:	Well, uh um, they're both– You try to find the number so they both, so they both, they both times by the number that they are (??) the same.
09	Teacher:	So you want to make the same on both sides.
10	Laura:	So like, uh um–
11	Teacher:	Like here I have the four weights on three. ((Moves four-screw weight on the three-unit distance.)) Where would you put it? ((Holds up a two-weight.))
12	Laura:	Uh um, probably on the six.
13	Teacher:	Why would you put it on the six?
14	Laura:	Uh um, two times six is twelve and four times three is twelve.
15	Teacher:	Did you hear that Leanne?
16	Leanne:	I still don't get it.
17	Chantal:	°But it's, twelve has to do with it.°
18	Leanne:	What has *twelve* got to do with it?

19 Daniel: Just trust it, it works.

Following my request, Laura began by articulating a rule that did not take into account the concrete case that I currently had set up in front of the class. She talked about a number and about something occurring on both sides or in both instances, and about something that is "timesed," yielding something that is the same (line 08). The next turn constituted mediational work: Laura's talk was too distant from the actual experience and so I rephrased, "So you want to make the same on both sides." Laura hesitated and I quickly moved the four-unit weight into the position that was three-unit distances from the fulcrum (line 11). I asked again where she would put it, hoping that with this new situation, Laura's way of talking may become intelligible to Leanne and others with similar difficulties.

As previously, Laura initially provided a laconic answer. Again, I encouraged her to provide a reason (line 13). Laura provided another situational description of the way in which one can arrive at the distance in question, "two times six is twelve and four times three is twelve." Called upon whether she heard what Laura had said, Leanne responded that she did not get it; Chantal could be heard saying that the twelve figuring in Laura's answer indeed had something to do with the problem. But Leanne now appeared to question Chantal, what the twelve had to do with this situation. In response, Daniel suggested trusting it, presumably the description Laura had provided.

20 Leanne: I know, but I would like to understand.
21 Daniel: Well, I don't know why it works but that it works.

The conversation then moved on, as other students provided descriptions of how to predict when the balance will be equilibrated. At the end of the second whole-class conversation relating to balancing the lever, I suggested:

22 Teacher: I want to summarize Laura's law. She says multiply the load by the
            distance ((Writes on the overhead)) and that has to equal what?
            Laura?
23 Laura: That equals the effort times the distance.

The result of the two whole-class discussions was posted as "Laura's law." In a similar way, the ratio rule for doing balance beam problems was posted as "Riley's rule," which consisted in dividing the two weights and finding a distance so that the inversed division of distances corresponding to the weights would yield the same number.

Further Opportunities

Later, during a lesson on second-class levers, I asked students how one could
know the force needed to hold up a class II lever, which, in this class, we called
the "wheelbarrow lever" (figure 6.6). Using familiar names and structural resemblances with familiar objects was part of my attempt to take students' own
pre-unit language as the starting point and not force language changes faster
than the students as a collective could handle. Shamir, referring to the posting of
Laura's law, got up and read it to the class. Using the posting as a resource, he
paraphrased, "Multiply the load by the distance and you get a number, then find
the distance for the effort so when you multiply them, you get the same number
so, effort times distance, and load times distance." In the following exchange,
Shamir drew on this way of talking to provide his response to a question that I
asked as part of my repeated attempts to ascertain that the linguistic patterns of
standard science actually were resources salient to the students.

24   Shamir: Four.
25   (2.0)
26   Teacher: Because?
27   (1.7)
28   Don't just say four! Four, be*cause*–
29   (1.3)
30   My answer is four *because*–
31   Shamir: Four because, hmm, six times two is twelve, and then four times
               three–
32   Leanne: Uh um, I made a mistake, I think it's six because I thought it was
               three on the–
33   Teacher: No, this is a two.
34   Leanne: I thought it was three.
35   Teacher: And so, what is your reasoning be*cause*–

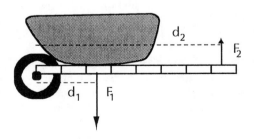

Figure 6.6. Students conducted planned investigations with a second-class lever, which
was also exemplified as a wheelbarrow in an attempt to provide family resemblances
between their familiar language and the formal language concerning simple machines.

36 Leanne: I think it's six, because Laura's thing is (.) two times six is twelve, and six times two is twelve.

Shamir simply stated the number of unit-distances at which the three-unit weight needed to be placed to balance the two-unit weight placed on six-unit distances from the fulcrum (line 24). There was a pause, in effect asking Shamir to continue, but he did not. I therefore requested such a continuation (line 25). My "Be*cause?*" asked not for a continuation but also for an explanation. There was no response. I then uttered an admonition, "Don't just say four!" following it with a pattern to be followed, "Four, be*cause*." Again there was a pause so that I reiterated the pattern to be followed, "My answer is four *because–*" (line 30). Shamir then framed this situation before them drawing on the linguistic pattern developed by Laura, that is, by calculating the product moments on each side, that is, weight times its distance from the fulcrum. In response, Leanne, who had earlier said that the answer was "three," revised her response. When I asked, she too multiplied weight and distance for one of the two sides, and then explicitly denoted the pattern "two times six is twelve" as "Laura's thing."

Something else is notable in this excerpt. Repeatedly I asked students to articulate rationales, emphasizing the word "because." At this point, we were still early in the unit. There was no culture in this class or the school more generally that held students accountable for their answers, that is, a culture in which students would provide explanations for their answers or would be asked by the teachers to do so. One aspect of my teaching was devoted to the development of a linguistic pattern whereby students provided explanations of their answers, which are also descriptions of how to arrive at the answers.

Students provided further applications of the rule during the discussion of "catapult" (third-class) levers, where the entire class hypothesized the size of effort given the load and the distances. Students also built levers into their machines. Natasha and Erin built a crane-like structure in which a 100-gram mass as load on the end of a long arm was counterbalanced by a heavy weight including a hammer and sandbag (figure 6.7). Maryam and Jessica produced a similar design. Four groups (eleven students) also employed levers as central parts of their final, integrating project. In these projects, the relationship between the weights and their distances from the fulcrums needed exact calibration for the devices to work properly. Thus, the students had ample opportunities to explore levers and their relationships in more detail.

There were further opportunities for talking about various lever problems. During the students' final project, a "review" of the lever activities allowed students to hypothesize and test, in whole-class situations, further problems; when called upon, students described how to derive their answer. Various students used the product moment rule that was, again, associated with its creator Laura. In another whole-class conversation about pulleys, I showed how Laura's prod-

Figure 6.7. Natasha (*right*) and Erin present their crane-like structure in which a heavy load (a sandbag) is counterbalanced by a lighter force (a hammer) placed at a larger distance from the fulcrum.

uct moment rule could be applied to pulleys by using a diagram that highlighted the structural similarities between pulleys and levers.

Despite these opportunities, we have to be careful about thinking that because students had opportunities for solving mechanical problems in their designs, they would develop better ways of talking about to the product moment rule, that is, "Laura's law." The problems of getting the calibration right can be done without invoking the product moment rule; it is a matter of adjusting one's material practice until the chosen situation behaves in the desired way—much like a football quarterback does not need to know the laws of motion to get the ball to the desired player despite rain, wind, or slippery ground. Rather, the situation was quite different so that it was expected that students would use different structuring resources to resolve the contingent problems in the design and construction.

Levels of Appropriation

At the end of the unit, my research team and I assessed how students had changed their ways of talking in the context of simple machines. We designed opportunities for writing, speaking, and acting, in accordance with my commit-ment to the notion of learning as an increasing generation of and participation in material and linguistic practices. Prior to and at the end of the unit, students pre-pared semantic maps, wrote responses to application questions, discussed their written answers, and modeled solutions to practical problems using physical materials. Detailed comparative analyses and microanalyses showed that stu-dents' responses to items differed greatly across formats on both pretest and posttest (e.g., McGinn and Roth 1998).

On both pretests and posttests, there were variations in performance even when problems were structurally equivalent from a scientific perspective. For example, during pretest interviews, we asked students questions using levers with and without rules marked on both arms. From students' talk, gestures, and pointing, eight different solution strategies were identified that varied in degree of mathematization. These strategies included: (a) "calculating with scientific formulas" using product moment or ratio rules; (b) "cross matching weights and distances" when the unit weights matched the unit distances; (c) "number crunching," based on combining given numbers with arithmetic operations in nonscientific ways; (d) "referencing locations," based on using numbers as ref-erents to describe locations for placing weights; (e) "measuring distances with their fingers" and placing weights at the measured location; (f) "'eyeballing' distances" to estimate the appropriate placement of weights; (g) "trial and error," that is, moving the weight until the lever balanced; and (h) "haphazard guess-ing" involving multiple trials with little apparent learning between subsequent trials.

These eight solution strategies were not equally represented when students solved problems with ruled and unruled levers (table 6.1). Students' strategies with levers that were not ruled included measuring distances with fingers, "eye-balling" distances, using trial and error, and haphazard guessing; with ruled lev-ers, students' strategies included referencing locations to place weights, "num-ber crunching" with arithmetic operations, cross matching weight and distance, or calculating with scientific formulas. Haphazard guessing was the only answer category that occurred across the two formats. Thus, even a seemingly minor change in the available materials (adding numbers to the lever) produced notice-able effects on observed practices; once the numbers were available, all student responses incorporated numbers in some way.

On the posttest, there existed similar variations: across three parts of the as-sessment (writing, talking, and using levers), students adopted diverging re-sponses that were unrelated to their earlier responses (table 6.2). When talking about and manipulating actual levers, students generally exhibited a qualitative understanding of the inverse relationship between load and effort and the dis-tances associated with them. However, the paper-and-pencil test, which asked for numerical results, encouraged numerical strategies. Mathematical language arose from whole-class discussions and was proposed by students; these strate-

Table 6.1. Pretest transition matrix of response patterns on class I lever problems across two situations

Unruled Lever Strategy	Ruled-Lever Strategy				
	Calculat-ing with Formulas	Matching Weight and Distance	Number Crunching	Referenc-ing Loca-tions	Guessing
Measuring	1	1	1		
Estimating			1	2	
Trial and Error	1			3	1
Guessing			1		

Note: $N = 12$. One student provided an answer only for the unruled lever.

gies were not an explicit goal of instructions that all students were to achieve—that is, formulas were not marked as things to be memorized for a test. Given the various learning problems described above, the appropriation of qualitative discourse and material practice were deemed sufficient learning goals, and these goals were met by all but a couple of students. Here, ten students correctly used the product moment and ratio language (see equations in table 6.2) to calculate problems based on integer ratios of weights and distances on class I levers, and eight did so on class II levers. Five students incorrectly used multiplicative and ratio language to arrive at their solutions for class I levers, and seven used it on class II levers. Other students used additive language or combinations of the languages. This competence compares well with that of much older college students, most of whom cannot do class I lever problems even if they involve integral multiples of weights or distances (Roth 1991). Many years later, I also found out that the high school students in an engineering course could not spontaneously do the kinds of problems my sixth- and seventh-grade students had come to do.

During the posttest interviews, students evoked the names of the rules and laws posted, but they had difficulties using the associated language to describe how to balance the equal arm levers or how to find the effort in a second-class lever:

Well, anyways I, okay, I'll go, I got my answer by timesing fifty by six 'cause fifty's there and six is what it's on, okay, and that gave me three hundred grams, same as Sylvia's. (Kian)

I did weight times the distance, like Laura said on, well while we were doing our lessons, she said that the weight times the distance would be, so I timesed fifty by six and got three hundred as well. (Sylvia)

Well, no, that's kind of what, I was going to do, but I guess I kind of, I guess I divided it by the six, but I . . . 'cause like Laura had hers. (Amanda)

Table 6.2. Posttest responses to paper-and-pencil and hands-on problems on class I and class II lever problems

Problem Type	Answer Frequencies				
	Quantitative (paper-and-pencil)			Qualitative (hands-on)	
"How hard do you have to pull to balance the lever?"	$F_1 \cdot d_1 =$ $F_2 \cdot d_2$ $d_1 : d_2 =$ $F_2 : F_1$	Incorrect multiplications, ratios, etc.	Additive rules	Correct IF $F_1 > F_2$ THEN $d_1 <$ d_2	Incorrect
class I lever	10	5	11	23	3
class II lever	8	7	11	20	6

Such ways of talking can be interpreted as having covered half of the way to the language legitimated by school science. The three girls appropriated only part of the description provided by those students who intentionally used the language for providing an answer (Laura, Don, Bella, Riley, and Daniel).

Sometimes, "Laura's law" was simply a term denoting something students did not understand or know how to do. This became clear when students indicated that a particular problem could be solved applying this law, but could not actually apply it in the situation. Similarly, during a whole-class discussion on second-class levers, Shamir answered my question about how to figure out the effort, knowing load and load distance and effort distance, by walking to the bulletin board and reading aloud the text that stated "Laura's law." As such, the law denoted a resource that was easily available, and students knew that it was posted as such.

We gathered similar evidence in other situations such as the conceptual difference between pulley configurations. During the introductory discussion, I had employed the letters "A" and "B" to distinguish the drawings of two different pulley configurations, one provided a mechanical advantage (MA) of one (MA = 1), the other a mechanical advantage of two (MA = 2). Students later used the labels "A-pulley" and "B-pulley" as convenient denotations. In several situations, students later used the the terms "A-pulleys" and "B-pulleys" to help them whether or not the pulley configuration decreased their effort. Here, the students' answers to a problem were mediated by the enunciation of a label rather than by a straightforward description of the system itself. "A-pulley" and "B-pulley," posted copies of transparencies, and the transparencies in my binder with the curriculum were resources for students' practice to talk about and build pulley configurations. Again, while these resources were rapidly available, the associated (linguistic and material) practices were less rapidly appropriated.

TEACHER-INTRODUCED LANGUAGE

In this section, the language about mechanical advantage is used to illustrate students' rapid appropriation of a language even though I had introduced it and its token to the class. The process of appropriation was roughly divided into four periods. First, I introduced the new language about mechanical advantage. Then, students made their first steps in this new linguistic practice during whole-class sessions where I could observe their first attempts. Third, structured small-group activities provided students with situations in which they could try to use the mechanical advantage language on their own. Finally, the students collectively populated their own intentions and orientations with the language surrounding (mechanical) advantage, in a reversal of an often-cited slogan according to which students populate language with their own intentions.

Introducing the New Language

To introduce mechanical advantage, I began one lesson by asking students about the purpose of machines. This question previously had been the topic of an extended class discussion. Several students responded again that the purpose was to make life easier. I then introduced a formal way of assessing how many times the effort becomes easier. This definition was at the same time formal, the ratio of load and effort, and an operational definition of how to measure load and effort.

> So if you take the load and divide it by how much effort it takes you, the load that you hang on your machine divided by the effort. Now, if the mechanical advantage is greater than one, if you take your grams, that you hang on your machine divided by the grams you have to crank or pull, then you get the mechanical advantage, if it is greater than one ((Teacher writes "MA > 1" on overhead)), you have a mechanical advantage. If it is less than one ((Teacher writes "MA < 1" on overhead)), you have a disadvantage.

Here, the possibility of associating the formal definition of mechanical advantage with the everyday notions of advantage and disadvantage was provided. I explicitly made a connection between a mechanical advantage smaller than one (i.e., MA < 1) and the word "disadvantage." My next example tied the present discussion to Aslam's presentation on the previous day, further encouraging this linguistic bridge: "Aslam showed us a machine that had seventy-five grams as a load, and then it took us one hundred grams for the effort. Now if you divide one hundred into seventy-five, you get?" After students performed the calculations and provided the numerical answer, I continued:

> It's less. Now let's go back. If it's less than one, the mechanical advantage, less than this means, less than one you have a disadvantage. So this is the same way that we can look at all of your machines, after you presented and to take some engineering criteria to your machine.

The immediately following presentations of student-designed machines provided opportunities for employing this language and for students to engage in this practice. Subsequent lessons provided further opportunities for using the term "mechanical advantage" in the context of student- and teacher-designed machines.

First Participation in Linguistic Practice

The whole-class conversations following the students' design and construction activity provided many opportunities to engage in the practice of measuring mechanical advantage and to refine the associated discursive practices (figure 6.8). In presenting the machines they designed, students also talked about the mechanical advantage these provided. They measured load and effort forces as part of their presentation, and the audience calculated the mechanical advantage. I wrote the results of these calculations on the chalkboard (visible in figure 6.8) or overhead. This episode, recorded during Daniel and Shamir's presentation, clearly illustrates this. They had used Lego blocks, gears, and wheels to design a transporter. In the whole-class discussion, their peers held them accountable for what they had done, particularly with respect to the mechanical advantage their machine was to deliver.

```
01   Maryam:  OK, where is your advantage? and=
02   Daniel:  =Right here, see this, I geared this down, this ⌈is a gear box.⌉
              ((He points to the gear box.))
03   Maryam:                                              ⌊OK, let's measure⌋ it
              and see what your effort is.
04   Daniel:  Our effort ⌈we can't, it is not possible.⌉
05   Shamir:            ⌊There is no effort, all       ⌋ we have to do is let it go.
```

((Shows how load is released.))
06   Maryam: Then it's not, there has to be an effort, or else it is not like everybody
              else's.

Maryam's opening comment (line 01) illustrates an initial way of talking about mechanical advantage, "Where is your advantage?" However, in response to Daniel's pointing to a part of his machine, she repaired her earlier phrase and suggested a measurement of mechanical advantage. Her comment in line 06 shows that Daniel's and Shamir's ways of describing mechanical advantage conflicted not only with her own ways but also with those that she articulated as being commonly used in the classroom, "it is not like everybody else's" (line 06). This critique was further sharpened when other students in the audience refused to accept pointing to the gearbox to describe mechanical advantage.

07   AJ: What's the mechanical advantage?
08   Daniel: Right here. ((Points to gear box.))

Figure 6.8. In presenting the machines they designed, students talked about the mechanical advantage these provided. They measured load and effort forces as part of their presentation, and the audience calculated the mechanical advantage, which I noted on the chalkboard (or overhead).

09 AJ: *No, no*, measure it!
10 Leanne: People asked you why your mechanical advantage was, he said it was
            this. ((Walks to the front and points to gear box.)) But in everybody
            else's machines, the mechanical advantage was a number.

Here, AJ followed Maryam's rephrased line of inquiry; he asked, "What's the mechanical advantage?" rather than "Where is the mechanical advantage?" (line 07). In her rejoinder, Leanne made it quite clear that for most class members, the shared way of talking about mechanical advantage required it to be expressed as a number (line 10).

In this way, more and more members participated in the new language about the mechanical advantage of machines. I encouraged students not only to talk about and assess mechanical advantage but also to describe current problems reducing the mechanical advantage and to suggest modifications improving it. Sometimes I directed students' attention to specific aspects of the design that brought up the idea of friction that decreased the mechanical advantage. Later, various students began to offer suggestions for how to overcome the friction problem. In one situation, the mechanical advantage was two (MA = 2). Although this satisfied the criteria for a machine decreasing effort, I asked students how they could improve the design to increase the mechanical advantage. In the subsequent conversation between presenters and the audience, various students suggested:

Well, if you use, if the car was part of your machine, if you wanted it lighter it would be a better mechanical advantage, if it was like plastic or something light, it's wood so like it takes away some advantage. (Aslam)
    When you are pulling the string, and if it was a big machine, and you were pulling it, that takes off some mechanical advantage, and also when you are pulling the string, your little car over there. (Shamir)
    A better pulley, because, like here, Claire had to hold it so the string wouldn't come off, so it something that lifts over it so that the string wouldn't come out. (Kian)

First Private Attempts during Structured Activities

The small-group activities organized around artifacts that I had designed and worksheets provided first opportunities for students to deploy new language on their own. (All previous opportunities were in whole-class discussions and in my presence.) Here, students could talk about their differences and develop ways of talking that were shared within the small groups. There were ample opportunities to stabilize this talk.

11	Erin:	What is the mechanical advantage of your pulley system? ((Reads from instructions.))
12	Aslam:	There *isn't* one.
13	Erin:	There isn't one? I'm gonna say it was a disadvantage. ((She begins to write an answer.))
14	Aslam:	What are you doing? Erin, *no, no, no!*
15	Erin:	Just say it was none.
16	Aslam:	You have to put like something divided by something.
17	Erin:	OK, it was fifty over a hundred.
18	Aslam:	No, a hundred, no a hundred and (.) two.

In this conversation, Aslam and Erin articulated a way of describing two pulley configurations in terms of mechanical advantage. Although Aslam began by noting that there was no mechanical advantage (line 12), he later changed this description to "a hundred and two," after having suggested that mechanical advantage involved "something divided by something." In this, he rejected Erin's formulation, "Just say [mechanical advantage] was none" (line 15), and supported a mathematical way of formulating mechanical advantage. He inverted Erin's suggestion (line 17) to arrive at the standard form of load divided by effort. In this class, formulas were not practiced nor required of students. Students did not engage in routine calculation of numbers. Rather, the students' analysis of mechanical advantage was more a comparison of load and effort rather than algorithm based, that is, a definition-based calculation of the fraction load over effort. Erin's "it was fifty over a hundred" has to be read as the convention to write load above effort. This episode also illustrates the presence of the everyday discourse in Erin's utterances "disadvantage" and "there was none," and the emergence of a new language in Aslam's utterance "something divided by something." "Something" constituted two yet-to-be-specified variables.

While I observed students develop this new way of talking, I understood that a full appropriation of the new language in this class would only be expressed when students deployed it in the pursuit of their own intentions. Students had many opportunities for such a development of a shared language during their design and construction activities.

Widespread Use

The students rapidly incorporated the new language surrounding the mechanical advantage of machines. That is, I consider the successful adoption not merely a problem of getting students to calculate load over effort under certain conditions but especially a broad adoption of linguistic and material practices of which the calculation of a number or the comparison of weights is an integral part. Building on students' definition of a machine, I encouraged them to design their machines in such a way that "it makes it easier for [them] to move the load." Without further emphasis on mechanical advantage, I asked students to begin designing a machine that could move heavy loads over a large distance. The model of the device designed and constructed by the students was to be able to move a load of at least 100 grams over a minimum distance of two meters. In the course of this activity, there were many opportunities to observe students' concern for mechanical advantage, both as a linguistic practice (designing machines that decrease the amount of effort, and designing tests) and a material practice (building the machines, and conducting tests). That is, the point is to get students to go beyond just parroting some phrase or linguistic pattern. Full-scale integration of the language is indiscernible from the competent navigation of the design world. Competent linguistic practice is achieved when the boundary between knowing the language associated with mechanical advantage and knowing one's world around the world of designing machines more generally has disappeared.

While I do not have evidence for all groups that the boundary disappeared between parroting the calculation of mechanical advantage when asked and knowing their way around designing machines that exhibit a mechanical advantage, my videotapes show many students for whom the following episode during the planning of the transporter was typical.

19 Don: Is that your model of your model? *Don't* Dan! *No*! But do you know what I'm saying. We could use that old one and then you could crank it up and then slide down into the truck.
20 Dan: But see that wasn't a mechanical advantage. ((He starts erasing the drawing again.))
21   Up here could be the warehouse. Hook the weight onto there, it slides down there, hits that and slides into the truck.
22 Don: But it needs to be a mechanical advantage instead of pulling it. We need to get it up there somehow.

In this episode, Dan and Don were both oriented toward designing their machine on paper, looking at each other's earlier sketches. They called one another's attention to the problem of designing a machine that had a mechanical advantage. Don proposed to employ a design element used in their previous model (line 19). Dan responded by pointing out that their previous tests showed that the element did not to provide a mechanical advantage (line 20). A few moments later, Dan proposed a design for their transporter, but Don critiqued this design in terms of mechanical advantage. Here, we see one of the many examples where students used the language of mechanical advantage to analyze and improve their design; they used it for their own intentions rather than parroting a teacher statement or filling in some blank where this would be the required canonical and teacher-appraised answer. Designing machines, building prototypes, and talking mechanical advantage had become indistinguishable; they

Figure 6.9. Dan (left) and Don are working on their transporter. At the moment, there are neither pulleys nor the low-friction rope they would use later. However, using replacement parts prior to completing the prototype allowed the pair to test the design in different configurations.

were all part of the same orientation in and toward a world of designing (figure 6.9).

This evidence, however, does not provide the entire picture. I repeatedly observed students who accurately analyzed situations on paper and provided descriptions compatible with the standard language promoted by the curriculum. At the same time, they had not yet developed an equivalent competence in their material practice that would allow them to actually construct a pulley configuration that would increase the mechanical advantage. That is, they could talk mechanical advantage but could not build a prototype exhibiting mechanical advantage. However, during the design and construction activities following the introduction of mechanical advantage, this language became a mediating element that provided students with feedback and therefore began to mediate their access to the material world. That is, the orientation to the world associated with the language of mechanical advantage mediated what they were doing with the materials; it provided them with a form of feedback, which they used to adapt their designs or material practice.

There were increasing instances in which students' concern for mechanical advantage was registered. Some approached me to report that their machines provided some specific amount of mechanical advantage, and they provided me with specific factors that increased the mechanical advantage in their model. For example, Laura and her group had chosen an arborite surface for moving objects because this "increased slippage." Most student groups began to test their designs, typically after they had finished their construction activities. They used the spring scale available on a specified desk as a resource. Over time, many students used Bella's set of keys, which was known to have a mass of 100 grams, as a reference object to be used in measurements of mechanical advantage.

While constructing machines of their own design, students maintained their concern for mechanical advantage. Some students, including Don and Dan, began their tests even before the entire model was in working condition. Don called on Dan soon after the photograph in figure 6.9 was taken:

> Dan, what we should do is a twenty-five-gram weight and then just get a piece of string and right now just see if it is a mechanical advantage. I just want to do this to try it. Let's just do this to test it. I just want to test it.

Dan agreed and they prepared a test for the model at its current state of development. As they set up their test, Don and Dan already identified possible problems with their model in the current state.

23	Don:	We shouldn't use shoelaces!
24	Dan:	Well we're just measuring it. ((Dan attaches the wooden block to the shoelace and it stretches down to the ground.))
25	Don:	°Tie a knot. Yeah. And then like, yeah, whatever.° (1.1) Okay now we need the scale again. (1.0) Move that up. ((Both try bringing the lower part of shoestring up and raise the block off the ground.))
26	Dan:	Well there's going to be pulleys.
27	Don:	We won't know, but it can't be dragging against the ground. (1.2) ((Both try to bring block off the ground.))
28	Dan:	I know, we're just using it to see.

They attributed the decrease in mechanical advantage to the thickness of the shoelaces (line 23), the lack of pulleys as support for the moving lace (line 26), and the fact that the load dragged on the ground (line 27). But Dan repeatedly encouraged Don to view this as a preliminary test (lines 24, 28). Their test showed a disadvantage (MA = 0.3), which provided Don and Dan with a context to talk about the weak points in their present model, derived mostly from friction caused by various features in their test. They called it a "disadvantage" elsewhere. Subsequently, they talked about replacing the currently used popsicle sticks with pulleys so that the central part of their model, a string, moved with less friction; they also discussed replacing the shoelaces with finer string that was to be strung more tightly so that they would reduce friction with the support and eliminate dragging of the load on the base. Dan and Don implemented these changes which improved the performance of their machine about seventeen-fold so that they achieved a mechanical advantage of five (MA = 5).

NETWORKS OF RECURRENT CONVERSATIONS

In this chapter, I have clarified the notion of control and appropriation of orientations to the world and, with it, the associated linguistic and material practices. The data illustrate rather widespread adoption of the language about mechanical advantage and its recurrent use in conversations held in different locations and for different purposes. A central mediating factor in this adoption may be the presence of advantage and disadvantage in many everyday situations. Advantages and disadvantages were common aspects of students' language in and out of school prior to being made the focus in this science class. The shift in language from articulating and talking about "advantage" to articulating and talking about "mechanical advantage" is small. The associated mathematical discourse requires the comparison between effort and load, that is, two measurements. Even if students did not calculate mechanical advantage at first, they could easily assess whether their machine provided an advantage or a disadvantage. With repeated use during whole-class conversations over and about students' models and the teacher-designed pulley configurations and transparencies, students quickly appropriated the new language. That is, in the case of mechanical advantage, the classroom community had the opportunity to develop a "special network of recurrent conversation" (Winograd and Flores 1987, 158). Across situations—small-group and whole-class conversations, design activities, and structured investigations—mechanical advantage became a central aspect of the language for articulating and talking about simple machines.

This, however, cannot be the whole story. Notions such as "force" and "velocity" are also recurrently used in everyday language. Yet it has been shown that physics students at the secondary and tertiary level alike have difficulty developing ways of talking that have a family resemblance with those ways employed by physicists and physics textbooks. That is, the situations that are typically associated with the corresponding language vary between everyday life and physics classrooms and physics laboratories. Throughout this book, there are examples that show that it takes extended, motivated effort to move from the everyday to the physicists' way of orienting to, articulating, and talking about, for example, force and velocity as things different from other things.

The introduction and appropriation of the mechanical advantage language is different from the language denoted by "Laura's law," "Riley's rule," or "Aslam's rule." Their deployment in formal language to the tasks at hand was more limited. When levers were involved in the design of a machine, other concerns predominated in the language that did not require any of the formal, mathematics-based rules as linguistic resources. Thus, there were few opportunities for an emerging network of recurrent conversation equivalent to the mechanical advantage case. Laura's law (and all other laws, for that matter) was not usually evoked as a resource when students were articulating entities and processes while designing. Although most students had evolved a qualitative language about levers (shown in the posttest conversations), the quantitative language never became part of other activities. That is, Laura's law, for example, did not become part of the orientation toward designing a machine and articulating salient entities and processes. It was limited to the few whole-class and small-group activities especially designed for lever talk, and those situations that I had set up for the specific purpose of doing or reviewing lever tasks.

In this case, in spite of the fact that a student was the originator of a description, and in spite of repeated opportunities to engage in this way of talking, it was not taken up widely in the classroom community. Ownership in its narrow sense, as a description of who generated a language, does not constitute an appropriate explanation. It can be argued that most of the students have not had the opportunity or interest to appropriate the language, to make it their own in the sense of populating their own intentions with this way of talking. Thus, "Laura's law" existed as a linguistic resource; when asked, students could refer to the posted copy of the transparency where it had been noted. Some students knew that it described the way of finding the required information on lever problems, but were not using this way of talking when presented with a relevant situation on the posttest. That is, the language surrounding Laura's law did not become a part of the recurrent conversations in the classroom in the way that the talk surrounding mechanical advantage became.

We are now in a position to understand the enormous time and effort required to bring about a community of "triangle" language: students (a) had no prior language for designing with "triangles" and (b) lacked opportunities and encouragement to build and engage a shared way of talking. First, in contrast to the closeness of the talk about advantage and the more technical mechanical advantage, the fourth- and fifth-grade students in my previous study did not bring an equivalent language about bracing using triangular configurations to class. Second, there were few public discussions in which structures were tested and analyzed in terms of weak points. There were therefore no opportunities for a network of recurrent orientations and conversations to arise in which a suitable language would be a consistent part.

In contrast, if the sixth- and seventh-grade students did not raise relevant issues, I encouraged them to discuss and test mechanical advantage for every project presented. Moreover, the discussion did not end with measuring mechanical advantage; I encouraged students to talk about features of the presented models that decreased the (mechanical) advantage and to suggest changes that would increase it. This increased the number of opportunities for talking mechanical advantage, articulating simple machines, and making distinctions between better and poorer designs. Thus, the students collectively engaged in linguistic and material practices associated with mechanical advantage. They evolved an orientation to the design world in which telling apart poorer from better designs by means of the mechanical advantage language became a key aspect. The initial gap between students' and my pre-unit language was narrow; thus, (mechanical) advantage (and its correlate of disadvantage when MA < 1) provided an opportunity for a common language to emerge. A corresponding context in which common ways of articulating the world and talking about design was to be developed did not exist in the fourth- and fifth-grade case of triangular bracing, which I described at the beginning of this chapter. A similar observation was made in a second study in an entirely different school context, region of the country, age level, and course. In the qualitative physics course (chapter 2), "This arrow is forcing it that way" was a crucial step in forming a new language about the effect of force and velocity on the motion of a particle. The students' everyday talk about "forcing" became a stepping-stone, a pivotal move in the shift that allowed students a convergence of their language with that of standard science.

Closeness of critical situations and language for developing language forms that students bring and teachers want to develop seems to be a central issue. The notion of ownership, which I thought was tied to bringing about a linguistic practice, turned out not to be a suitable way of describing the process of community formation. However, the notion of ownership may have been too simplistic. One can claim that this notion still operates, but now with respect to the appropriation of new ways of talking. Ownership may reside in students' ability to make a language their own, whether or not they invented it, that is, in the ability to express their own intentions and orientations with new ways of talking. In other words, I suggest reversing the way in which Bakhtin (1981) is frequently cited, whereby students will appropriate a language when they can populate it with their intentions. I suggest that we need to theorize language evolution by beginning with students' intentions and orientations. They will populate their orientations and intentions when there are places and needs, from their perspectives. These needs are not brought about by a form of discrepant event or other data that themselves do not have a place in the orientations students currently take—competing scientific theories, too, are not evaluated on the basis of data, for they often differ in the ways in which they appreciate something as data. Rather, when new orientations and intentions evolve from students' practical actions, new linguistic needs may coemerge and coevolve, which can be populated by existing language currently unknown or unfamiliar to students.

In the past, researchers and teachers often assumed that if students are allowed to invent and use their own scientific and mathematical language, they will automatically take ownership. In this chapter I began to separate ownership (control) from the inventing of a particular way of talking. We now look not simply at whether activities allow students to invent and deploy their language but also at whether activity structures and artifacts in the students' and teachers' experience allow them to build common ways of talking.

Curriculum designers (including teachers) face the same problems that have been described for the designers of computer systems. One of the hardest challenges is to design the participants' environment in such a way that they can create and deploy language that makes sense to all. Professional curriculum designers and teachers are the playmakers who set the stage for participation in situations where particular ways of talking are intelligible and fruitful. They have to find and support ways in which students and teachers can, collectively, develop new ways of articulating things and situations, and then evolve language that is about them. It is from the initial articulation in activity that talk about the objects and events, and therefore ways of talking science both sensible to students and legitimate to the teacher, can emerge. The starting points have to be situations and orientations sensible to both; these starting points are chosen such that they solicit particular ways of articulating objects, events, situations, or explanations. Then the collectivity can evolve new and more viable ways of talking. In this effort, it is not important whether the artifacts that serve as conversational topics mirror real things, but whether they encourage interaction and reflection. These new ways of talking enable students to articulate the world in new ways or new worlds in familiar ways. And because children coparticipate in establishing and maintaining these new forms of talking, they are populating their intentions and orientations with linguistic resources provided to them by the teacher.

7

Mediation of Language: Space, Physical Orientation, and Group Size

Talking is equivalent to taking an orientation and taking up a position in the world. However, if talking is taking an orientation and taking a position, considered in both physical and metaphorical ways, then the physical arrangements, group size, and focal artifacts are probably mediating the talk, because all human activity is taking place in a physical and social context. Thus, how people interact and how they talk is mediated by the "physical arrangements, the spatial layout of a setting, the arrangement of the furniture, the open spaces, walkways, coffee niches, doors to the outside, and so on" (Jordan and Henderson 1995, 74–75). The talk that I overheard and recorded on the airplane (see the introduction) was structured by the arrangement of seats along narrow aisles, which allowed the stewardess to walk backward without the risk of falling, while moving her eyes from row to row and passenger to passenger. Even the approaching sound of her voice is part of the situation, structuring the interaction such that in some situation, a stretched-out hand is sufficient for requesting a goblet of water, or a slight shift of the chin sufficient to note that one does not desire anything at the moment.

Everyday talk is structured by physical arrangements, layout of a setting, group size, and so forth. These factors mediate the participation in material and linguistic practices and therefore mediate knowing and learning. That is, the constellation of focal artifacts, social configurations, and physical arrangements determines who learns and to what extent. It therefore comes as a surprise that educators generally have not paid attention to these dimensions. Some readers may ask, "But how does one address the mediating influence of these factors even if one were to know what these are and how they mediated the interactions in the classroom?"

Recent workplace studies (e.g., Heath and Luff 2000) show that physical arrangements of interactional settings and the artifacts used therein are important resources that participants draw on to manage their interactions. These studies increasingly focus on knowing and learning as they arise from the mediational effects that artifacts (tools, representational devices), social configurations, and physical arrangements have on conversations. For example, team navigation is accomplished by groups of people such that there is a complex interplay of required tools (e.g., gyrocompass, nautical slide rule, alidade, three-scale nomogram, maps), social configuration of team members, and physical arrangements that interface with the career progress of individuals and afford safety-assuring redundancy in the system (Hutchins 1995). Artifacts also provide anchors or bridges across varying discourse communities, and across different physical, geographical, and social organizations of participants—but they may lead to different practices in different communities. Whereas existing workplace studies recognize relationships of interactions and practices with artifacts, social configurations, and physical arrangements, equivalent work in cognition and instruction has merely begun. In this chapter, I will show how these aspects pertain to science classrooms. I will analyze a variety of factors that mediate the structure and content of the conversations; the data derive from the same sixth- and seventh-grade classroom that featured in the previous chapter.

FOCAL AREA

In the study of knowing and learning through design activities, I had used four activity structures that allow me to analyze how different constellations of focal artifacts (overhead transparencies, instructions, summary sheets, and models of corresponding simple machines), social configurations (e.g., group size, division of labor, hierarchies), and physical arrangements mediated the content and structure of conversations. The four activity structures arise from the crossing of two factors: designer of the focal artifact (teacher, students) and size of the group oriented toward the artifact (small group, whole class). There were whole-class discussions over and about student- (designs and prototypes) or teacher-designed artifacts (models, overhead transparencies); and there were small-group conversations over student- (prototypes being designed and built) and teacher-designed artifacts (structured tasks using simple machines provided to students). My analyses reveal that the mediational effects on content and structure of ways of talking are associated with the size of the focal area, that is, the area where the events take place that coparticipants orient to and deem to be salient. The focal area was determined by the size of the focal artifact, social configuration (whole class, small group), and physical arrangement of members (who may have different roles). This focal area was normally comediated by the focal artifact and task structure. During whole-class settings, these focal areas included presenters (students or teacher) and artifacts; during small-group activities, the focal area included all students in a group. Members within the focal area (teacher, presenting students) controlled the conversations both structurally and topically. Furthermore, the focal artifact (teacher- or student-designed physical models, worksheets, diagrams) and people in the focal area influenced development of the current topic. Thus, members' roles and levels of participation in classroom conversations were a function of their position relative to the focal area, and this influenced consequent changes in the nature of discourse.

WHOLE-CLASS ACTIVITIES

In whole-class activities, the interactional space was ordered along an axis from focal artifact to audience. Members in the focal area (students or teacher) determined who from the audience should participate in the ongoing conversation. Characteristically, members in the focal area did considerably more of the talking than others. In most situations, someone in the focal area took every second turn. Those in the focal area mediated any participation from the audience. This, then, limited the number of students who could actively contribute. (Here, this

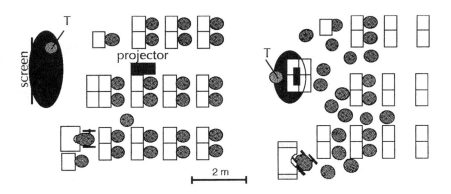

Figure 7.1. In whole-class situations, speaker, central artifact, and representational medium define a space. Whoever is within this space has considerable control over the conversation. The teacher (T) conducts whole-class discussions centered on a projected transparency (*left*) and an artifact placed on his desk (*right*).

Figure 7.2. In this whole-class situation, I conducted a discussion centered on a projected transparency. The orientation was toward the projected image, which could be viewed from anywhere in the classroom without obstruction.

sometimes gave rise to opportunities for students in the audience to engage in other activities.)

The physical arrangement of the audience was in part determined by the nature of the focal artifacts. Transparencies were projected against the screen or some segment of the wall and thus visible from most locations in the classroom. When such a transparency was the sole focal artifact, students often remained in the seats assigned to them in their other subjects (figure 7.1a). When presentations included a physical model of a simple machine, however, visual access was limited; students interested in seeing the artifact therefore pulled up their chairs (figure 7.1b). In both situations, the problematic of the physical arrangement became evident. Because of their distance from the focal area, most students were relegated to audience and their participation was limited to watching and listening.

Teacher-Designed Artifacts

During whole-class conversations around teacher-designed artifacts (figure 7.2), the students' roles as participating audience were clearly defined. For whole-class discussions solely based on drawings projected by an overhead transparency, students often remained in their normal seats assigned for other classes. Here it became clear that participation in conversational activities was higher from students sitting near the front and lower from students sitting further away. The videotapes show my repeated attempts to draw students into participation in the ongoing conversations. I moved closer to the students in the back, selected the next speaker, and then immediately returned to the focal area. (I analyze my

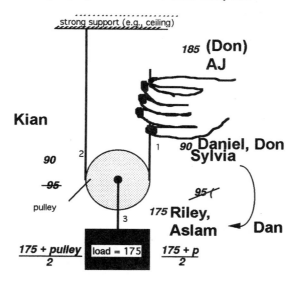

Figure 7.3. During the whole-class discussion, I recorded different students' conjectures about what a scale in different parts of the pulley system (1, 2, or 3) would show as measure. After making the measurement, the whole class discussed the outcome in terms of their previously stated predictions. After class, the transparency was photocopied and then posted on the science bulletin board.

actions as these were available from the videotapes, and therefore to any analyst; I do not describe intentions, which are not available in the tapes. Most actions were neither preplanned nor conscious to me while in the classroom.) There, I gestured or referenced the projected image rather than the actual inscription to elaborate a student utterance. My move from the focal area closer to the audience can be read as inviting students to participate. Sitting toward the back of the audience discouraged participation in the conversations and therefore in the discursive practices.

Whole-class conversations around teacher-designed artifacts—physical devices such as pulleys, levers, block and tackle, and transparencies with diagrams thereof—were associated with my control of the structure and topic of conversations. Although the lessons required neither recitation nor correct answers, the focal artifact(s) provided a strongly mediating structure to the topic of the conversation. I tended to select the next speaker, recapitulated difficult-to-hear contributions by members of the participant audience, summarized longer contributions, and provided links between temporally separated contributions. In the following episode, the conversation was about the forces in a system including a moving pulley (suspended from a ring stand) that carried a load; a sketch of the system (figure 7.3) was projected against the screen behind the focal area (defined by the constellation that included the pulley system and me) similar to the photograph in figure 7.2. The following episode began with my question to the class about whether others agreed with Dan's or with Daniel's answer, which were quite different. There was a pause, which many readers will recognize it as wait time I, the time allowed for students to think about an answer before speaking, and then the selection of a student, Don, who had raised his hand thereby asking for a turn at talk.

01 Teacher: Do you agree with Dan or Daniel? There are two opinions here.
02   (3.0)
03   Don?
04 Don: I agree with David, because the ceiling will take some of that.
05 Teacher: You agree with, so Daniel has some support from Don, other people?
              Jennifer?
06 Jennifer: I agree with Daniel, because, like Don, the ceiling does take some
              weight off.
07 Teacher: Okay, did you hear? Uh um, Jennifer argues that the ceiling takes
              some, and she agrees with David. Mac?

Prior to this episode, two students, Dan and David, had offered their hypotheses and explanations about the tension in one string: the support and the person carry the load. Each hypothesis and the name of the student were recorded on the transparency. Here, I solicited further support for Dan's or David's hypotheses or explanations. First I stated the two options (line 01), and then I asked specific students (those with raised hands) to respond (lines 01, 03, 05). After Don responded, I repeated that he had agreed with Daniel, thereby supporting this answer. I then called for others to respond (again, readers will recognize this as part of wait time II, the time allowed so that a number of students can articulate their answers) and selected Jennifer among those students with raised hands (line 05). She, too, agreed with Daniel. Again, I repeated part of her answer, a move that has the potential to make this part of the answer more salient than other things that had been said as seen in the case of the term "Mercedes star" analyzed in chapter 4. After each student's contribution, I recorded his or her name next to the hypothesis they supported, which was David's in this case (figure 7.3). Don and Jennifer supported the hypothesis that the downward force was balanced by both the support and the person pulling; it was not clear though, whether "some of that" denoted an equal distribution of the load across the two forces F_1 and F_2. This episode was typical for this type of conversation. On the one hand, I tended to encourage students to develop and appropriate a language over and about pulleys beginning with their pre-unit language so that much of the conversation was determined by students' contributions. On the other hand, because I took the responsibility of mediating speaking turns, I ended up with every second turn, though frequently only to select the next speaker.

Parenthetically, I note that in this episode students used the linguistic structure "ANSWER, because . . ." or "I (dis-) agree with X, because . . ." that I had introduced to the school culture in general and to this class in particular. As shown in chapter 6, early on in the unit I had to continuously solicit students to provide an explanation. Such patterns in language do not come about naturally, but need to be continuously encouraged until they become "second nature," a way of patterning one's talking in actions where others see and say different things. Because such patterning is external to the ways of talking students bring to the classroom, whole-class situations constitute resources that have two advantages: similar to interactions in small groups, the teacher has the opportunity to correct individual students and model the speaking patterns, and the number of students who witness the modeling and therefore come to know about the pattern is much larger.

The conversational topic and its evolution were considerably constrained by the focal artifact. Although I could not predict the contents of the conversation, the transparency imposed form on the conversation's evolution. Independent of the various contributions of students, the three forces (F_1, F_2, and F_3 in figure 6.3a, which are indicated by the numbers 1, 2, and 3 in figure 7.3) would almost invariably be talked about. On the other hand, the structure of the drawing constrained the evolution of the conversations. For me, these drawings were resources for asking questions. While the interactions were not in the traditional teacher initiation–student response–teacher evaluation format, the overall sequence of questions was nevertheless scripted to a considerable degree by the needs of the curriculum about simple machines.

Artifacts structured not only the interactional physical space but also the temporal evolution of the activities. They were scenarios for actions and unfolding conversations insofar as they determined topics and structured conversations: students first stated hypotheses, I recorded students' hypotheses, data were collected using the physical device, students were asked to explain any discrepancies between data and hypotheses, and claims were summarized and recorded on the transparency. I prepared the transparencies such that students' conclusions could be recorded and associated with the name of the student who first or most convincingly defended an explanation ("X's Rule"). An example of a transparency was that for the single pulley (figure 7.3); a matching physical model of the situation accompanied it. The labeling of the drawing made it clear that there were three forces to be measured: that on the axle (tension 3) and those in the string on either side of the pulley (tensions 1, 2). As the conversation unfolded, I recorded students' hypotheses and names. In this way, a transparency was an accomplishment of a conversation and provided a trace of the conversation participation; the transparency and the conversation were mutually constitutive. At the same time, the transparency became a record (like a videotaped play) of the conversation that was stored and posted for future reference (only the final claims, not individual hypotheses).

Student-Designed Artifacts

Whole-class conversations about student-designed artifacts shared many similarities with those about teacher-designed artifacts. The students who presented were in the focal area and therefore controlled, to a large extent, the interactions and topics (see, for example, figures 6.7 and 6.8). Other students who wanted to add to the conversation had to wait their turn until selected by one of the presenters. As long as the conversation appeared to be trouble-free, I remained outside the focal area or became part of the audience. My distance and relative position to the focal artifact determined the level of my participation in, and the nature of, classroom discourse. Depending on my position, my role in the conversation differed (figure 7.4). When part of the audience (locations 1, 4, 8), my role in the conversation was similar to that of other students in the audience. I raised my hand and waited to be called upon. Presenting students were in control of who spoke and what the conversation was about. In case of trouble (such as a stopped presentation, difficulties answering a question, or problems with measuring mechanical advantage or starting a machine), I progressively moved closer to the presenters. From intermediate positions (3, 6, 10), I prompted, directed without being called upon, or quickly moved to the focal area.

The following excerpt from the student presentation represented in figure 7.4 occurred while I was standing at position 6, in the wings so to speak. From this position, I entered the conversation only to assist in turn taking (line 14) after the main "trouble maker" in class, Shamir, had challenged the presenting group, which a number of the students had greeted with laughter (line 12). Devin, Jennifer, and Laura presented the prototype of a machine designed to move heavy loads over a considerable distance (see figure 6.1). The episode began when Devin responded to Sylvia's question, about where the group had gotten its design idea, in particular, how the idea of using arborite had emerged.

```
01   Devin:      When Laura brought this in, when sh:– Before we said, you could
                 just move along this, the pulleys (way?) with the ar:⌈::b o r–⌉
02   Jennifer:                                                       ⌊Carla?  ⌋
03   Devin:      Whatever that is.
04   Carla:      As a big machine, why would you need these pulleys and stuff, you
                 could, can just ⌈like–⌉
05   Devin:                      ⌊that ⌋ would make it easier.
06   Carla:      Instead of just turning the chain, and driving it.
07   Kian:       No it has to be hand pulled because, in case the battery runs out or
                 something.
08   Jennifer:   Leanne?
09   Leanne:     If it was a big machine, and it was up high, and it went, how, if it was
                 at this side ((toward pulleys)) how would it be able to go back?
10   Jennifer:   Well, since this is like a little car, we put the car in reverse. Shamir?
11   Devin:      Shamir?
```

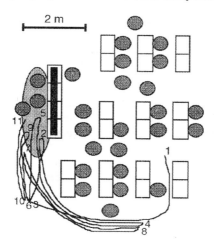

Figure 7.4. During a typical whole-class conversation about a student-designed artifact, I had positioned myself in three distinct locations—directly next to the presenting students, to the side ("in the wings"), and in the back of the classroom. Depending on my location with respect to the focal area, I influenced conversations to different degrees.

12 Shamir: Instead of pulling the string why don't you just drive it? ((Laughter in the class.))
13 Devin: Because it is not (?).
14 Teacher: Okay, did *you* ((Turns to Laura)) want to say something about?
15 Laura: If you want it back, we can always have like a crank here, it might not be as much of a mechanical advantage, and attach a string right here and just crank it back up. (2.0)
16 Shamir: That's ah– ((Raises hand to get selected.))
17 Jennifer: Chantal?
18 Chantal: If you pull it, it might fall at the end.
19 Jennifer: No!
20 Chantal: Let's see!

The transcript shows how the presenting students managed the conversation, taking questions (lines 01, 05, 10, 13) and assigning the next individual to question or comment (lines 02, 08, 10, 17). I had asked students to be responsible for the unfolding conversation and attempted to absent myself from it. This is noticeable in the transcript, where I entered only once (line 14) to encourage Laura to answer more fully to Shamir's challenge than her partner Devin had done (line 13). Laura then articulated a longer response, associated with pointing gestures that showed where and how improvements to her machine could be made, though she also suggested that the resulting mechanical advantage would not be as high.

When in the focal area (positions 2, 5, 7, 9, 11), I helped students setting up, getting started with their presentation, or mediating some conflict that may have arisen with a particular question asked in some aggressive manner. During the following episode, recorded at the beginning of the presentation by Devin, Jennifer, and Laura, I was standing with the three students on center stage (position 2 in figure 7.4). Previously, I had asked students to evolve a set of specifications for deciding the quality of a design. At this moment, I attempted to move the lesson to the next stage, the presentation and the associated discussion and critique session.

21	Teacher:	Talk about your machine, can we sort of hold it up?
22	Jennifer:	Laura, hold it up!
23	Teacher:	Laura, hold the cart. Can you give us sort of an explanation of what the positive aspects are of your machine, and what some of the design aspects–?
24	Jennifer:	Well, we have two pulleys here that are turning to help, to have better slippage, and the ground is really slippery. And that's a two hundred gram weight ((Points to the load)) and we pull here ((Points to the place where she pulls)) and we have a string attached to this (.) nail ((Points to the nail)) so that it would work better, and keep in the middle, and we have railings so that it doesn't slip off.
25	Laura:	And also, the slippery part is called arborite, and it really helps. Plus the wheels on this, and the pulley right here, is like a free-moving pulley–
26	Teacher:	So, can you explain to us, do all these pulleys do the same kind of help?
27	Laura:	It does (.) no, actually, this pulley helps to stabilize and move along and the same with the wheels, and those pulleys are to give it a little more an advantage and slippage, and– (7.0) Devin?

Just as the group finished setting up its prototype design, I asked the three students to talk about the machine and to hold it up so that all students could see it (line 21). The students were slow to start, so I asked the students to explain the positive aspects of their machine and some of its design features (line 23). Jennifer and Laura provided a first exposition, but Laura appeared to stop midsentence after having described one of the pulleys as "free moving." At this point, I asked her to explain to the audience ("us") whether all the pulleys had the same function (line 26)—some were simply changing the direction of the rope within the system.

This episode features me as central participant in the conversation. In my contributions, I asked students, for example, to "explain" or "give us an explanation." Such contributions, therefore, ask for elaboration of the issues at hand, which, when enacted by the students, would allow me to step back, relinquish the control and leave it to the students to talk, question, critique, elaborate, explain, and justify. One may assume that the relationship between position and talk is a typical pattern for teachers. Interestingly, similar patterns were observed when students changed their location and entered the focal area. That is, the relationship may have a much deeper origin in the way human beings orient to others during interactions given different spatial positions that they may take in a room or set of rooms.

With changes in my position, language, content, and language structure also changed. These changes occurred simultaneously at several levels: When I moved to the focal area, I took greater control of the ongoing discourse, and discussion of scientific and technological topics increased. While I was away from this area, the discussion focused on issues about the origin of the idea ("Where did you get the idea?"), the strength of the model ("Can you sit on it?"), or the amount of time it took to complete the project ("How long did it take to make it?"). By moving into the focal area and directing the conversation, I moved the conversation toward those issues that constituted the curriculum content: simple machines, mechanical advantage, forces, or rules for balancing levers. That is, there was a clear shift in conversational topic associated with a shift in position and orientation.

During whole-class conversations around student-designed artifacts, some combinations of social configurations and physical arrangements could shift the focal area, and with it, the course of the ongoing conversation. Some students in the audience came to sit so close to the presenters' table that they could touch it and the artifacts displayed (figure 7.5); they were able to enter the focal area and thereby to wrestle control over the turn talking away from the presenters. In such situations, the focal area changed, mediated by the new social configuration and physical arrangement (figure 7.6). In one situation, Daniel (D), Riley (R), and Shamir (S) sat very close to the artifact presented. When the presenters opened for questions and comments, the three made themselves so present (through interjections, contact with the presented artifact, and continuous questions) that the focal area shifted to include them (A2), while all other students remained in the audience. This is exemplified in the following episode that occurred at the very end of the presentation, most of which the presenters had managed quite well.

28	Riley:	Okay, no one would buy this, because with this surface it would cost so much money, to get a big piece o f ⌈i t – ⌉
29	Jennifer:	⌊Yes, but⌋ they could use ice instead.
31	Shamir:	I said it.
32	Daniel:	But ice ⌈melts.⌉
33	Laura:	⌊It's up⌋ ⌈north.⌉
34	Riley:	⌊But if⌋ it's in the Bahamas?
36	Chris:	⌈But it's up north.⌉
35	Jennifer:	⌊It's not in the Ba⌋hamas.
37	Kian:	It's not, it's up north.

Figure 7.5. Here, some of the students sit so close to the presenters' table that they can touch it and the focal artifacts; they are thereby able to take control of the conversation.

38		((Several others, "Up north."))
39	Mac:	Can't you read?
40		((Several overlapping comments in class away from camera.))
41	Jennifer:	It's not up north!
42	Riley:	But if it's shifted to another company?
43	Teacher:	I hate to be interrupting but we should have at least one more group today.

Riley began by charging that the kind of surface chosen by the three designers would cost too much. As Jennifer and Laura attempted to defend their design choice, Riley and Daniel, both with their hands posed next to the artifact, continued what is perceived as an unfriendly critique. Mac and Chris, also sitting in the front, contributed to the emergent situation. All of a sudden, there were many students talking at the same time so that I literally stepped in, walking onto the stage (figure 7.4, position 11), apologized for the interruption, and suggested having one more group to present their design (line 43). Jennifer selected the next two speakers.

44	Jennifer:	AJ and Sylvia.
45	AJ:	What if a tree fell down, that won't–
46	Aslam:	Oh my god!
47	AJ:	You never had a rainstorm? ((Some other voices in the background.))
48	Jennifer:	Pssh.

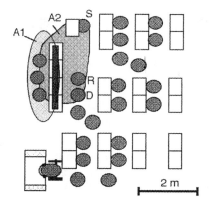

Figure 7.6. When student audiences sat very close to the central artifacts, the focal area could actually shift to include them. In such a situation, these students also became central to the conversation.

49 Teacher: Okay, Aslam, the last comment.
50 Jennifer: No.
51 Teacher: Okay, Sylvia and then Aslam, and then we close up.
52 Sylvia: I think your project is very nice and it has a great advantage, and I think if people just stopped making up little things so it could be not that great, like AJ, they have tree falling down, it's gonna be a storm?
53 Aslam: Okay, you guys fit all those criteria, right? You guys fit all the criteria?
54 Shamir: No.
55 Aslam: Okay, so you did that. You wrote up the best machine in the whole class.
56 Jennifer: Thank you.
57 Chantal: How do you know?
58 Aslam: How do you know? I know they do, because it really looks nice compared to some others that I have seen, so–
59 Shamir: Like yours.
60 Aslam: I mean, so it's really good you guys had a mechanical advantage, next project please. ((He is speaking over several other voices.)) ((Lots of laughter in the class.))
61 Teacher: I think they deserve applause.

The first student called, AJ, proposed another scenario that the designers may not have considered. Aslam uttered one of his frequent "Oh my god!" interjections as a sign of exasperation when one peer or another attempted to argue for argument's sake. AJ continued, but I eventually stepped in to move the conversation into its final stage (line 49) by calling on Aslam. However, Jennifer, who had previously selected Sylvia, contradicted me; I revised my request and asked for Sylvie and Aslam to have the final input. After both had made comments with appeasing function, Shamir, again posing his hand on the presenters' table, responded negatively to the question of whether the group had fulfilled all design criteria. Although Aslam returned with another comment to appease the situation by congratulating the designers, first Chantal and then again Shamir attempted to keep the critique alive, in the latter case turned against Aslam.

This episode shows how the students who were sitting in the front, close enough to the presenter to make physical contact with the table and, on occasion, with the artifacts by touching them, came to have a tremendous part in the conversation, whereas other students, sitting in the back and without the physical contact, were marginalized. I tested the working hypothesis about the relationship between physical arrangements and domination of the discourse in this social configuration (including conversations around teacher-designed artifacts). After several instances, in which students such as Daniel and Shamir shifted the focal area, I moved them to the back of the classroom. Simultaneously, I moved some of the other students (Amanda, Kian, Ian, and Jessica) to the front. My hypotheses were confirmed in that Shamir and Daniel no longer held the stage after these moves in "social engineering." The participation in conversations of the formerly quiet students increased significantly, as indicated by the number and length of their contributions in the transcripts, when they moved near the focal area. This is exemplified in the following episode during a teacher-centered whole-class discussion focusing on the question of which of two carts, A or B, held at the same height but on differently inclined planes, would travel farther. As usual, I had projected a representation of the situation in addition to showing an actual experimental setup (figure 7.7). If there were no frictional forces, both cars should travel the same distance, given that they have the same amount of potential energy.

62   Teacher: The first question is, which goes farther on the plane, I mean on the plane area not on the incline, but on the flat, and explain why? (4.2) Okay, this one is Jennifer, no Sylvia?
63   Sylvia: Well B, because it gets to go down further and faster.
64   Teacher: So you say B, because it goes down farther, and (.) that's why it goes down further (.) Jennifer?
65   Jennifer: I also think B because it has like more of a start, it can go faster, because it's got more like of a start (.) faster start.
66   Teacher: Okay, some others, there where some others, Amanda?
67   Amanda: I think B because it can go up higher, so it will come down faster.
68   Teacher: Okay, it's higher. Now the question is, you said it will be B, the question is (.) why? (1.1) It's the why, what makes this situation (0.9) but gives that situation something to the car that actually goes down farther? Jennifer?
69   Jennifer: I think B, because uh um it's lifted up farther, and if it's lifted up farther it can go down faster and further.

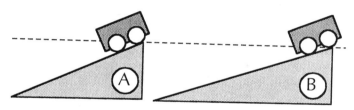

Figure 7.7. An overhead transparency displayed a representation of the experiment that was conducted on the front desk. Students were asked to predict in which configuration, A or B, the cart would travel farther.

70 Teacher: But what does it have, what does the car have that makes it go down farther? (2.2) First Kian.
71 Kian: Well, it has less friction, because when it's lower, it just goes, and it goes just like a little bit, 'cause it didn't have very much far. It's got le– less friction.
72 Teacher: So you got something there. (1.2) Aslam?
73 Aslam: I think B, because the gravity pulls it down to the bottom.
74 Teacher: Okay, B, because gravity is pulling it down, that is what everyone says. And you say (.) there is something else. Um. ((Nods toward Ian.)) Go ahead, Ian.
75 Ian: I'd say B, because when it goes down, it goes the same distance as how high it is.
76 Teacher: Okay, so you say, what is the height, what does that height give you, give that car? ((Points toward Jennifer.))
77 Jennifer: It has wheels so that it can go down faster.

This whole-class conversation included Amanda, Ian, and Kian, three students identified as learning disabled by their school, who had never spoken up when I arrived in the classroom. At that time, they were sitting toward the back of the classroom. Now that they were sitting up front, they had begun to raise their hands, indicating the wish to contribute. They were selected as next speakers and were attributed turns at talk that they did not have previously. Concomitant with these changes, we sometimes observed dramatic changes in the competencies of their linguistic and material practices, especially for the special needs students in the class. I also observed that Leanne, a student who was successful in traditionally taught classes, and Maryam both decreased their participation in the whole-class discussions as they moved to the back. There, they engaged in conversations unrelated to science and other disruptive behavior. Readers will note again how, in this episode, students used the structural pattern of justification, "I think X, because . . ." or, equivalently, "It has X so that . . ." that I had consistently encouraged to emerge.

The social configuration and physical arrangements not only determined the level of control over the conversation but also its topic. During whole-class student-centered conversations, my contributions decreased in number. The presenters selected the next speaker and, sometimes, spontaneous audience-centered conversations began. However, while students did ask questions or made comments—e.g., about how to improve a design, what the mechanical advantage was, which design feature it came from, or how it could be improved by decreasing the friction—they often did not explore those issues that science teachers normally value. In such cases, I asked questions or made comments to focus on issues important within an orientation that scientists or engineers would take in the particular instance.

In whole-class, student-directed conversations, the focal artifact mediated the topic and structure of conversations. When students presented, they had the artifact available as a resource for their presentation. But the focal artifact did not determine the structure of whole-class conversations in the same way as during teacher-directed situations. In student-directed conversations, there was no specific order to either presentation or questions: the artifact constituted a scenario for improvisation. In the following exchange from an earlier episode, Jennifer, Laura, and Devin presented their second machine, which was intended to haul heavy loads over a certain distance. (The physical arrangement of the class at that time is presented in figure 7.4.)

24   Jennifer: Well, we have two pulleys here that are turning to help, to have better slippage, and the ground is really slippery. And that's a two hundred gram weight ((Points to the load)) and we pull here ((Points to the place where she pulls.)) and we have a string attached to this (.) nail ((Points to the nail)) so that it would work better, and keep in the middle, and we have railings so that it doesn't slip off.

25   Laura: And also, the slippery part is called arborite, and it really helps. Plus the wheels on this, and the pulley right here, is like a free-moving pulley–

26   Teacher: So, can you explain to us, do all these pulleys do the same kind of help?

27   Laura: It does (.) no, actually, this pulley helps to stabilize and move along and the same with the wheels, and those pulleys are to give it a little more an advantage and slippage, and– (7.0) Devin?

Here, Jennifer and Laura began talking about the features of the project that they considered important: low friction (slippage, arborite, wheels, pulleys), a 200-gram load, a "free-moving pulley," and features to stabilize the vehicle. These features arise, in part, from the class's jointly elaborated evaluation criteria that the model should lift a load greater than 100 grams, move the load more than 200 centimeters, and have a mechanical advantage greater than one. As such, the student-built model and the posted evaluation criteria were resources for their presentation. The students had correctly identified the sources of friction, pulleys that increased the mechanical advantage, and the pulleys that only changed the direction of the forces. They also correctly measured load and effort, and correctly calculated the mechanical advantage.

After the initial presentation, the focal artifact—here Laura, Jennifer, and Devin's machine—structured and provided an orientation for the audiences' questions and critical comments. For example, student-designed artifacts led to contingent queries. In the following episode, Carla and Leanne asked the presenters to defend specific design choices. At issue were problems that could arise during the process of scaling up from the model to real applications. We return to an earlier episode:

```
04  Carla:     As a big machine, why would you need these pulleys and stuff, you
               could, can just ⌈like–  ⌉
05  Devin:                    ⌊ that ⌋ would make it easier.
06  Carla:     Instead of just turning the chain, and driving it.
07  Kian:      No it has to be hand pulled because, in case the battery runs out or
               something.
08  Jennifer:  Leanne?
09  Leanne:    If it was a big machine, and it was up high, and it went, how, if it was
               at this side ((toward pulleys)) how would it be able to go back?
10  Jennifer:  Well, since this is like a little car, we put the car in reverse. Shamir?
```

In these conversations, the physical models were resources for talk and action. That is, the conversations were not about just any topic related to simple machines, but about the particular machines before the children. Here, Carla (turns 04, 06) and Leanne's (turn 09) critique focused on the "pulleys and stuff" that were part of *this* machine and about how *this* machine could be scaled up to real-world requirements. Thus, the particular form and components of a machine together mediated what presenters might address in their presentations and what audience members might address in their questions. In this sense, the physical models were resources for sustaining conversations about specific topics. Thus, the artifacts were resources that (in a weak sense) scripted the conversations of the children. Therefore, because of the wide differences, the physical models constituted different scenarios that gave rise to different topical orientations of the whole-class conversations. Variations in students' designs provided variation in contexts that gave rise to different concerns voiced in the presentations and conversations. All artifacts, however, allowed members to participate in talk about machines and to raise their concerns about aspects of the specific machine presented—concerns relevant for one machine were irrelevant in the context of another.

The presented artifact also structured my questions. I used the model as a resource for questions that would encourage students to talk about the different types of pulleys they used (decreasing effort, changing direction). Questions and students' responses were then opportunities to link the present discussion with past discussions about simple machines—in this case, the pulley—and thereby invoke the correct physics concepts. Sometimes, I made this link explicit by showing transparencies from past discussions. Laura's explanation included two references to past discussions, "free-moving pulley" and "slippage," which were aspects of the developing language about simple machines. Here, "slippage" is a term from the children's vernacular that later was replaced by the scientifically equivalent but opposite "friction." We have seen in the previous chapter that similar transitions occurred for other vernacular expressions such as from "advantage" and "disadvantage" to "mechanical advantage" with an associated use of the correct measurement and calculation practices. In another situation, and by making reference to the same prior conversation, I asked students to compare the pulleys in Chris, Daniel, and Leanne's "crane" with those from an earlier class discussion.

In summary, although whole-class conversations were set up to elicit students' active use of language, only a limited number of students could participate actively by contributing to the conversations. There is much evidence in my data of students in the audience who appeared frustrated because they were not selected as next speakers; there were many hands raised so that it took considerable time to select everyone. Depending on the length of wait, some students abandoned their attempts to contribute; a few held out as long as it took to get their turn. Some students (especially those most removed from the focal area) stopped following the conversation and engaged in other activities. There were also complaints that it took too long to ask everyone and that we should simply get on with the lessons.

SMALL-GROUP ACTIVITIES

Small-group activities were organized by (a) teacher-prepared models of machines with associated instructions for investigations or worksheets requesting students to describe and explain a physical situation previously discussed in a whole-class discussion or (b) students' design and construction activities. In these situations, there were as many focal areas as there were groups. The focal areas were defined by physical arrangements of artifacts and members' locations. During these small-group activities, participation in linguistic and material practices was high; as evidenced in our video recordings and the fieldnotes collected, all students contributed in their groups to the ongoing conversations, manipulation of materials, and tool use. That is, all students engaged in material and linguistic practices of the classroom. Each student in the self-selected group had physical access to the artifacts—thus opportunities to manipulate the artifacts, participate in related activities, contribute to the organization of the activity, and coparticipate in orienting and talking by drawing on various resources in the environment.

Small-Group Activities with Teacher-Designed Artifacts

Figure 7.8 shows the situation for two groups during the class-I-lever investigation. In this situation, the activities were centrally organized around the artifact. After selecting their partners, students usually remained at the site they had designated for doing the activity. This site determined the focal area in which the small group of actors played out the activity. Although the groups were in close proximity, the activities were independent. Anyone who wanted to engage one or all of the students in a group had to physically enter their focal area. When Shamir (S) wanted the neighboring group (comprised of Aslam, Bella, and Leanne) to answer some questions, he had to enter their focal area by turning around and touching Leanne's desk. In a similar way, I interacted with different groups upon entering their focal area, but remained an observer in other situations where I was out of this area.

The artifact also determined preferred orientations of the interactional space. For example, Aslam (A) and Bella (B), who were to operate the lever, set it up closely and in front of themselves. When Leanne (L) wanted to operate the lever, she got up, walked around the desks, and moved next to Bella. Aslam turned the lever, so that he didn't have to look at it from the side. He also turned the worksheet in front of Leanne, permitting him to engage with her in a negotiation as to the nature of the task. Bella, however, could not read the instructions from her position and participated only as operator of the lever in spite of her general orientation to academic and task achievement.

Artifacts in the focal area not only constrained students' participation in

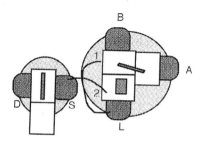

Figure 7.8. Aslam (A), Bella (B), and Leanne (L) sit around three individual desks that they had pushed together for this collective task. They have in front of them a simple equal arm balance, many nuts, and worksheets. Shamir, who works on the next desk, is so close to their focal area that his simple hand movement onto their desks disrupts them.

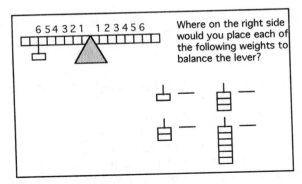

Figure 7.9. Aslam, Bella, and Leanne have in front of them a simple equal arm balance, many nuts, and the worksheet partially displayed here. Their task is to find answers and subsequently describe a pattern that allows them to predict where to put a particular number of nuts to balance the beam.

conversations as a function of their orientation but also determined discourse topics. For example, worksheets laid out scenarios for students' interactions over and about some model of a simple machine. Figure 7.9 illustrates a part of the worksheet titled "Is there a pattern?" that accompanied a model of a class I lever. The following episode highlights the scenario and resource functions of the artifacts that I had designed for this student-centered task.

01 Leanne: First you put this one on the six. ((She points to the single nut.))
02 Aslam: Oh!
03 Leanne: No, we only need one, put it on the six. ((Bella puts on some
             weights.)) (7.3) ((Bella puts more weights on the balance; Aslam and
             Leanne watch.)) That's balanced, right? Hold on. Yes it is.
04 Bella: So what do we do?
05 Leanne: Hold on, it's balanced, right?
06 Aslam: Look, wait a second. ((He looks at the sheet.)) It says– There's four
             questions!
07 Leanne: Yeah, this is six, right. (3.0) Okay, now, put, put the two, put another
             one on there (.) and put another one, okay, no, we only need two (.)
             and–

Here, the worksheet structured the interaction in that it served as a scenario. Leanne read the inscription in figure 7.9 as instructions to balance the lever with one nut on the left using first one nut on the right (line 01), then two metal nuts (line 07). In this way, they proceeded to answer all twelve questions. Aslam also used the sheet as a resource for understanding the task: "there's four questions" (line 06). His statement was a clear answer to Bella's question, "What do we do?" The inscription's template form further enhanced its function as a scenario, for the blank spaces "requested" information. Here, the conversation contains few scientific terms and rules; students' talk shows a concern for getting the activity completed in an appropriate manner. Their orientation was toward completing the task, and their talk in action pertained to this orientation. This changed when students engaged in searching for patterns and in summarizing their results, that is, when they engaged in stating observation categoricals based on the simple observation sentences noted on their sheets. The blanks following the label "Our pattern is" invited students in a similar way to make sense of the data they collected. Thus, students were invited to fill the blanks: The sheets acted as scenarios for courses of actions that would lead to the filling of the blanks. The transcripts illustrate that in these situations, students' talk was more about turning instructions into action rather than describing and explaining the phenomena under investigation.

Small-Group Activities with Student-Designed Artifacts

During design activities, artifacts and social configurations gave rise to varying physical arrangements within groups and with the classroom as a whole. During artifact design, the entire classroom became a design studio. There were focal areas for individual groups, but these frequently moved according to the task at hand. A casual observer to the classroom would see that there were no fixed locations where students worked, though they were loosely associated with their seats. But, because they worked in groups with peers not necessarily their usual seat neighbors, the physical arrangements had little to do with the ordinary classroom set up. The classroom re-created a workshop, with students working where they had the required space and tools. Groups articulated their plans when others inquired, allowed them access to their materials, tools, and skills in doing particular things.

The specific setup of the classroom, with two large and stable tables for doing heavy-duty work such as sawing, increased the amount students traveled and interacted with others. Although groups sometimes chose their usual seats as work sites, the designation of the two special heavy-duty work sites shifted students' work locations. There was a large table mounted with protecting particleboard for cutting, drilling, and sawing (figure 7.10); a smaller worktable designated for using the glue gun (figure 7.11); and a sink for jobs involving water (for locations, see figure 7.12). Movement throughout the classroom became necessary when students sought additional materials or tool support from other students. Figure 7.12 illustrates the high degree of movement for two groups throughout the classroom on a typical construction day.

Dan and Don, two sixth-grade boys, began their work at their usual desks (A_a). As part of their activities, they repeatedly left their workstation to get supplies from their boxes (A_4), use the glue gun (A_8), and saw some wood (A_2); to

Figure 7.10. Around the table with a protective layer, where all heavy-duty jobs had to be done, there were always large numbers of students, which provided many opportunities for engaging in conversation with others.

evaluate their design midway through the construction, they went on forays to get a spring scale for determining mechanical advantage (A_5) and a measuring tape (A_3). Finally, they left their construction site on four occasions to observe other projects or talk with other students (twice each to A_1 and A_6). Later, to be closer to their supplies and the glue gun, they shifted their construction site to A_b. However, moving through the classroom was not the only opportunity to communicate with other students. During the fifty-minute period, eleven other students (seven of whom were seventh-grade students) came to see Dan and Don to request tools or materials (ten occasions), to chat, or to watch (four occasions).

01 Don: Oh Dan, use a ruler okay? ((Dan bends down to find his carpenter's pencil.))
02 Leanne: Do you have a screwdriver?
03 Don: *No!*
04 Leanne: Yeah, yeah, yeah! Please?!
05 Chris: Can we have a hammer? ((Don hands Leanne the screwdriver.))

06   Don: Okay? No *wait, wait, wait!* Okay, how big do we want to make them?

In this way, the two boys were constantly barraged with requests, which they sometimes rejected and at other times fulfilled. At the same time, when they acceded to a request, they also contributed to the repartition of collective resources and skills. Similarly, two seventh-grade girls, Leanne and Chantal, moved about and shifted their focal area to achieve different goals (locations B).

Artifacts had an effect on topic content and structure even if they only emerged from, and were the results of, students' interactions. Conversations were local; the few times when someone tried to make an announcement to the entire class, it was obvious that not all students attended to the announcements. That is, teacher control of communication was low in this situation. In earlier discussed configurations, the interactions followed (to different degrees) scenarios constituted by inscriptions and physical models. The situation changed during the design and construction of models. Here, students' actions were the least determined: students had to script their future actions on their own, and decide what their courses of actions should be. Much student conversation was about planning and converting designs into models, and only a minor part was devoted to "conceptual" talk (using scientific concept words). Prior to the following episode, Dan and Don had decided to test their model as it was, even before completion, and even before installing the pulleys central to their design. (At that

Figure 7.11. The glue station attracted many students. Here, they interacted with others about designs and encountered different ways of dealing with problems.

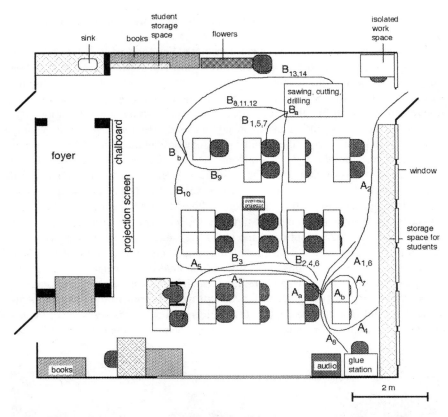

Figure 7.12. During the design and prototype construction tasks, students moved considerably around the classroom to access various resources, including the station for sawing and drilling. Locations such as the glue gun station or the table for cutting, sawing, and drilling gave rise to many student–student interactions.

time, the two were seated at A_a in figure 7.12.) Don had suggested testing to see if their model already provided a mechanical advantage ("what we should do is a twenty-five-gram mass and then just get a piece of string and right now just see if it is a mechanical advantage"). For a long stretch, neither Dan nor Don spoke (line 07). Then they began the test. We return to an earlier episode.

07   (38) ((Dan ties a hook to the wooden block. Don adjusts the shoe-
            lace.))
08 Don: We shouldn't use shoelaces!
09 Dan: Well we're just measuring it. ((Attaches the wooden block to the
            shoelace. It stretches down to the ground.))

10 Don: °Tie a knot. Yeah. And then like, yeah, whatever.° (1.1) Okay, now we need the scale again. (1.0) Move that up. ((Both try to bring the lower part of shoelace up and raise the block off the ground.))
11 Dan: Well there's going to be pulleys.
12 Don: We won't know, but it can't be dragging against the ground. (1.2) ((Both try to bring block off the ground.))
13 Dan: I know, we're just using it to see.

Although much of the students' conversation during design and construction was devoted to establishing plans and converting them into actions, their discourse included some concerns for conceptual issues (e.g., forces, mechanical advantage, and friction). In the present case, although Dan and Don did not utter the word "friction," their concerns for it were implicit in their exchange. In this test, they identified three problematic issues that decreased the mechanical advantage, all related to friction. First, they used a shoelace instead of the string they had planned and ultimately used (line 08); second, at present, they only used popsicle sticks to support and guide the string rather than the planned pulleys (line 11); finally, the test load (a piece of wood) dragged on the ground (line 12). At the end of this segment, Dan reasserted that this was merely a test. This initial test revealed a mechanical advantage of about 0.3, but Dan's description that they were "just using it to see" suggests that they envisioned an improvement of the mechanical advantage. In the end, they achieved a mechanical advantage of MA = 5.

In summary, table 7.1 provides an overview of the opportunities and constraints arising from the different social configurations and physical arrange-

Table 7.1. Opportunities and constraints arising from task structures

	Whole Class		Small Group	
	Teacher Artifact	Student Artifact	Teacher Artifact	Student Artifact
Emphasis on students'				
- everyday talk	moderate	high	moderate	high
- own pace	low	moderate	moderate	high
- personal interest	low	high	moderate	high
- scientific concepts	high	moderate	moderate	low
Teacher control	high	moderate	moderate	low
Teacher monitoring of individual understanding	moderate	moderate	high	high
Hands-on	almost none	almost none	high	high
Student talk	low	low	high	high
Distance to artifact	large	large	small	small
Gestures	almost none	almost none	many	many

ments. Small-group activities allowed all students to participate in the material and discursive practices. At the same time, because of decreased teacher control, students' conversations often did not include the scientifically more significant aspects of the curriculum. Whereas student-centered activities around teacher-designed artifacts controlled the activities and to a small degree the conversational topics, student–centered activities around student-designed artifacts allowed the greatest deviations from scientifically correct language. The important functions of the transparencies and instructions became apparent when they were compared with the models. The latter lack both explicit instructions and template function. In addition, the drawn transparencies highlighted specific features that are of importance to scientific considerations but may be hidden in the actual model. Furthermore, when students presented the models they constructed, others focused more on external aspects rather than those important in scientists' discourses. Thus, students frequently asked questions such as "Where did you get the idea to make that?" or "Where is your advantage?" rather than asking the almost standard scientific question, "What [or how large] is your mechanical advantage?")

ARTIFACTS AS MEDIATIONAL TOOLS

Chapter 1 showed that gestures, pointing, and nonverbal communication are important attributes of orienting in activity. In the previous section, artifacts played important roles in structuring participation according to members' relative positions with respect to focal artifacts and in structuring discourse content and developing conversational topics. In this section, I provide answers to the question, "To what degree does the setting support participants' nonverbal communication, gesturing, and pointing?" Here, the notion of mediational tool plays an important role. Mediational tools are those that support and facilitate conversations. They do so because they afford gestures, pointing, and indexical expressions so that only part of what a person says is expressed in propositional form. (Indexical expressions are words such as "this," "there," and "here," which require additional information so that the listener or reader knows what the referent of the utterance is.) Access to drawings or models provided opportunities for student talk to contain increased levels of indexical expressions, gestures, and pointing; they could draw on the affordances of the artifacts as mediational tools. For example, a student might not know or may have forgotten that "fulcrum" designates the point around which a lever turns; when the student talked in the presence of a lever, however, he or she could simply point to that part of the lever and continue in their argument. Furthermore, *because* they could gesture or point to particular features and processes of their simple machines when they were in close proximity, utterances that might have been ambiguous became less equivocal. Thus, close proximity to artifacts mediated conversations in that students could maintain conversations before they fully understood the subject matter and avoid potential ambiguities by grounding their talk in less equivocal, local references. Others, who did not have access to the artifact (e.g., drawing or model) had to explicate the situation they were describing in propositional form, which is much more cumbersome. In this case, the artifacts were resources and mediational tools to a much lesser extent (or not at all).

Physical arrangements of speakers relative to focal artifacts facilitated or constrained communication. During whole-class conversations about teacher-designed artifacts, I had access to diagrams that afforded indexical talk. Videotapes and transcripts clearly illustrate my use of this access. The following transcript of teacher talk recorded during the whole-class conversation over and about the projected drawing of a pulley can be understood only with additional visual information. During this conversation, the corresponding pulley setup was also available. However, students and I talked to the drawing rather than its physical equivalent. (Numbers in square brackets refer to the locations of forces as marked in the figure.)

> If we pull here [1] and measure, here [3] we have load and here [1] is my effort, I have to pull here [1]. How much do I have to pull just to make it stand here [3]?
>   This [3] weighs 175, this [3] is pulling down, how hard do I have to pull here [1] (.) just to make it stand here [3]?

In this excerpt, "here" refers to different locations on the drawing. Pointing to these locations on the drawing allowed me to reduce the specification of locality to "this" and "here." For those who listened to the talk and perceptually followed the pointers, the referent of "this" and "here" in each case was unambiguous. At the same time, because of their physical distance, few students had the same opportunity. They had to describe each location in some way understandable to the audience: "where you're pulling," "the ceiling," "the roof," "where you pull up," "if the pulley was on the ground," "the part that is attached to the ground"; one student stated, "I agree with Dave, the *top* Dave," to refer to the ideas of that person recorded further up on the acetate, which I would have been able to designate simply by pointing to the name. In a similar way, proximity to the physical devices such as a block and tackle afforded gestures and pointing, whereas distance forced speakers to provide explicit descriptions of things, properties, locations, actions, and so forth.

When speakers approached focal artifacts and thereby changed physical arrangements, changes in conversations became apparent. For example, when students suggested modifications to design drawings on the chalkboard, their descriptions no longer sufficed. They had to enter the focal area to change the

drawings themselves, that is, to indicate the operation or modification they
wanted to propose by pointing directly to the appropriate spot on the transparency or projected image.

In the episode below, we return to a conversation wherein I introduced pulleys to the students (figure 7.3). I had asked students for predictions and explanations for the reading of the scales when the load was, as previously measured,
a 100-gram mass. Shamir began to answer, but, as if aware of the limitations of
talk alone, walked up to the overhead projector and pointed to the image.

01 Shamir: If the pulley wasn't tied to the string, you see if it was like this
                  ((Walks up to the projected image and points)) and then this string
                  came down under then–
02 Teacher: But I want to test it like this? Aslam?
03 Aslam: If the thing was attached to the ceiling on the overhead there, if you
                  turned it all around, and the part that is attached is on the ground,
                  then it is harder to pull it up than to pull it down, so it'll be harder,
                  like it will be a better support if it is stuck to the ground. (0.8)
04 Teacher: Which one, you mean that pulley?
05 Aslam: Like if you turn that around. ((Approaches projector and turns trans-
                  parency around.)) And see that ((Points to pulley)) is on the ground,
                  and see the support is on the ground already, so that would be a bet-
                  ter, so you could pull down so that would be better, you could pull
                  down. ((Gestures pulling.))

Shamir proposed to change the setup, but at that moment, I wanted to have
the pulley tested in the configuration at hand (line 03). I called on Aslam, who
produced a longer response. However, it was difficult to understand what he
said, because he used so many indexical and generic terms ("it," "the thing,"
"there"). Pointing to one of the pulleys, I asked whether he was talking about it.
Like Shamir, Aslam got up and walked to the overhead projector; then he turned
the transparency around and, pointing, began his explanation.

Here, both students found that they could explain better by referring directly
to the drawing than by making such references explicit in the talk itself. Rather
than, as many other students, referring to "the string you're pulling at" or "the
string that is attached to the ceiling," Shamir pointed to the string he was talking
about and uttered "if *this* string came down." In the same way, Aslam's initial
explanation (line 03) was quite difficult to understand. Aslam approached the
projector and with a single movement turned the transparency upside down.
Now, it was apparent what aspect of the drawing he described as "ground," what
he wanted to articulate by "support," and where he suggested pulling. The new
configuration changed the nature of Aslam's contribution to the discussion.
While his utterances in line 03 had been incomprehensible to students and
teacher alike—he did not elaborate his description and was too far away to reference the objects of his talk through pointing or gesture—his talk was immedi-

ately elaborated through indexing in line 05. Here, talk and object of talk mutually elaborated each other.

The difficulties in communicating when speakers had no access to the representational device also existed when students talked to students—the problem of understanding was therefore not just mine. For example, following the tug-of-war (chapter 1), I discussed with the students alternative uses of the block and tackle. Early in the discussion, I had drawn some of the configurations on the chalkboard as instructed by students. However, Shamir talked about a configuration that I could not understand. Don shouted out that he understood what Shamir attempted to say, and I asked him to come to the chalkboard and draw the configuration for the still-seated Shamir (line 09).

```
06   Shamir:   Move the banister on the other side.
07   Don:      I know what he means.
08             (3.0)
09   Teacher:  Do you know what he means? ((Handing him the chalk.))
10   Don:      Well, okay, if you had the (.) banister thing, the railing goes like that
                ⌈then ⌉ the string and then there would be a pulley
11   Teacher:  ⌊Yeah.⌋
12             (1.5)
13   Don:       Am I doing this right to you?
14   Shamir:   Yeah.
15   Don:      And then this *((figure 7.13a)) would, we don't *((figure 7.13b))
               think about that.
```

Even such simple instructions as "move the banister on the other side" (line 06) were becoming difficult to understand. Don had already drawn the first three elements of the pulley system, and correctly so, as Shamir's feedback indicated (line 14), when he first waved at Shamir with his right hand (line 15) and then bent down as if ready to place the chalk in the tray (figure 7.13c). In the speaking pause, he then completely turned around stretching out his arm, tendering the chalk in Shamir's direction (figure 7.13d). Don evidently wanted Shamir to draw the configuration he proposed. Shamir got up and walked toward the chalkboard despite my earlier indications to stay in his seat, and I no longer prevented him from doing so. The communication simply had become too difficult, verbal expressions alone were just too cumbersome to move the discussion along.

The social configuration and physical arrangements of small-group work—particularly with resources such as drawings, instructions, tools, and other artifacts—afford forms of communication not available to many students in the whole-class situation. Compared to the class discussions, students in small groups used an increased amount of pointing and gesturing to explain their ideas or to remediate trouble when different understandings surfaced. In the following example, we return to an earlier situation (figure 7.12, A_a). Dan and Don had

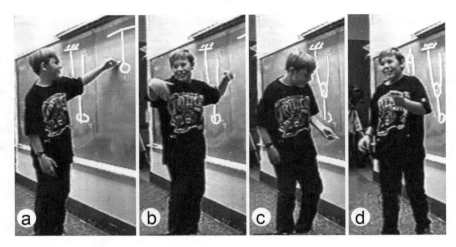

Figure 7.13. Don initially said he knew the pulley configuration that Shamir was talking about and had begun to draw it (left). But then, he simply waved to Shamir, thereby inviting him to walk up to the chalkboard and draw his pulley configuration.

just begun the design of their second machine; their model was to be able to transport a load of 100 grams or more over a distance of at least two meters. Initially, there were no drawings, and Dan articulated an idea by using his ruler and his gestures as resources to elaborate his talk—his talk and resources together constituted the idea for the first time in a public forum. The ruler stood for the lever and the pivoting movement he described, his fist for the load that was moved onto the lever, and the direction of his fist's movement indicated where the pulley was to be. Based on their initial utterances, Dan began to prepare a drawing.

16 Dan: See Don, like this, you pull it up and this goes up– ((Points to his
             drawing, then moves his finger along some lines to the top of the
             sheet.))
17 Don: =I know.
18 Dan: and then the truck goes underneath, and then down ((Gestures and
             points to his drawing)) a truck moving underneath the lever and then
             we can have this ((Gestures something falling down and into his
             truck)) really big ((Spreads his arms as much as he can)) like 200 me-
             ters ((Stretches, reaches high up to indicate tallness)) this high. ((Gets
             up and gestures about five feet.))

In this episode, Don used the existing drawing as a resource in addition to gestures in the air, which were intended to communicate the actual size of their project. Here, pointing, gesturing, and talking against the background of drawing and previous conversation were integrated to constitute designing and communicating designs. This situation differed in significant ways from whole-class conversations where the pointing and gesturing of members in the audience were disconnected from the artifacts. Because of the physical distance that rendered referents ambiguous, pointing and gesturing could not be used to elaborate the meaning of the artifact (or parts of it), and the artifact did not elaborate the speaker's movements. However, communication over and about artifacts was not necessarily trouble-free. Students sometimes realized that what they said was understood in a different way. When alternate understandings did become apparent, the nature of physical arrangements allowed them to use contextually available resources to remediate their different understandings. Using gestures, elaborating movements by describing the appropriate actions (e.g., "cut it"), or displaying facial expressions and making other noises were resources that brought about mutual understanding.

Focal artifacts had important structuring roles in interactions. For one, they constituted scenarios for the various activity structures. That is, the artifacts ordered the activities in terms of the topic, physical space, and temporal development. The nature of the artifacts as scenarios was clearly evident for those that I had designed. Here, the artifact was designed to pose only those problems that students were to engage with so that they functioned as scenarios for human–human interactions. I purposefully designed artifacts to guide myself in raising specific questions and to offer for discussion only those elements of physical situations that were important for developing suitable discourses. Artifacts, brought about by particular actions, self-reflexively structured these actions, that is, artifacts structured events. However, these scenarios functioned like other plans of action in that they largely underdetermined what happened. This was most apparent in the different conversations and actions that developed when several small groups used the "same" instructions. Thus, whereas artifacts have structuring effects on conversations, they cannot constrain content development enough to guarantee that students will talk standard science in small-group situations.

Artifacts had mediational and supportive functions to conversations, as these had been in the context of the computer-based Newtonian microworlds (see chapters 1, 2, and 5). Individuals who had access to an artifact pointed, gestured, and physically manipulated the artifact to elaborate their talk. In this way, they expressed what was difficult or too lengthy by means of verbal description alone. For transparencies, the situation was somewhat different. Because of their public visibility, transparencies afforded, at least partially, the coordination of conversation over distance—even in the absence of direct physical access. My transparencies functioned as context support systems. However, because physical arrangements limited access for students, transparencies did not provide the same conversational support to students as they did to me. For some aspects of the conversation, visual access alone was not enough. In these episodes, some students spontaneously sought access to the inscription to remediate the complexity of situation descriptions associated with verbal expressions alone (other students opted out of the discussion).

ACTIVITY STRUCTURES AND WAYS OF TALKING

In chapter 6, I described the growing competencies students exhibited from pretest to posttest. The assessments also revealed considerable variations in performance across assessment settings for individual students. These learning outcomes cannot be understood independently of the instructional setting in which students learned. However, not all activity structures afforded students' participation in conversations and learning in the same way and to the same extent. There were mediating effects due to the interaction of focal artifacts, social configurations, and physical arrangements of members and artifacts. Mediating effects of these interactions were particularly apparent in relation to students' discursive practices. Thus, what, how, and the extent to which individual students participated in and developed standard ways of talking engineering and physics was mediated by the three elements of the setting with which we are concerned here: artifacts, social configurations, and physical arrangements.

The four activity structures researched were characterized by the origin of the focal artifact (teacher designed, student designed) and the social configuration (whole class, small group); these activity structures, different in the orientations and intentions that they ask of students, mediated degrees of participation and language content and structure. In whole-class conversations around teacher-designed artifacts, I controlled the conversation and turn taking. Because I had access to the artifact, I could use indexical expressions. I mediated students' access to the conversation; their access to the focal artifact was limited so that they had to articulate and elaborate their reference to specific parts of the artifact in verbal form. In whole-class conversations about student-designed artifacts, the communicative patterns were similar but now the presenting students were largely in control. The audience's participation in the conversation and access to the artifacts were still limited.

In small-group activities, the situation changed. Now all students had access to the artifacts and could actively participate in material and discursive practices. The artifact only partially mediated the development of conversations around teacher-designed artifacts. In design conversations, students prepared their own scenarios and controlled their discussions and activities.

It would be naive to assume that students will spontaneously engage in or develop the linguistic and material practices characteristic of some formal discipline—the case studies in chapters 2 and 3 provide ample evidence for this contention. The activity structures presented here provide students with a range of opportunities to develop and practice new ways of articulating and talking about simple machines. Depending on the designer of the conversation's focal artifact, the issues raised included physics concepts or highlighted mainly students' interests (not necessarily the same as the teacher's). Activity structures allowed students to participate in ongoing conversations according to their preferences and confidence. But each of these activity structures related focal artifacts, social configurations, and physical arrangements in different ways and therefore afforded something particular to students' learning so that we recommend a balance of all activity structures.

First, small-group conversations about student-designed artifacts (which started each cycle through the four activity structures) allowed students to begin instruction with their root language, on topics of their interest, and mostly at their own pace and to communicate as much as they wanted with their partners and other groups in the community. Their proximity (inherent in the physical arrangements) provided opportunities for articulating sense as students oriented to the artifacts. However, other than through initial constraints on the artifacts to be produced, there was little guarantee that conversations would focus on scientific concepts specified in the curriculum. Small-group conversations over teacher-designed artifacts provided similar opportunities to conversations that arise from proximity in the physical arrangement, but conversational topics were constrained by the scientific concerns embedded in the artifacts. Whole-class conversations about student-designed artifacts focused again on students' concerns and interests, but often included scientific concerns when they addressed my questions. Whole-class conversations around teacher-designed artifacts provided the greatest control in terms of topic development and content and form of argument, but also provided the least amount of time per student to talk. Whole-class activities limited contributions from the student-audience and were dominated by those in the focal area. Having the opportunity to work in a mixture of the four activity structures, students could design simple machines, articulate salient objects and events, and still have the opportunity to interact with the teacher.

DESIGNING FOR CHANGING WAYS OF TALKING

Artifacts, social configurations, and physical arrangements of class members' relative position and orientation to one another and to focal artifacts had differential effects on the ways of talking and what participants talked about. My ethnographic research suggests that there was a link between the levels to which individual students could engage (when they wanted to) and their evolution of a suitable language. Science curriculum planners can learn from computer systems designers about changing material and discursive practices. Systems which force users to radically change their ways of doing things (including their ways of talking) are often doomed to fail, while those designs that draw on the users' ways of doing, articulating, and talking about things prior to the new system are particularly successful. This point is convincingly illustrated by the success of the Xerox-Macintosh interface which uses icons based on traditional office practices: desktop, trash cans, file folders, paper stacks, and documents. The artifacts allowed office personnel to move from their precomputer workplace language to the workplace language of computer-enhanced workplaces. They continued to say "put the memo in the project folder," "put this file in the trash can," or "leave the file on the desktop" rather than having to change to "copy the file into the project directory" or "delete the file" or having no equivalent. Each of these required changes in the way office workers were telling what to do and how to do it might appear minor, but as whole they demanded a change in one's life-world, which the workers were not willing to or could not easily make, as the evident success of the visual interface and its copycats suggests.

During whole-class conversations, the levels of individual participation from those in the audience were lower than in small-group work, and the direct access to artifacts was more limited, thereby reducing the opportunities those artifacts provided to mediate the actions of students and teacher. On the other hand, the possibilities for controlling the creation of and changes in language were high in whole-class conversations, as were my opportunities for providing feedback. During small-group conversations, the possibilities for individual participation were high, as were opportunities for creating and exploring new ways of talking away from my watchful eyes. In these situations, especially during open design and construction, students had experiences that they could later use as resources for more formal discussions. However, students did not necessarily use standard ways of talking science about the salient issues when they worked in unassisted ways, even in the presence of specific artifacts (diagrams, models). This, of course, was the same in the tenth-grade unit on chaos theory (chapters 3 and 4) and the twelfth-grade unit on Newtonian physics (chapters 2 and 5).

Once new forms of language become available in public forums, individual members need to have opportunities to participate in conversations they consider safe. They can then use appropriate new ways of talking through active participation designing and the associated telling and doing in action. In the present case, these opportunities existed in the small-group structured investigations and unstructured design and construction activities. Only through the perpetuation of changes by many members of the collective can we expect the group language to change. Levels of participation in ongoing conversation also contribute to the rate of change in language. During design and construction, I often found high levels of interaction within and between groups and an associated rapid adoption of material and linguistic practices after they had been invented or introduced by some students. That is, because students interacted so much with each other, they learned to use devices, tools, and new scientific words from each other in ways that they found more intelligible and useful; they evolved new ways of talking much more easily and rapidly than during whole-class sessions where they were mainly listening and watching.

For example, chapter 6 shows in great detail how the practices related to mechanical advantage—measuring load and effort, calculating the proper ratio, setting up pulleys and levers such that they provide a mechanical advantage, analyzing machines that do not provide a mechanical advantage—were largely acquired within the class, and from student–student interactions. On the other hand, there are downsides to the social configuration in small groups. Despite repeated discussions about pulleys and mechanical advantage, there were students who maintained a particular way of talking about pulleys: Saying, for example, "Pulling down is easier than pulling up," even when pulling down actually required twice the effort. Here, the personal orientation to actual pulling experiences goes with a language that is not consistent with what I wanted to teach at the moment. The overriding factors in students' arguments were personal experiences with pulling; they were overriding, despite students' knowledge that the measured effort was less than the load. The small-group configurations appeared to have supported the maintenance of current language rather than providing strong enough incentives for change.

I began this section with the example of the Xerox-Macintosh interface, which allowed office workers to easily move from their precomputer to computer workplace. This interface can therefore be thought of as a tool designed for legitimate peripheral participation (Lave and Wenger 1991), easing users' transitions into changing worlds. When we ask students to learn science, we in fact ask them to transit into new worlds, for which they must articulate and evolve new sociomaterial practices. Artifacts consistent with the metaphor of legitimate peripheral participation must be well designed to allow students continuous trajectories from their vernacular to formal language. But there are no "idiot-proof" artifacts that prevent all but one language to evolve. The case studies in chapters 2 and 3 show that such trajectories are not self-evident and that it is more likely for a variety of ways of talking to emerge—none of which resembling the one the teacher intended—rather than the one that the school curriculum legitimates. As classroom teachers, we operate under the constraint of our mandate: to teach subject matter knowledge. For science educators, this implies that we do not encourage the development of just any language, but one that shows considerable *family resemblance* to some standard defined in relevant policy documents under the auspices of scientists. Artifacts that invite and support students' participation constitute an important part of discourse generation and appropriation. Well-designed artifacts also must encourage members to engage and must enable and empower them to increase the depth of participation in science conversations in proportion to their competencies. This chapter shows not only how communicative practices depend on the artifact but also that the interaction of artifacts, social configurations, and physical arrangements create differential opportunities and constraints for participation.

There are two constraints on learning new ways of talking, which underscore why the theoretical concept of legitimate peripheral participation is not directly applicable to school situations, nor, for that matter, are the concepts of community and community of practice. First, new forms of talking have to emerge as much as possible from telling in action, where students draw on the linguistic resources with which they are thoroughly familiar. In the present case, a number of scientific ways of talking arose from their vernacular counterparts, including friction (from slippage) and mechanical advantage (from advantage and disadvantage). Second, to appropriate specific forms of talking, one needs to participate in conversations where those forms of talk are recurrently used and where the sites and opportunities for talking form an intelligible network. School science, however, cannot be entirely viewed as legitimate peripheral participation in or enculturation to science because the usual ratios of newcomer to oldtimer are not maintained, nor are the corresponding mechanisms of participation. One therefore has to view science classrooms as collectives that are provided with opportunities to change their language about specific objects, and, equivalently, to change the ways in which they orient to, articulate, and experience the world. In this chapter, I showed how artifacts and concomitant social configurations and physical arrangements afford different levels of participation and feedback as well as access to and control over focal artifacts.

Case studies like the present one do not easily lend themselves to supporting generalizations that are transportable to other school contexts and learning environments. In my experience, the extent to which students learn scientific ways of doing and talking in design activities depends on the school culture, student population, and makeup of a specific class. Based on the results of the present study, I have already changed the way in which I structure activities when I teach. My primary design considerations are: salience of focal artifacts, ease of access to the artifacts, and maximum opportunity to contribute to ongoing conversations. My teaching now provides opportunities for increasing the focus on the construction of artifacts that are appropriately sized to allow easy physical access in small groups and easy visible access in whole-class situations so that I can work with the same artifacts in both social configurations.

For example, in a study of learning about the physical properties of water, students built, in small groups, particle models of water in its different states from five- to ten-centimeter Styrofoam balls; these models were large enough to be accessed by all students working in a group of three students and to be held up and discussed by the whole class (Roth 2002). After conducting an experiment—for example, the melting of ice and freezing of water—students refined their models so that they could explain the outcome of their experiment. Through successive cycles of conducting experiments and refining the design of their models, students were afforded many opportunities to engage in science-related material and discursive practices. In a similar way, I provided large copies (18 x 24 inch and newsprint size) of graphs, maps, and other representations when I wanted students to construct interpretations and claims drawing on language that had a high *family resemblance* to science talk; I asked students in turn to construct newsprint-sized representations of their work so that these could easily be shared with the whole class. In other situations, I arranged overhead projectors such that they were easily accessible from all parts of the classroom and therefore afforded quick access to those who wanted to contribute to the emerging shared representations; or again, I used shared electronic whiteboards with groups of five to ten members because of their affordances to physical arrangements with respect to the artifact and other participants.

Epilogue

Language and Science

Throughout this book, I have developed and taken a pragmatic perspective that views learning and development as contingent processes, arising from the dialectic of who a person is, as the current endpoint of his or her biography, and the situation he or she confronts at present. We talk as part of going about our daily business, at home or in schools, as teachers or students practice. This talk, however, generally is not talk *about* some aspect of the world, it is not explanatory talk; rather, the talk is part of the actions that continuously transform the present situation as we move into the future and leave the past behind. Thus, a when I say to my wife in the process of pruning our trees, "Give me the bigger ones, please!" I am not talking *about* the size of the shears I am holding as too small. I am not re-presenting the shears or the branches I want to cut. I am not even re-presenting and talking *about* the fact that I want the shears. And I do not have to articulate to her that I want the larger pruning shears rather than something else. Being attuned to the same situation, standing there about one meter away from me, she does not have to interpret what I said but instantly hands me the other shears. But when we bought the shears, we talked about them, the different sizes and mechanisms, the material they are made of, the quality of manufacture, and so forth. Although oriented again toward making decisions about which shears to buy, our talk is about the shears qua object and their different properties. Our verbal gestures therefore exist with other gestures in a setting to which we are oriented and which presupposes a common world where it unfolds and develops its sense.

Utterance is inseparable from attunement and understanding. Intelligibility is articulated before it is expressed in interpretation. Speech is the articulation of intelligibility. Intelligibility expresses itself in speech, comes to terms with itself. Words do not receive meaning nor is the meaning of words constructed. Rather, words accrue to meaning. To express, my whole body becomes the thinking or intention that it signifies (Merleau-Ponty 1945). It points and points out; it speaks. Meaning therefore exists in the living body, extends itself to the entire sensible world. Utterances are the excess of our existence over the natural world. As soon as people use language to establish a living relation between themselves and others like them, language is no longer an instrument, no longer a means, but a manifestation, a revelation of the intimate being and of the psychological link that unites us with the world and those that are like us.

Once we conceive of language in this way, as contingent achievement constitutive of and constituted by the situation in which it is used, then the contingent nature of students' language does not surprise. Once we give up the idea that language has the function only of re-presenting something that is not there itself, once we give up the notion that the world is somehow self-evident rather than contingent, the question "How come students don't get this?" no longer makes sense because it is as contingent as any other way of articulating the world.

Such a position allows us to accept that there is no inherent reason why students should develop *one* way of talking, the one canonized in and sparsely represented by their textbooks, over any other way of talking. In the process, we abandon the practice of abstracting language from the heterogeneity of linguistic and other behavior in the attempt to formalize what is essentially a dynamic and indeterminate structure. To utter a sentence without a place in a familiar language cannot be confirmed or disconfirmed—it can only be a savored or spit out. If it is savored, repeated by the same and other persons, it may become a sentence that is now possible within the familiar language, become a part of the familiar language. Wittgenstein's point is this: you cannot give meaning to a sentence by confronting it with a nonlinguistic meaning, by something other than already familiar language. Heidegger, who suggests that you cannot give or attach or construct the meaning of words, makes this point: words accrue to meaning. From the two philosophers we can learn that language and what it articulates and what it is about are inextricably bound up with one another. There are no presences behind language, meanings attached and belonging to words. Whatever we consider to lie "behind" language is inseparable from further language as far as we can articulate it, and then fades into the background of our unarticulated experience and practical understanding of how the world works. That is, whatever words are said to mean in particular situations is related to their always insistent actual habitat; this is not, as in a dictionary or encyclopedia, simply more words and more definitions, but includes gestures, prosody (vocal inflections), facial expression, bodily position, and in fact the entire existential setting in which the spoken word always occurs. This, therefore, leads us to understand that language is both a tool and part of the terrain (world) that the tool articulates and describes. Language, whether spoken or written, ultimately is an aspect of the material world, of which we, human beings with bodies, are also a constitutive part. Language is simply the name for a part of the material continuum that humans sometimes use to refer to and articulate other parts of the material continuum. It allows us humans to get around this world, and mastery of using language constitutes mastery in getting around a particular part of this world, as mastery of using the human body allows us to get around this world. All differences between knowing a language and getting around the world are erased, a way of viewing language and language acquisition in a new and radically different way.

LOOKING BACK

Theories about language are generally based on the assumption that speakers have some conception or ideas about the domain that they are talking about. Thus, children and students are said to have misconceptions about the phenomena that a researcher has asked them about without ascertaining whether the individuals involved have ever had the opportunity to talk about this segment of the world. That is, there is a general assumption embodied in theoretical models whereby some semantic model seated in the brain or mind drives the speech production. However, the fact that speech and gesture are not always consistent should give us occasion to question traditional models of language; furthermore, the fact that students frequently do not see what a teacher or researcher sees in the situation (see chapters 2 and 5, in particular) should give us further reason to question traditional ways of thinking about science language. In chapter 1, I suggested that rather than being the expression of ideas, mental models, or conceptions, the production of structure in perception, gesture, and speech is part of a more general attempt to orient and take position in the world. The video of students in the process of learning gives testimony to the considerable work involved until structure emerges at all three levels, as shown by the analyses in chapter 2. The confluence of perceptions, gesture, and speech in activity forms an expression rather than being the expression of something else behind.

The data in this book support the contention that rather than driving gestural and verbal expressions (representations), semantic models, if they exist at all, are the outcome of processes where the students not only organize the expressive means (language, gesture, and other [written] representations) but also develop a structure for the content. When students began their investigations, they had to manipulate objects to foreground events and create phenomena with which they were not familiar. During the initial stages of an investigation, they did not know yet how to structure the perceptual field into figure and ground.

That is, they could not extract those features that are required for producing the observational and theoretical descriptions that the curriculum foresees. However, as students investigated, their perceptions, gestures, and language mutually adjusted until they arrived at a stage where the three modes of expression were consistent. In short, they gradually constructed a semantic model (chapters 2 and 3).

Interaction participants frequently do not make reference in talk or gesture to that which is perceptually available to everyone. How they are oriented with respect to the salient artifacts (chapters 1 and 7) and how far they are away from them make a difference as to how the language is used (chapter 7). Consequently, it is necessary to develop a theory of language development that includes the immediate, perceptually accessible setting as one modality of communication. Furthermore, any framework that usefully explains the emergence of new language has to allow for the description of the evolution from not seeing and knowing a phenomenon to the presence of a fully fledged, socially negotiated and accepted explanation of the phenomenon now perceptually available to the participants.

Gestures and language are also available to the teacher in the class. As such, he or she has many opportunities for identifying the entities that are salient to students, and how these are represented in talk (chapter 5). Moreover, mismatches between gestures and talk can be used to make inferences about individuals' current understandings. During transitions, gestures precede verbal means in communicating the new understandings. Thus, teachers who pay attention to and read students' gestures can help facilitate (i.e., scaffold) the emergence of appropriate language because its precursors already exist in sensorimotor re-presentations of objects and events. In this respect, the role of the teacher is of particular importance, for there are no criteria available for selecting one way of talking over another before these ways actually exist. Students have no way of judging the appropriateness of their ways of talking until some later point. Only from the vantage point of a consistently viable language is it possible to point out the problems arising from earlier forms of talk. Teachers, however, already know the observational and theoretical language that students are to learn. Through their interactions with students, assisted by their reading of gestures, they can scaffold students in their development of new forms of (protoscientific) language outlined in the curriculum.

Throughout this book, I have provided examples of students in the process of investigating phenomena or designing artifacts. As part of the process of learning, they talked. But in many situations this talk had very little in common with anything that science teachers and science educators suppose science language to look like, even though students drew on words that have their place in a language characteristic of science. But their language also had very little in common with the students' habitual ways of speaking outside of the classroom, although, again, there were elements in students' ways of talking in the classroom that resembled their normal ways of talking. The muddle that we observe is due to the fact that students do have neither a semantic model nor a practical experience of the world that would allow them to talk *about* phenomena. Rather, their utterances are a form of articulating the world in action, which has as its main function a coordination of orientation, an articulation of the sensible world, and moving the investigative process ahead. It is out of these early articulations in action that patterned ways of talking emerge, which in the best of circumstances subsequently become talk *about* the entities, observation sentences, observation categoricals, and theory statements, that is, various levels of *talking science*.

Learners frequently not only talk about the world in terms that differ from science but also experience worlds that are different; they articulate the world differently from their teachers in perception and action. We therefore need to theorize learners as individuals in the dark, individually or collectively groping to structure the setting and articulating this structure for one another. It is in the process that they come to articulate the world in new ways; they make observation sentences, observation categoricals, and entire theories. Because the world does not tell students how to structure it and which language to speak, these new ways of talking are as contingent as are all forms of language. What we therefore need is a theory that explains equally well why students arrive at the Foucault pendulum as an explanation for the chaotic pendulum as why they arrive, if they in fact do, at a language that has a greater family resemblance with the one that chaos scientists characteristically speak. What we further need is a theory that explains how students learn particular ways of talking (and writing) in situations that are very different from those outside schools where people do develop new languages, but always when newcomers come to existing communities of practice rather than when there is a predominance of newcomers that is supposed to approach in their practice one person in their midst. The theory also needs to explain the role of body and gesture in the development of language, and the role that particular social configurations and spatial arrangements have on the orientations people take and the ways of talking that they develop in the process of inhabiting the particular spaces that they do.

Laboratory activities are said to play an important role in science learning. However, we know relatively little about how manipulating materials and tools and acting in laboratory settings allows students to appropriate language that is more similar to the scientific language intended by the curriculum than the familiar ways of talking that students have evolved in the course of their everyday lives and bring with them to science class. Claims about the value of traditional laboratory activities are largely unexamined. It is unlikely that we will arrive in this way at more definitive answers to our questions about the pedagogic value of laboratory work for the appropriation of scientific language; rather, to make progress, we need to focus more sharply on what students are actually doing and saying in the laboratory. School laboratory activities are therefore largely ill conceived, confused, and unproductive. Many students learn little of or about science and do not engage in doing science.

Throughout this book, I have provided examples of opportunities that science laboratory activities provide over lectures. The social, material, and historical dimensions of laboratory settings allow students to anchor their utterances in multiple ways in their experiences in the world, ways that engage not only their talk, but also their hands, arms, and bodies. That is, I have shown how familiar ways of talking, inherently experienced as meaningful by speakers, emerge from and are grounded in the dialectical relation of sense and reference, themselves emerging as dialectical relations of activity and action, and action and operation, respectively. It is not merely a matter of a polar "hands-on versus minds-on," but hands, eyes, bodies, and talk contribute to what observers can discern as cognition and learning. Students' material actions are deeply integrated and co-constitutive of the collective language they develop for articulating the world, pointing out these articulations during interactions, and moving from observation sentences to observation categoricals. For example, Chris and Rani's use of "labile" and "stable" were grounded in the examples with the pencil and the steel ball in the plaster bowl that they enacted. Understanding of stability therefore is not just a matter of developing a way of talking, but also comes from the sense one gets from holding a pen that topples over. The meaning of saying "stable" does not just lie in another word functioning as a synonym of the first but also resides in the bodily and perceptual experience in a world of objects already understood. Thus, from the perspective developed here, there is a lot of value in Katrina's analogy of the chaotic pendulum and drawing of a ball (chapter 3). All students' bodily enactments were resources for articulating the invariant structures in the different focal situations. Her cognition therefore has to be understood as arising from the intricate relationship of bodily experience, gesture, and discourse.

In showing the importance of social, material, and historical dimensions of the situation to talk, I am not simply making some point about the importance of nonverbal aspects in communication. Researchers often use the term "nonverbal communication" as a way of denoting a variety of signs (e.g., gestures, indexical reference through some form of pointing, body orientation) that tell an additional something and thereby is supposed to give meaning. In this book, I presented gesture, body position, voice inflections, and other physical expressions as integral parts of communication, not as distinct and partially overlapping systems.

The student activities presented here revealed that there exists an integration of materials (apparatus), actions, and utterances, an integration that has been a mangle of practice (Pickering 1995). I understand this mangle as the process by means of which the dialectical relations of sense, reference, and meaning come to be intertwined. Students' ways of articulating their world, which leads to observational and theoretical language, cannot be understood independent of the material actions they engage in. From highly situation-specific talk, in part exploring talk itself, emerge tentative observation descriptions that are *about* physical phenomena. Students' new ways of talking are tied to their actions and the materials they use. The outcomes of students' actions initially are little more than tentative observation sentences bound to a specific materials and configurations. Students' utterances are at first revocable, but become firm as students evolve other, confirming observation sentences. At this point, they evolve tentative generalizations, that is, simple observation sentences shift to become observation categoricals. This research concerned with understanding the discursive and physical actions of people in complex laboratory settings suggests that knowing and meaning ultimately bottom out in physical experience. Being in a common physical world is then a fundamental and necessary condition for intelligent language production and use. The microanalyses in this book point out different ways in which the grounding of discourse (i.e., symbols) is achieved through the agency of students in the physical and social worlds constituted by their school science laboratories.

TALKING SCIENCE, WRITING SCIENCE, AND CONCEPTIONS

Throughout this book, there are situations in which students found expressions as they interacted with their setting. They talked, but initially, this talk had very little in common with the science of textbooks and scientific journals, or scientists' presentations during conferences. I use "muddle" as a positive term to denote the highly unstable forms of talk that one can observe when students engage with unfamiliar objects, producing phenomena that they have not seen before and which they come to perceive differently in the course of their engagement with the segment of the world. Uttering words is part of structuring situations, a structuring that the students in the present book engaged in together, each being part of the structure of the other. The transcripts used here document the differences between spoken language and the written language students are supposed to use according to the respective curricula. Spoken language is but one way in which humans project their world. Orality is empathetic and participatory, identification with the known, "getting with it," first-person identification of narrator with the things or protagonists. In oral discourse, it is the here and now of the situation that provides the ultimate reference. If we cannot point to the thing about which we speak, we can at least situate it in relation to the unique spatiotemporal framework that is shared by the interlocutors.

My own research shows that the way in which scientists talk at their workbenches is not much different from the way in which the students in this book talked (e.g., Roth 2004c). Scientists' talk is highly indexical and disconnected, but suitable for the tasks at hand. It is their way of articulating the laboratory world, the job to be done, and the interactions among different participants. When they account for what they have done and why, scientists' language changes. Their language is no longer a tool to articulate the salient aspects of laboratory work, but is *about* the entities that are of interest from the perspective of their scientific community. It is a way of talking that has family resemblance with the language they use for publishing, a very different way of using language. It now has a tool quality, it is *about* the world, and it mediates scientists' access to the world in very specific ways. At the moment, there is no research that articulates the relationship between the two languages and what is required to make the transition from one to the other. (Given the high rejection rates in some journals, one can presume that science educators, too, experience the drastic change between doing research and communicating it in written form to their peers.)

All of this, of course, makes a face-to-face conversational framework problematic for the teaching of scientific languages (Gee 2004). How do students move from their laboratory talk—which uses incomplete sentences, spiked with deictic terms ("this," "there," "here"), vague references, and ambiguous sentence structures that are resolved by the shared context—to the language characteristic of formal talk and written language *about* scientific entities? This privileging of written language forms is only an expression of where our culture has gone more generally. In the following, I take a critical look at existing work about talking science, writing science, and conceptions, all of which are questioned by the framework developed in this book.

The author of the seminal work on *talking science* provided a definition of this concept and practice that is more extended then simply speaking:

> Learning science means learning to talk science. . . . "Talking science" means observing, describing, comparing, classifying, analyzing, discussing, hypothesizing, theorizing, questioning, challenging, arguing, designing experiments, following procedures, judging, evaluating, deciding, concluding, generalizing, reporting, writing, lecturing, and teaching in and through the language of science. (Lemke 1990, 1)

Lemke suggests that language is not simply a medium that stands between students' minds and the world but that the language of science is a constitutive aspect of the activities of observing, describing, comparing, and so on. Many science educators who focus on language refer to Lemke's *Talking Science* in support of curricula that allow students to converse in science classrooms. There exists a contradiction, however, in that students who are new to a situation clearly do not use the language of science if language is understood as a structured way of deploying a specific set of words (i.e., the science concepts). They may use words, but there is little family resemblance between what students say and how they say it and what and how scientists talk about the same situation. Students' utterances during initial inquiries in a domain resemble groping one's way in an unfamiliar, pitch-black setting where we run into things that are completely unfamiliar. While we still speak in such situations, the utterances may have very little in common with our normal ways of dealing with the world (including speaking), which are associated with our familiar settings, nor with the eventual way of speaking, which will be appropriate for our newfound ways of coping in a new world. There is therefore a need for more clearly articulating what "talking" and "science" mean, and to distinguish, as I have done, articulation in action from talking *about* something. For someone to talk about something, it needs to exist in a more or less identified form that one actually can talk about, an aspect of the world already articulated in action (perception, manipulation). The very existence of something, as something *about* which we speak, implies that we had previously articulated it in action and had found ways of telling it apart from other things.

Lemke's definition of talking science also includes writing. The language that appears in science textbooks and scientific journal has been, and still is, taken as the paradigm for scientific language. Clearly however, writing is very different from speaking. Writing restructures consciousness, because, from a sociological and a psychological point of view, the written text must "'decontextualized' itself in such a way that it can be 'recontextualized' in a new situation—as accomplished, precisely, by the act of reading" (Ricœur 1991, 83). The mumbles, stumbles, tics, vague deictic references, malapropisms, seizures, or metaphors that characterize everyday talk, even that of teachers, have been completely eliminated from texts.

Writing renders the text autonomous with respect to the intention of the author. With writing, the situation changes and with it, the forms of thinking that are dialectically related to the ways of using language: there is no longer a context common to author and audience, and the concrete conditions other modes of structuring no longer exist. The freeing of the written material with respect to the dialogical condition of situated activity is the most significant effect of writing. That is, the written text distances itself from the author *in the process* of writing; it becomes autonomous. This distanciation is constitutive of the phenomenon of writing. Distanciation requires work, and the amount of effort that this work takes, even if a student has mastered talking in situation, has yet to be investigated. The passage from speaking to writing affects language in other ways as well. Most importantly, reference is changed profoundly when it is no longer possible to identify the thing spoken about as part of the common situation of the interlocutors. The world of the text is not the world of everyday language; everyday talk is concretely realized in time and in presence, whereas written texts and language more generally exist outside of the temporal constraints of lived time. Although written texts can contain indexical terms, these refer to something on the inside. A scientific text has to be able to stand on its own, not refer to the situation of the student, of any student, and at the same time has to provide opportunities to be appropriated into all situations and by all students.

Most of us do not use science in much of our everyday lives, even if we have been educated as scientists. We marvel at a rainbow and articulate its colors rather than explaining it as the effect of refraction and internal reflection. We enjoy a sunrise pointing it out to our spouses rather than talking about the revolution of the Earth that makes the Sun appear above the horizon. We ask a co-worker to close the door to keep the heat in rather than talking about convection currents that take the heated air outside in exchange for the cold air from the outside. If we want science to be for all, we may have to rethink what we want students to be able to do—participating in conversations allowing us to deal with the contentious science-related issues of the day or expressing ourselves as scientists do in their conferences and journals. Ong (1982) calls on us to free ourselves from a typographic and chirographic bias in our understanding of language. Perhaps now may be the time to follow his lead and to rethink how we want students to participate in science-related conversations. I am aware of the difficulty that such rethinking will face in the science education community given the ideological nature of our commitment to viewing language in terms of the written word.

In the science education community, it is common to think about science and scientific knowledge in terms of conceptions that people are said to have or hold. There is an extensive literature on so-called misconceptions and how these interfere with the instructions that students are to receive; by engaging in conceptual change, students are said to restructure their cognitive frameworks in slight or radical ways; and by drawing on metacognition, learners are supposed to be able to monitor, integrate, and extend their own learning and select good learning behaviors. In this approach, which is independent of the particular framework researchers pledge allegiance to, language is an intermediary between the conceptions in someone's head and the world outside, or equivalently, plays the dual role of *expressing meaning* and *referring to the world*. Even scholars who develop discourse-oriented theories make language a medium for expressive actions such as sharing ideas, expressing meaning, and highlighting certain features for future thoughts. Students' talk is then a medium of externalizing thoughts and conceptions from the computational hardware to the public (social) forum. All of these approaches have in common that the student is a rational actor who makes choices about what to learn, how to learn, which language to deploy, and so on.

It is evident that these approaches are at odds with the perspective on language that I am articulating here. Such theories are inappropriate for the data presented here because of the considerable variations in the talk, which would have required constant changes in the underlying the so-called conceptions.

There are some proposals for abandoning the notion of stable knowledge structures and stages during conceptual change episodes and for assuming intermittent periods or stages of confusion; others propose varying numbers of traditional intermediate stages. All of these positions therefore require different *types* of knowledge that students appear to acquire as they are faced with science lessons. The approach I am articulating here does away with the notion of fixed conceptions and transitions into different (intermediary) conceptions and confusion. A less stringent assumption is that talking is part of a more general movement to taking position in the world, and consistent ways of talking characterize moments of stability usually associated with times when we are moving about in familiar worlds. Stable and recurrent patterns of talking no longer make sense when we get ourselves into new, unfamiliar situations, which require that we find ways of positioning ourselves and orienting, including appropriate ways of articulating the world surrounding us in activity until new stable and recurrent patterns have established themselves. In the meantime, students' utterances do not have a place in a (temporarily) fixed form of language. But utterances that do not have a place are neither true nor false, for they cannot be confirmed or disconfirmed, argued for or against. Viewing language in this way, we have done away with the need for conceptions and the structural changes they have to undergo. Talking in situation does not have to be structured and therefore can undergo minute changes as new semantic and syntactic resources are brought into and become part of situations. These minute changes can be documented in a continuous fashion. It will turn out that some were only momentary blips; others became more stable resources to the persons in activity. Eventually, new more or less stable recurrent ways emerge.

The approach I am proposing with this book does away with the need for mental representation of the situation, for students evolve initial articulations, among others, into situated observation sentences and observation categoricals. Being in the situation does away with the need of re-presentation, for people are there, knowing that they can articulate, pick up, and talk *about* anything that they might need. These situated utterances are ephemeral and may be forgotten in the next instance; subsequent sentences may in fact be incompatible with earlier ones without that the students ever experience an inconsistency, discrepancy, or contradiction. But some observation sentences will stabilize within a group and then become consistent resources that students will recurrently deploy and which last beyond the immediate activity.

Appendix

Transcription Conventions

The following transcription conventions are used throughout this book.

*	The asterisks, which appear as part of the utterances, indicate the point where speech coincides with the visual representation placed to the right of or above the verbal transcript.
Is [straight up] [Gravity is]	Left and right brackets in consecutive utterances indicate the extent to which two speakers overlap in their speech.
((Points.))	Double parentheses enclose the analyst's comments, including actions relevant to the situation analyzed.
that	Italicized words indicate verbal stress, which is usually heard in conversation as emphasis.
°But it's°	Words between degree signs are uttered with a much lower speech volume, almost to the point of being inaudible.
why::	Each colon represents a lengthening of the preceding phoneme by about one-tenth of a second.
(1.6)	Length of a pause in speaking, in tenths of a second.
(.)	The period in parentheses marks a hearable pause of 0.1 seconds or less.
–	En-dash indicates a sudden stop in speech without the change in intonation that normally marks the end of an utterance.
.;!?	Punctuation marks are used to indicate intonations rather than as demarcation of grammatical units.

=   Equal sign indicates "latching," that is, the normal pause between two speakers does not exist but there is no overlap.

THIS, BAnister   Capitalized words and parts of words are spoken with a louder than normal voice in the setting.

References

Bakhtin, M. M. 1981. *The dialogic imagination.* Austin: University of Texas.

————. 1993. *Toward a philosophy of the act.* Austin: University of Texas.

Buber, M. 1970. *I and thou.* New York: Simon & Schuster.

Chapman, D. 1991. *Vision, instruction, and action.* Cambridge, Mass.: MIT Press.

Churchland, P. S., and T. J. Sejnowski. 1992. *The computational brain.* Cambridge, Mass.: MIT Press.

Crowder, E. M. 1996. Gestures at work in sense-making science talk. *Journal of the Learning Sciences, 5,* 173–208.

Davidson, D. 1986. A nice derangement of epitaphs. In *Truth and interpretation,* ed. E. Lepore, 433–46. Oxford, England: Blackwell.

Decety, J., and J. Grèzes. 1999. Neural mechanisms subserving the perception of human actions. *Trends in Cognitive Sciences* 3: 172–78.

Derrida, J. 1988. *Limited inc.* Chicago: University of Chicago Press.

————. 1998. *Monolingualism of the other; or, The prosthesis of origin.* Stanford, Calif.: Stanford University Press.

diSessa, A. A. 1993. Toward an epistemology of physics. *Cognition and Instruction* 10: 105–225.

Eco, U. 1976. *A theory of semiotics.* Bloomington: Indiana University Press.

————. 1984. *Semiotics and the philosophy of language.* Bloomington: Indiana University Press.

Fox-Keller, E. 1983. *A feeling for the organism: The life and work of Barbara McClintock.* New York: W. H. Freeman.

Frost, R. 1915/1966. The road not taken. In *British and American classical poems,* ed. L. Herrig, H. Meller, and R. Sühnel, 112. Braunschweig, Germany: Georg Westermann.

Garfinkel, H., M. Lynch, and E. Livingston. 1981. The work of a discovering science construed with materials from the optically discovered pulsar. *Philosophy of the Social Sciences* 11: 131–58.

Gee, J. P. 1996. *Social linguistics and literacies: Ideology in discourses.* 2nd ed. London: Taylor & Francis.

———. 2004. Language in the science classroom: Academic social languages as the heart of school-based literacy. In *Establishing scientific classroom discourse communities: Multiple voices of research on teaching and learning,* ed. R. Yerrick and W.-M. Roth, 19–37. Mahwah, N.J.: Lawrence Erlbaum Associates.

Gentner, D., S. Brem, R. W. Ferguson, A. B. Markman, B. B. Levidow, P. Wolff, and K. D. Forbus. 1997. Analogical reasoning and conceptual change: A case study of Johannes Kepler. *Journal of the Learning Sciences* 6: 3–40.

Giroux, H. 1992. *Border crossings: Cultural workers and the politics of education.* New York: Routledge.

Goldin-Meadow, S., M. W. Alibali, and C. B. Church. 1993. Transitions in concept acquisition: Using the hand to read the mind. *Psychological Review* 100: 279–97.

Gooding, D. 1990. *Experiment and the making of meaning: Human agency in scientific observation and experiment.* Dordrecht, The Netherlands: Kluwer Academic Publishers.

———. 1992. Putting agency back into experiment. In *Science as practice and culture,* ed. A. Pickering, 65–112. Chicago: University of Chicago Press.

Gregory, B. 1990. *Inventing reality: Physics as language.* New York: Wiley.

Hanks, W. F. 1992. The indexical ground of deictic reference. In *Rethinking context: Language as an interactive phenomenon,* ed. A. Duranti and C. Goodwin, 43–76. Cambridge, England: Cambridge University Press.

Heath, C., and P. Luff. 2000. *Technology in action.* Cambridge, England: Cambridge University Press.

Heidegger, M. 1977. *Sein und Zeit.* Tübingen, Germany: Max Niemeyer.

Hutchins, E. 1995. *Cognition in the wild.* Cambridge, Mass.: MIT Press.

Johnson, M. 1987. *The body in the mind: The bodily basis of imagination, reason, and meaning.* Chicago: University of Chicago Press.

Jordan, B., and A. Henderson. 1995. Interaction analysis: Foundations and practice. *Journal of the Learning Sciences* 4: 39–103.

Lakoff, G. 1987. *Women, fire, and dangerous things: What categories reveal about the mind.* Chicago: University of Chicago Press.

Lakoff, G., and M. Johnson. 1999. *Philosophy in the flesh: The embodied mind and its challenge to Western thought.* New York: Basic Books.

Latour, B. 1987. *Science in action: How to follow scientists and engineers through society*. Milton Keynes, England: Open University Press.

———. 1993. *La clef de Berlin et autres leçons d'un amateur de sciences*. Paris: Éditions la Découverte.

Latour, B., and S. Woolgar. 1986. *Laboratory life: The social construction of scientific facts*. Princeton, N.J.: Princeton University Press.

Lave, J., and E. Wenger. 1991. *Situated learning: Legitimate peripheral participation*. Cambridge, England: Cambridge University Press.

Lemke, J. L. 1990. *Talking science: Language, learning, and values*. Norwood, N.J.: Ablex.

———. 1998. Multiplying meaning: Visual and verbal semiotics in scientific text. In *Reading science*, ed. J. R. Martin and R. Veel, 87–113. London: Routledge.

Leont'ev, A. N. 1978. *Activity, consciousness, and personality*. Englewood Cliffs, N.J.: Prentice Hall.

McGinn, M. K., and W.-M. Roth. 1998. Assessing students' understandings about levers: Better test instruments are not enough. *International Journal of Science Education* 20: 813–32.

McGinn, M. K., W.-M. Roth, S. Boutonné, and C. Woszczyna. 1995. The transformation of individual and collective knowledge in elementary science classrooms that are organized as knowledge-building communities. *Research in Science Education* 25: 163–89.

McNeill, D. 1992. *Hand and mind: What gestures reveal about thought*. Chicago: University of Chicago Press.

McNeill, D., and S. D. Duncan. 2000. Growth points in thinking for speaking. In *Language and gesture*, ed. D. McNeill, 141–61. Cambridge, England: Cambridge University Press.

Mikhailov, F. 1980. *The riddle of self*. Moscow: Progress.

Merleau-Ponty, M. 1945. *Phénoménologie de la perception*. Paris: Gallimard.

Nemirovsky, R. 1993. Students making sense of chaotic behavior. *Interactive Learning Environments* 3: 151–75.

Nöe, A. 2002. On what we see. *Pacific Philosophical Quarterly, 83*, 57–80.

Ochs, E., P. Gonzales, and S. Jacoby. 1996. "When I come down I'm in the domain state": Grammar and graphic representation in the interpretive activity of physicists. In *Interaction and grammar*, ed. E. Ochs, E. A. Schegloff, and S. A. Thompson, 328–69. Cambridge, England: Cambridge University Press.

Ong, W. J. 1982. *Orality and literacy: The technologizing of the word*. New York: Routledge.

O'Regan, J. K., and A. Noë. 2001. A sensorimotor account of vision and visual consciousness. *Behavioral and Brain Sciences* 24: 883–917.

Pickering, A. 1995. *The mangle of practice: Time, agency, and science*. Chicago: University of Chicago Press.

266   References

Quine, W. V. 1995. *From stimulus to science*. Cambridge, Mass.: Harvard University Press.

Ricœur, P. 1991. *From text to action*. Trans. Kathleen Blamey and John B. Thompson. Evanston, Ill.: Northwestern University Press.

Rorty, R. 1989. *Contingency, irony, and solidarity*. Cambridge, England: Cambridge University Press.

Roth, W.-M. 1991. The development of reasoning on the balance beam. *Journal of Research in Science Teaching* 28: 631–45.

———. 1995. Affordances of computers in teacher-student interactions: The case of Interactive Physics™. *Journal of Research in Science Teaching* 32: 329–47.

———. 1996a. The co-evolution of situated language and physics knowing. *Journal of Science Education and Technology* 5: 171–91.

———. 1996b. Thinking with hands, eyes, and signs: Multimodal science talk in a grade 6/7 unit on simple machines. *Interactive Learning Environments* 4: 170–87.

———. 1998. *Designing communities*. Dordrecht, The Netherlands: Kluwer Academic Publishers.

———. 1999. Discourse and agency in school science laboratories. *Discourse Processes* 28: 27–60.

———. 2000. From gesture to scientific language. *Journal of Pragmatics* 32: 1683–1714.

———. 2001. Phenomenology and mathematical experience. *Linguistics and Education* 12: 239–52.

———. 2002. *Being and becoming in the classroom*. Westport, Conn.: Ablex.

———. 2003. Gesture-speech phenomena, learning, and development. *Educational Psychologist* 38: 249–63.

———. 2004a. Im Dunkeln Tappen. *Zeitschrift für Qualitative Bildungs-, Beratungs-, und Sozialforschung* 2004/2.

———. 2004b. Emergence of graphing practices in scientific research. *Journal of Cognition and Culture* 4: 595–627.

———. 2004c. Perceptual gestalts in workplace communication. *Journal of Pragmatics* 36: 1037–69.

Roth, W.-M., and R. Duit. 2003. Emergence, flexibility, and stabilization of language in a physics classroom. *Journal for Research in Science Teaching* 40: 869–97.

Roth, W.-M., and D. Lawless. 2002a. Signs, deixis, and the emergence of scientific explanations. *Semiotica* 138: 95–130.

———. 2002b. When up is down and down is up: Body orientation, proximity, and gestures as resources for listeners. *Language in Society* 31: 1–28.

Roth, W.-M., and Y.-J. Lee. 2004. Interpreting unfamiliar graphs: A generative, activity-theoretic model. *Educational Studies in Mathematics* 57: 265–90.

Roth, W.-M., and K. B. Lucas. 1997. From "truth" to "invented reality": A discourse analysis of high school physics students' talk about scientific knowledge. *Journal of Research in Science Teaching* 34: 145–79.

Roth, W.-M., M. K. McGinn, C. Woszczyna, and S. Boutonné. 1999. Differential participation during science conversations: The interaction of focal artifacts, social configuration, and physical arrangements. *Journal of the Learning Sciences* 8: 293–347.

Roth, W.-M., C. McRobbie, K. B. Lucas, and S. Boutonné. 1997a. The local production of order in traditional science laboratories: A phenomenological analysis. *Learning and Instruction* 7: 107–36.

———. 1997b. Why do students fail to learn from demonstrations? A social practice perspective on learning in physics. *Journal of Research in Science Teaching* 34: 509–33.

Roth, W.-M., C. Woszczyna, and G. Smith. 1996. Affordances and constraints of computers in science education. *Journal of Research in Science Teaching* 33: 995–1017.

Snow, R. E. 1992. Aptitude theory: Yesterday, today, and tomorrow. *Educational Psychologist* 27: 5–32

Suchman, L. A., and B. Jordan. 1990. Interactional troubles in face-to-face survey interviews. *Journal of the American Statistical Association* 85: 232–44.

Winograd, T., and F. Flores. 1987. *Understanding computers and cognition: A new foundation for design.* Norwood, N.J.: Ablex.

Wittgenstein, L. 1974. *Philosophical investigations.* 3rd ed. New York: Macmillan.

Name Index

Subject Index

About the Author

Wolff-Michael Roth is Lansdowne Professor of Applied Cognitive Science in the Faculty of Education at the University of Victoria. He has taught in middle and high schools for the better part of twelve years until beginning his university career. Even then, he continued teaching entire terms at the elementary, middle, and high school levels—always exploring new ways of teaching science in a variety of settings and based on his emerging understanding of science as a particular way of life, characterized by its own discursive and material practices.

While teaching physics at a college preparatory school, he began to conduct investigations into learning and teaching with a particular focus on how language is used. His research has been published not only in educational research journals generally and science education journals in particular but also in other disciplines, including linguistics, history and philosophy of science, and applied cognitive science. His books include *Being and Becoming in the Classroom*, *Toward an Anthropology of Graphing*, and *Rethinking Scientific Literacy* (with A. C. Barton).

The interests of Wolff-Michael Roth are broad and interdisciplinary but always focus on knowing and learning in science with particular focus on the way language and other representations are used in practical settings in formal learning environments—including kindergartens, schools, and universities—in the

workplace—e.g., fish hatcheries, scientific laboratories, scientific fieldwork)—
and in other everyday activities (e.g., environmental activism, local meetings).